The Townsend Thematic Reader

Christopher G. Hayes

UNIVERSITY OF GEORGIA

Patricia J. McAlexander

UNIVERSITY OF GEORGIA

TOWNSEND PRESS

Books in the Townsend Press Reading Series:

Groundwork for College Reading
Ten Steps to Building College Reading Skills
Ten Steps to Improving College Reading Skills
Ten Steps to Advancing College Reading Skills

Books in the Townsend Press Vocabulary Series:

Vocabulary Basics
Groundwork for a Better Vocabulary
Building Vocabulary Skills
Building Vocabulary Skills, Short Version
Improving Vocabulary Skills
Improving Vocabulary Skills, Short Version
Advancing Vocabulary Skills
Advancing Vocabulary Skills, Short Version
Advanced Word Power

Other Reading and Writing Books:

Everyday Heroes
A Basic Reader for College Writers
Voices and Values: A Reader for Writers
English at Hand

Send book orders and requests for desk copies or supplements to:

Townsend Press Book Center
1038 Industrial Drive
West Berlin, New Jersey 08091

For even faster service, contact us in any of the following ways:

By telephone: 1-800-772-6410
By fax: 1-800-225-8894
By e-mail: TownsendCS@aol.com
Through our website: www.townsendpress.com

Contents

1 / Making Choices

The Monsters in My Head   *Frank Langella*   3
> The creature creeping in his son's bedroom window reminds
> the author of the terrors that stalk us all.

Tickets to Nowhere   *Andy Rooney*   9
> Lotteries make a few people rich overnight; they make mil-
> lions poorer, in every sense of the word.

Anxiety: Challenge by Another Name
James Lincoln Collier   14
> Turning down a golden opportunity out of fear taught the
> author a lesson he's never forgotten.

To Get a Story, I Flimflammed a Dead Man's Mother
Bob Teague   20
> If you think TV news is ugly, says the author, you ought to
> see what goes on behind the scenes.

The Bystander Effect   *Dorothy Barkin*   29
> What explanation is there when a brutal crime is committed
> in full view of witnesses, and nobody lifts a finger to help?

A Crime of Compassion   *Barbara Huttmann*   37
> Which is the crime: allowing a man to die, or reviving a
> living corpse?

2 / Education and Learning

3 / Family Life

6 / The Light Side of Life

Alternate Table of Contents

Illustration

Process Analysis

Comparison-Contrast

Division-Classification

Argument-Persuasion

Preface

In the more than forty years the two of us, combined, have been teaching introductory college composition, we have used scores of thematic readers and have reviewed dozens more for consideration in our classes. Time after time, we found many of the anthologies lengthy and unwieldy, their size daunting to instructor and student alike. We also felt guilty when we used these collections because we covered a fraction of the selections—and our students wondered why they spent so much for a book from which they read so little. Moreover, because of their length and complexity, we found a good number of the selections intimidating to first-year college students. Since our aim has always been to spend more time encouraging students to write and revise and less time discussing and explicating readings, these lengthy and often complex pieces turned out to be inappropriate for our purpose. But perhaps our greatest dissatisfaction with many of the texts was that the readings were not interesting and relevant to our students. And, of course, no matter how well-written a selection may be, if it doesn't engage the beginning college student, its value in the classroom and in the student's life remains unrealized.

The Townsend Thematic Reader bears a striking dissimilarity to the thematic readers described above. That's because we designed it to be:

- **Compact.** The book contains 34 selections (grouped into six thematic units), yet numbers a manageable 256 pages. Because of its conciseness, *The Townsend Thematic Reader* sells for a low net price of only $12.00. It can, then, be easily paired with a rhetoric or handbook to create a complete, cost-conscious package.

• **Accessible.** The book's selections are manageable in length (the average runs five pages). Students can read and reread most selections in a single sitting, with an occasional longer piece lending variety and challenge.

• **Engaging.** Even the most reluctant students will be stimulated by the book's selections. Issues such as date rape, generational conflict, ethnic identity, alcohol abuse, and overcoming fears touch directly on students' lives. Timely and provocative, the readings encourage students to think, discuss, and write about matters of importance.

• **Versatile.** In addition to grouping the selections by themes, the book offers an alternate table of contents that arranges readings according to the standard nine rhetorical patterns (description, narration, illustration, process analysis, comparison-contrast, cause-effect, definition, division-classification, and argument-persuasion). *The Townsend Thematic Reader* can thus accommodate a variety of instructional approaches and course plans.

The Selections

The book's readings are grouped into six themes: "Making Choices"; "Education and Learning"; "Family Life"; "Television, Movies, and Entertainment"; "Human Connections and Disconnections"; and "The Light Side of Life." As the themes suggest, the selections exemplify varied purposes and voices—from nostalgic recollection ("Dad") to vigorous argument ("A Crime of Compassion"), from how-to advice ("Let's Get Specific") to light-hearted social commentary ("Rudeness at the Movies"), from exhilarating childhood epiphanies ("The Chase") to tragic stories of violence on today's college campus ("A Dangerous Party"). A handful of selections can be considered classics (for example, "How to Mark a Book" or "Shame"), while a number have never before been anthologized (including "The Fine Art of Complaining" and "Is Sex All That Matters?"). Voices of women and men, Native Americans

and Asian Americans, African Americans and Hispanic Americans
are all represented in the selections. Although many selections res-
onate with students' current concerns (for example, "Will You Go
Out With Me?"), others challenge students' views and broaden their
outlooks (for example, "The Price of Hate"). Most important, all selections are well written and provide effective models of clear
organization, distinctive voice, uncluttered style, and engaging treat-
ment of subject matter.

Instructional Features

The Townsend Thematic Reader does more than present a collection of outstanding readings; it also helps students make sense of
those readings. It encourages them to relate the readings to their
own lives, to share their perspectives with those of their classmates,
and to write paragraphs and essays informed by those private re-
flections and public discussions. In short, the book's instructional
features are carefully crafted to develop students' reading, thinking,
and writing abilities.

Two pre-reading aids precede each selection. First, to spark
students' interest, a *Preview* provides contextual background for the
selection. Next, *Words to Watch* defines vocabulary that may be unfamiliar to students. By defining words that students will see again
in the selection, this feature lays a foundation for vocabulary development, a crucial skill for building both reading and writing
proficiencies.

Following each selection are four other instructional features.
These prompt careful thought about the selection's major points,
about the author's techniques, about the personal and social meanings
implied by the piece, and about how students might use their understanding of the author's ideas and craft to fashion their own essays.

- **Understanding Content** contains three questions that
  guide students in becoming close, attentive readers of text.
  The first question always asks them to identify a selection's
  main idea, either by pointing to a specific passage or by
  phrasing the idea in their own words. We ask this question
  first because being able to find or articulate the selection's

overarching idea helps students understand the frame that holds together the piece's supporting material. The remaining two questions help students to identify these supporting details and to draw valid inferences. The "Understanding Content" questions, then, draw students back to the text to reconsider their first interpretation of the selection and to revise and elaborate, if necessary, their preliminary construction of its meaning.

- **Understanding Technique** contains three questions that focus attention on each piece's dominant stylistic and rhetorical features. These questions ask students to consider choices writers must make about, for example, introductions and conclusions, sentence structure and style, tone and point of view, transitions and organization. Since these decisions are the same ones students must make in their own writing, the "Understanding Technique" questions both help students become more conscious of these decisions and enhance their repertoire of rhetorical options.

- **Thinking About Ideas** asks three questions that encourage students, individually and collaboratively, to explore the often complex concerns raised or implied by each selection. These questions lead students to place the selection's topic and its author's viewpoint within a larger social and personal context. In addition, the questions and the discussion they prompt often generate material that students can develop more fully in their own writing.

- **Writing About Ideas** presents three writing assignments. The first leads to a paragraph-length paper, while the last two call for essay-length responses. Four features guide these writing assignments. First, they are worded to remind students that their paragraphs and essays *must make and develop a point* ("Look over your brainstormed list, and select only the most convincing evidence in support of your position"). In other words, students are cued to consider the *purpose* of their writing.

Second, to keep students on track, the writing assignments often *include cautions* ("Be careful not to provide so much dialogue that you slow down the action") or *suggestions* ("Save your most significant piece of evidence for the final, emphatic position"). These hints not only help students shape their own material but also reinforce the qualities of effective writing highlighted in the "Understanding Technique" questions. Students thus see that their concerns are the same as those of professional writers.

Third, a number of the assignments call for *collaborative learning or investigation.* To gather material, to see various sides of an issue, to check the soundness of their thinking, students are encouraged to brainstorm with classmates, speak with friends, interview family members, or question "experts" on an issue. In this way, students are motivated to view writing not as a solitary act but as a community-shared practice within a particular context.

Finally, at least one of every three writing assignments is *linked* with another selection in the given thematic group. These linked assignments (indicated by a   ) help students see relationships among readings and, by broadening their perspectives, give them additional material to draw upon when they write.

Other Features

Many composition instructors emphasize that the traditional rhetorical patterns are strategies for helping writers meet their purpose. Such instructors need professional essays that illustrate real-world models of these patterns. To help instructors and students find appropriate models, *The Townsend Thematic Reader* provides an *alternate table of contents*, grouping selections according to the nine standard patterns of development: description, narration, illustration, process analysis, comparison-contrast, cause-effect, definition, division-classification, and argument-persuasion. Instructors who prefer to organize their courses according to these patterns will find that the book offers an engaging, high-interest collection of readings.

No matter how a course is organized, all instructors will appreciate the *Instructor's Manual* that accompanies the *Reader.* The manual provides a suggested syllabus, comprehensive answers to the "Understanding Content" and "Understanding Technique" questions, as well as possible directions the instructor might pursue as students discuss the "Thinking About Ideas" questions.

For years the two of us have have looked for an issues-centered reader like *The Townsend Thematic Reader.* With this book, we have a teaching resource that students like, use, and can afford. And we have found that the book makes it easier for students to acquire several gifts that will enrich their lives: an enjoyment of nonfictional prose, an ability to analyze and interpret writing, and an exuberance for writing about ideas that matter. We're confident that other students and other instructors will share similar success with *The Townsend Thematic Reader.*

Acknowledgments

Like others venturing on similar endeavors, we have received help—indirectly and directly—from colleagues and friends too numerous to name. For those individuals, we hope we have shown our appreciation in other ways and at other times. There are, however, three individuals from the always-astute and ever-patient Townsend Press family whom we must acknowledge by name. Carole Mohr and Amy K. Fisher provided invaluable assistance along the way, especially with questions and assignments. And we reserve special thanks for Janet Mendell Goldstein, whose editorial suggestions and clear, crisp design made this a far better book than it otherwise would have been.

Finally, we would be remiss and thoughtless if we did not acknowledge the support and various kinds of sustenance offered by our individual families. Our heartfelt thanks go to Sandra, Conor, Tim, Hubert, and Edward.

Christopher G. Hayes
Patricia J. McAlexander

1

Making Choices

The Monsters in My Head

Frank Langella

For a child alone in bed at night, a monster can seem as real as the room. You may remember your own nighttime terrors. Perhaps you recall lying in bed stiff with fear as you heard noises or saw shadows outside your bedroom window. In this essay, Frank Langella tells what he has learned about fighting night monsters and also explains that they are just the first in a series of "monsters" we must deal with, most of which appear in broad daylight. The following selection first appeared as an "About Men" feature in The New York Times Magazine.

Words to Watch

tufts (1): bunches growing together at the base
clapboard (1): a type of house siding in which long
                 narrow boards overlap each other
amorphous (7): without a definite form
summer stock (7): summer theater productions
aloft (9): overhead

I was sure he was coming to get me. First a hard step on the   1
gravel and then a foot dragging behind. Step-drag, step-drag. I lay
frozen in my bed. The long alleyway between our family house and
the neighbor's was hardly three feet wide. It was dark and covered
with black dirt, gravel and tufts of weeds and grass just barely able
to survive the sunless space. The two windows of my room faced

the clapboard wall of our neighbor's house, and Venetian blinds remained permanently closed against the nonview.

It was the mid-1940s. I had just seen a movie about a $\quad$ 2 mummy. I don't remember the name of it. Just the image, so powerful even still, of a man wrapped in grayish cloth around his ankles, legs, body up to the top of his head. Eyes and mouth exposed, one arm drawn up against his chest, elbow close to his side, hand clawed. The other arm dangling alongside the leg that dragged. Several strips of cloth hung loosely from that arm, swaying with each step-drag, step-drag. I don't remember where he was coming from or going to in the movie. It doesn't really matter. I knew that he was coming for me.

For so many nights I heard him as I lay alone in my bed. My $\quad$ 3 heart pounded as I waited for the good foot to land. A pause, then the slow drag. I would get up from the bed, pull the blind as little as I could away from the glass; and, with my chin just a little over the window ledge, I would stare hard into the dark alley. There were no outdoor lights, so I never could see him clearly. But he was there. He stopped when he saw me. I would get back into bed and wait. He usually left. Sometimes I fell asleep, and he returned, waking me. Other nights, he spared me and moved on.

I never told anyone about him. I don't know why. Shame, I $\quad$ 4 suppose. It was that he seemed to be my private terror, and as much as I was frightened of him, I was also frightened of losing him. One night, he deserted me forever, and I was not to think of him again for forty years, until my own son, this year, at age four, began calling out in the night: "Daddy, Daddy! There's a monster in my room. Come kill him." His room, several floors above the street, looks out over a New York alleyway to a brick wall. The windows are covered with louvered shutters. I found him sitting up in bed, eyes wide, staring at the tilted louvers, pointing at his monster. "He's coming in the window, Daddy. He's going to get me."

I grabbed a pillow and did a dutiful daddy fight with the mon- $\quad$ 5 ster, backing him up against the closet door, beating him toward the shutters, leaping onto the window seat, and driving him back out into the night. He was a sizeless, faceless creature to me. My son told me he was blue, with big teeth.

This ritual went on for weeks. Sometimes, several times a $\quad$ 6 night. I continued my battle, and, as I tucked him back under the covers, I explained that Daddy would keep the monster from him always. I was bigger and stronger; as long as I was there, no monster was going to get my boy. I was wrong. No matter how hard I battled, the monster returned when my son wanted him to. I was forced to accept the fact that my macho approach to protecting him from his fears wasn't working. My dad never told me he would save me from my monsters. I don't think he knew they existed.

As I thought back to my mummy and his eventual disappearance, I realized that he had never really gone away. He was with me still. He changed shapes as rapidly as I grew up. He became a wild bear at the foot of my bed. Then, later, an amorphous flying object swooping over my head. In later years, he was my first day at kindergarten, the agony of my early attempts at the diving board. He was hurricanes and the ocean, a mysterious death next door to us, my brother's ability to outdo me in all sports. He was my hypodermic needles, even early haircuts. Still later, my first date, my first night away from home, at sixteen, alone in a small boardinghouse as an apprentice in summer stock. The first woman to say no, the first woman to say yes. And then, he became my ambition, my fear of failure, struggles with success, marriage, husbandhood, fatherhood. There's always a foot dragging somewhere in my mind, it seems.

My son called out again. This time I went into his room, turned on the light and sat down facing him. His eyes were wild with fear, wilder than the earlier nights we had gone through this ritual. I asked him to listen, but he couldn't hear me. He kept screaming and pointing at the windows. "Kill him, kill him for me, Daddy!" he cried. He grabbed the pillow and tried to get me to do my routine. I felt I needed to speak to him without the ritual happening first. When, at last, I could quiet him, I said with trembling voice that I was never going to kill the monster again. I explained that this was his monster. He had made him up, and only he could kill him. I told him that the monster was in his head and leapt out whenever he wanted him to. I said that he could make him go away whenever he chose, or that he could turn him into a friendly monster if he liked. He sat expressionless. He had never stared at me so hard. I said again that I would no longer perform this particular battle for him, but that I loved him and would always love him. A slow and overwhelmingly beautiful smile that I shall never forget came to his face and he said: "You mean, I can make him do anything I want?" "Yes," I said, "you're in charge of him."

I went back to bed and lay there waiting for the return of the   9
monster. He didn't come back that night and has never again appeared in that form. Sometimes he's being driven from the living
room by my son with his He-Man sword aloft, its scabbard stuck
down the back of his pajamas as he cries out, "I am The Power."
And sometimes he is under the covers in the big bed when the
whole family plays tent. We just ask him, politely, to leave. He
stays for dinner now and then. He's everything from ten feet tall to
a small tiny creature in the cup of my son's hand. He's blue, green,
and sometimes he's a she.

As my son grows, I know we will be able to face his monsters   10
together. And now, when all I was once so sure of has become a
mystery to me, I'm hoping he'll be able to help me face the un-
known ones yet to visit themselves upon me.

Understanding Content

1. What is the selection's main idea? If it is stated directly, locate
   the relevant sentence(s). If it is implied, state the main idea in
   your own words.

2. Why does Langella describe as "macho" his method of protecting his son (paragraph 6)? Why doesn't the method work?

3. After Langella tells his son that he can make the monster go
   away himself, "A slow and overwhelmingly beautiful smile . . .
   came to [the boy's] face." Why does the boy smile? What does
   he realize?

Understanding Technique

1. In paragraphs 1–3, Langella describes in considerable detail his
   childhood environment and his childhood monster. What do
   those descriptive details add to the essay? How do you think
   Langella intends the details to affect the reader? How do they
   help Langella achieve his purpose?

2. Although Langella writes largely about his son's monsters, his title—"The Monsters in My Head"—refers to his own monsters. Why do you suppose Langella worded the title as he did? How does this wording reflect Langella's main idea?

3. What does the concluding paragraph add to Langella's essay?

Thinking About Ideas

1. Did monsters haunt you as a child? If so, how did you deal with them? Did you tell the adults in your life about the monsters? Why or why not? If you have children, are they ever afraid of monsters? If so, how do you help them deal with their fears?

2. Can you think of any situations in which fear could be helpful? Explain.

3. Nowadays the movies and television programs that children watch are much more graphic than anything Langella saw when he was a boy. Do you know any young children who watch frightening movies or television shows? If you do, what do the children watch, and how do they react? How do you feel about both their viewing habits and their reactions? Explain.

Writing About Ideas

1. Write a *paragraph* about a monster you experienced as a child. You might begin with a sentence like this: "I will never forget the monster that haunted me when I was a child." Then go on to tell when the monster showed up, how it looked and acted, how you reacted to it, and how it eventually disappeared. Select details that convey how frightening the monster was and how terrified you were. If you had no such monster, make one up—or, alternatively, describe one you saw in a horror movie.

2. As Langella suggests, fears surface throughout our lives. Write an *essay* about a current fear that you would like to overcome. Explain the fear in detail. Exactly what are you afraid of? Why? What experiences have you had with the fear in the past? Who

could help you face the fear? What could you do to rise above the fear? Possible topics to consider: going to the dentist, getting shots at the doctor's office, asking someone for a date, making a speech, going on a job interview, eating alone in a restaurant, ending a relationship, getting married. You may use a serious tone or a more playfully humorous approach. James Lincoln Collier's "Anxiety: Challenge by Another Name" (page 14) might give you some insight into the positive value of facing and mastering your fear.

3. Like Langella's son, most children need help, from time to time, dealing with difficult situations. They may have to contend with a schoolyard bully, overcome painful shyness, negotiate with an unfair teacher, get along with a strict stepparent. Select one such situation, and write an *essay* showing what adults can do to help children cope with this particular problem. To gather material for your essay, you may want to talk to several parents, teachers, and children. Use their suggestions as well as your own experiences and observations to develop your points.

Tickets to Nowhere

Andy Rooney

We've all heard or read about lucky people who have won millions of lottery dollars. One California man, for example, won over ten million dollars on his very first lottery ticket. Stories like that are enough to keep many people hopefully "investing" in the lottery week after week. But Andy Rooney, in this essay from his syndicated column, has another story to tell.

Words to Watch

his ship would come in (3): he would get lucky
slithered (6): slid from side to side
fidgeted (12): moved nervously

Things never went very well for Jim Oakland. He dropped   1
out of high school because he was impatient to get rich but after
dropping out he lived at home with his parents for two years and
didn't earn a dime.

He finally got a summer job working for the highway depart-   2
ment holding up a sign telling oncoming drivers to be careful of the
workers ahead. Later that same year, he picked up some extra
money putting flyers under the windshield wipers of parked cars.

Things just never went very well for Jim and he was 23 before   3
he left home and went to Florida hoping his ship would come in
down there. He never lost his desire to get rich but first he needed
money for the rent so he took a job near Fort Lauderdale for $4.50

an hour servicing the goldfish aquariums kept by the cashier's counter in a lot of restaurants.

Jim was paid in cash once a week by the owner of the gold-   4
fish business and the first thing he did was go to the little convenience store near where he lived and buy $20 worth of lottery tickets. He was really determined to get rich.

A week ago, the lottery jackpot in Florida reached $54 mil-   5
lion. Jim woke up nights thinking what he could do with $54 million. During the days, he daydreamed about it. One morning he was driving along the main street in the boss's old pickup truck with six tanks of goldfish in back. As he drove past a BMW dealer, he looked at the new models in the window.

He saw the car he wanted in the showroom window but unfor-   6
tunately he didn't see the light change. The car in front of him stopped short and Jim slammed on his brakes. The fish tanks slid forward. The tanks broke, the water gushed out and the goldfish slithered and flopped all over the back of the truck. Some fell off into the road.

It wasn't a good day for the goldfish or for Jim, of course. He   7
knew he'd have to pay for the tanks and 75 cents each for the fish and if it weren't for the $54 million lottery, he wouldn't have known which way to turn. He had that lucky feeling.

For the tanks and the dead goldfish, the boss deducted $114   8
of Jim's $180 weekly pay. Even though he didn't have enough left for the rent and food, Jim doubled the amount he was going to spend on lottery tickets. He never needed $54 million more.

Jim had this system. He took his age and added the last four   9
digits of the telephone number of the last girl he dated. He called it his lucky number . . . even though the last four digits changed quite often and he'd never won with his system. Everyone laughed at Jim and said he'd never win the lottery.

Jim put down $40 on the counter that week and the man   10
punched out his tickets. Jim stowed them safely away in his wallet with last week's tickets. He never threw away his lottery tickets until at least a month after the drawing just in case there was some mistake. He'd heard of mistakes.

Jim listened to the radio all afternoon the day of the drawing.   11
The people at the radio station he was listening to waited for news

of the winning numbers to come over the wires and, even then, the announcers didn't rush to get them on. The station manager thought the people running the lottery ought to pay to have the winning numbers broadcast, just like any other commercial announcement.

Jim fidgeted while they gave the weather and the traffic and 12 the news. Then they played more music. All he wanted to hear were those numbers.

"Well," the radio announced said finally, "we have the lottery 13 numbers some of you have been waiting for. You ready?" Jim was ready. He clutched his ticket with the number 274802.

"The winning number," the announcer said, "is 860539. I'll 14 repeat that. 860539." Jim was still a loser.

I thought that, with all the human interest stories about lottery 15 winners, we ought to have a story about one of the several million losers.

Understanding Content

1. What is the selection's main idea? If it is stated directly, locate the relevant sentence(s). If it is implied, state the main idea in your own words.

2. Why was Jim forced to slam on his brakes? What had happened to make him brake so suddenly? How did Jim react to what happened? What does this reaction reveal about Jim's approach to life?

3. Rooney states that "the last four digits of the telephone number of the last girl [Jim] dated . . . changed quite often." What does this comment tell us about Jim?

Understanding Technique

1. Which do you think Rooney intended readers to believe as they read Jim's story—that Jim would win the lottery, or that he would lose? Do you think that Rooney deliberately led his readers astray? Why?

2. Why might Rooney have titled his essay "Tickets to Nowhere"? How many meanings can you come up with for this title? How do these various meanings enlarge the scope of Rooney's essay?

3. Rooney uses direct quotations in only one spot in his narrative. Where does he use them? Why do you think he dramatizes that particular part of the story with exact quotations?

Thinking About Ideas

1. Do you know anyone who, like Jim Oakland, depends more on luck than on hard work or ability? Do you respect the person? Why or why not? Why do you think he or she relies so heavily on luck? What advice would you give to this person? What advice would you give to Jim Oakland?

2. Jim wanted to get rich by being lucky. If you could have a large sum of money at the end of five years, how would you prefer to get it—through a lottery or by having somehow earned it? Why?

3. Think about the positive and negative aspects of lotteries. On balance, do you think they do more harm than good or vice versa? Explain.

Writing About Ideas

1. Although most people don't waste their lives pursuing random chance, everyone appreciates good luck. Write a *paragraph* about a time you had good luck. Perhaps you found a twenty-dollar bill, met your future spouse by accident, or ran into a long-lost childhood friend. Whatever you write about, explain the circumstances fully, providing enough descriptive detail so that readers understand why the experience was such a fortunate one. Alternatively, you may write a paragraph about a time you had unusually bad luck.

2. Should state governments be in the gambling business? Write an *essay* persuading readers that states either should or should not

run lotteries. To support your claim, use your personal experiences with lotteries and gambling; examples drawn from people you know or know of; and any relevant statistics, facts, and opinions you can find. To help you define your position, you may find it useful to interview friends and family members who do or do not buy lottery tickets.

CD 3. Rooney uses just one example to illustrate his stand on a controversial issue. Like Rooney, write an *essay* in which you take a position that doesn't have broad acceptance. Perhaps you argue that high schools should distribute birth-control devices to students or that alcohol should be banned on your college campus. Defend your position by describing in detail the experiences of one person, being sure to include persuasive details that support your main point. In your conclusion, clarify, as Rooney does, that the one person you're writing about is intended to illustrate a general point. Barbara Huttmann's "A Crime of Compassion" (page 37) is another essay in which a single compelling example is used to support a controversial point.

Anxiety:
Challenge by Another Name

James Lincoln Collier

What is your basis for making personal decisions? Do you aim to rock the boat as little as possible, choosing the easy, familiar path? There is comfort in sticking with what is safe and well-known, just as there is comfort in eating mashed potatoes. But James Lincoln Collier, author of numerous articles and books, decided soon after leaving college not to live a mashed-potato sort of life. In this essay, first published in Reader's Digest, *he tells how he learned to recognize the marks of a potentially exciting, growth-inducing experience, to set aside his anxiety, and to dive in.*

Words to Watch

fabled (2): very famous
daunted (2): discouraged
proposition (3): offer
confronted (6): faced
wavered (7): went back and forth between alternatives
venture (10): uncertain task
corollary (15): an idea that follows from another idea
subsequently (18): later

Between my sophomore and junior years at college, a chance   1
came up for me to spend the summer vacation working on a ranch

14

in Argentina. My roommate's father was in the cattle business, and he wanted Ted to see something of it. Ted said he would go if he could take a friend, and he chose me.

The idea of spending two months on the fabled Argentine Pampas[1] was exciting. Then I began having second thoughts. I had never been very far from New England, and I had been homesick my first weeks at college. What would it be like in a strange country? What about the language? And besides, I had promised to teach my younger brother to sail that summer. The more I thought about it, the more the prospect daunted me. I began waking up nights in a sweat.

In the end I turned down the proposition. As soon as Ted asked somebody else to go, I began kicking myself. A couple of weeks later I went home to my old summer job, unpacking cartons at the local supermarket, feeling very low. I had turned down something I wanted to do because I was scared, and had ended up feeling depressed. I stayed that way for a long time. And it didn't help when I went back to college in the fall to discover that Ted and his friend had had a terrific time.

In the long run that unhappy summer taught me a valuable lesson out of which I developed a rule for myself: *do what makes you anxious, don't do what makes you depressed.*

I am not, of course, talking about severe states of anxiety or depression, which require medical attention. What I mean is that kind of anxiety we call stage fright, butterflies in the stomach, a case of nerves—the feelings we have at a job interview, when we're giving a big party, when we have to make an important presentation at the office. And the kind of depression I am referring to is that downhearted feeling of the blues, when we don't seem to be interested in anything, when we can't get going and seem to have no energy.

I was confronted by this sort of situation toward the end of my senior year. As graduation approached, I began to think about taking a crack at making my living as a writer. But one of my professors was urging me to apply to graduate school and aim at a teaching career.

2

3

4

5

6

---

[1]A vast plain in south-central South America.

I wavered. The idea of trying to live by writing was scary—a   7
lot more scary then spending a summer on the Pampas, I thought.
Back and forth I went, making my decision, unmaking it. Suddenly,
I realized that every time I gave up the idea of writing, that sinking
feeling went through me; it gave me the blues.

The thought of graduate school wasn't what depressed me. It   8
was giving up on what deep in my gut I really wanted to do. Right
then I learned another lesson. To avoid that kind of depression meant,
inevitably, having to endure a certain amount of worry and concern.

The great Danish philosopher Soren Kierkegaard believed that   9
anxiety always arises when we confront the possibility of our own
development. It seems to be a rule of life that you can't advance
without getting that old, familiar, jittery feeling.

Even as children we discover this when we try to expand our-   10
selves by, say, learning to ride a bike or going out for the school
play. Later in life we get butterflies when we think about having
that first child, or uprooting the family from the old hometown to
find a better opportunity halfway across the country. Any time, it
seems, that we set out aggressively to get something we want, we
meet up with anxiety. And it's going to be our traveling companion,
at least part of the way, into any new venture.

When I first began writing magazine articles, I was frequently   11
required to interview big names—people like Richard Burton, Joan
Rivers, sex authority William Masters, baseball great Dizzy Dean.
Before each interview I would get butterflies and my hands would
shake.

At the time, I was doing some writing about music. And one   12
person I particularly admired was the great composer Duke
Ellington. On stage and on television, he seemed the very model of
the confident, sophisticated man of the world. Then I learned that
Ellington still got stage fright. If the highly honored Duke
Ellington, who had appeared on the bandstand some ten thousand
times over thirty years, had anxiety attacks, who was I to think I
could avoid them?

I went on doing those frightening interviews, and one day, as I   13
was getting onto a plane for Washington to interview columnist
Joseph Alsop, I suddenly realized to my astonishment that I was looking forward to the meeting. What had happened to those butterflies?

Well, in truth, they were still there, but there were fewer of 14
them. I had benefited, I discovered, from a process psychologists
call "extinction." If you put an individual in an anxiety-provoking
situation often enough, he will eventually learn that there isn't anything to be worried about.

Which brings us to a corollary to my basic rule: *you'll never* 15
eliminate anxiety by avoiding the things that caused it. I remember
how my son Jeff was when I first began to teach him to swim at the
lake cottage where we spent our summer vacations. He resisted, and
when I got him into the water he sank and sputtered and wanted to
quit. But I was insistent. And by summer's end he was splashing
around like a puppy. He had "extinguished" his anxiety the only
way he could—by confronting it.

The problem, of course, is that it is one thing to urge some- 16
body else to take on those anxiety-producing challenges; it is quite
another to get ourselves to do it.

Some years ago I was offered a writing assignment that would 17
require three months of travel through Europe. I had been abroad a
couple of times on the usual "If it's Tuesday this must be Belgium"[1]
trips, but I hardly could claim to know my way around the conti-
nent. Moreover, my knowledge of foreign languages was limited to
a little college French.

I hesitated. How would I, unable to speak the language, to- 18
tally unfamiliar with local geography or transportation systems, set
up interviews and do research? It seemed impossible, and with considerable regret I sat down to write a letter begging off. Halfway
through, a thought—which I subsequently made into another corollary to my basic rule—ran through my mind: *you can't learn if you*
don't try. So I accepted the assignment.

There were some bad moments. But by the time I had fin- 19
ished the trip I was an experienced traveler. And ever since, I have
never hesitated to head for even the most exotic of places, without
guides or even advanced bookings, confident that somehow I will
manage.

————————

[1]Reference to a film comedy about a group of American tourists who visited too many European countries in too little time.

The point is that the new, the different, is almost by definition   20
scary. But each time you try something, you learn, and as the learning piles up, the world opens to you.

I've made parachute jumps, learned to ski at 40, flown up the   21
Rhine in a balloon. And I know I'm going to go on doing such
things. It's not because I'm braver or more daring than others. I'm
not. But I don't let the butterflies stop me from doing what I want.
Accept anxiety as another name for challenge and you can accomplish wonders.

Understanding Content

1. What is the selection's main idea? If it is stated directly, locate
   the relevant sentence(s). If it is implied, state the main idea in
   your own words.

2. According to Collier, how can we know from our emotions
   when to accept a challenge? At what point in his life did Collier
   learn to trust these emotional reactions?

3. In what way does Collier believe anxiety is positive? How, according to him, can we eventually overcome our fears?

Understanding Technique

1. Near the beginning of his essay, Collier explains that when he
   talks about anxiety, he's not "talking about severe states of anxiety or depression, which require medical attention" (paragraph
   5). Why do you think Collier provides this clarification early
   on? What is its value?

2. Collier uses several personal examples in his essay. Find at least
   three instances of these examples and explain how each helps
   Collier to further his main point.

3. Collier presents three life rules he has developed. How does he
   signal each of these rules? Why do you think he chose not to
   present all three rules at the beginning of the essay? What might
   have been lost had he done so?

Thinking About Ideas

1. Collier tries to persuade his readers to accept as a challenge those things that make them anxious. Do you agree or disagree with his point of view? Support your answer using incidents from your own experience.

2. What strategies have you developed to help deal with the anxiety you experience facing new or difficult situations?

3. Like most people, at one time or another, you probably decided not to take on the challenge of a new, anxiety-producing experience. How did you feel about yourself and your decision? Did the decision necessarily work against your best interests? Explain.

Writing About Ideas

1. Collier explains how his life experiences made him view the term "anxiety" in a new way. Write a *paragraph* in which you also redefine a term according to your own personal experience. You might want to write about a term such as "success," "failure," "disability," "homesickness," or "maturity." Consider beginning your paragraph with a sentence like this: "My first few months of college taught me a new meaning of _____."

2. Collier describes what is essentially his "philosophy of life"— the three rules by which he lives. In an *essay,* illustrate your philosophy of life. Start by sharing with readers the two or three central rules that guide your life. Then, devoting a separate paragraph to each rule, describe at least one experience that led you to develop that particular rule. End by explaining briefly the effect on you of your overall philosophy of life.

∞ 3. Like adults, children often have difficulty adapting to change. Focusing on a specific situation that tends to overwhelm children, write an *essay* explaining what parents and/or schools can do to encourage youngsters to accept new challenges. Develop your discussion by drawing on your own and other people's experiences. Frank Langella's "The Monsters in My Head" (page 3) offers one example of a father who helps a child rise to a challenge and master a fear.

To Get a Story, I Flimflammed a Dead Man's Mother

Bob Teague

No matter where we live or travel, we have a pretty good idea about what to expect from television news. We flip on the set and there they are again: the accident or murder victim, the grieving relatives, the compassionate yet professional reporter on the scene. What we don't see from our side of the tube is the pressure on the reporter to provide certain elements: the exclusive interview, the intimate emotion, the surprising side angle. In this excerpt from his book, Live and Off-Color: News Biz, *Bob Teague draws upon his twenty years with New York's WNBC-TV to describe the twilight areas of morality that reporters enter in order to get a scoop.*

Words to Watch

flimflammed (title): tricked
pathos (2): ability to arouse pity
rancor (12): resentment
speculating (21): guessing
tirade (22): long, forceful speech
vested interests (25): people with something to gain
protocols (25): customs and rules
circumvent (25): get around
perpetrated (26): committed
gaucheries (28): actions in bad taste

quid pro quo (37):   something given in exchange for
something else
mitigated (37): reduced
indiscretions (37): small sins

Working the street as a local TV reporter often makes it   1
necessary to grow a callus on your heart. When covering a murder,
for example, you have to delve into the gruesome details of the
bloodletting. If at all possible, you must also show the victim's
friends or family, preferably in a rage or in tears. If you are covering a political campaign, you must goad the candidates into spitting
obscenities at each other. Like: "He said you're incompetent and
unqualified. What's your reaction to that?"

Even when you feel that you are doing something disgusting,   2
or merely in bad taste—displaying insensitivity to the point of
being inhuman—you have to hang tough and follow through, like
sticking a mike under the nose of a weeping old woman whose
grandson has been stabbed to death in a New York gang rumble. I
did all that and worse. It came with the territory. If I failed to do it
for dear old Channel 4, some other streetwalker made of sterner
stuff would certainly do it for dear old Channel 2, Channel 5 or
Channel 7. And if my masters saw that kind of pathos on a competing station—they all had a shelf full of TV monitors in their
offices—they would ask me, "Where were you when Channel
Blank was getting the good stuff?" No one has yet devised a satisfactory answer to that one.

My friend Gloria Rojas of Channel 7 says that's exactly what   3
happened to her in covering the aftermath of a plane crash. While
other members of the Eyewitness News team blanketed the crash
site, Gloria was sent to the nearest hospital. "What a scene," she
told me. "Chaos all over the place. I just walked into the emergency
section with my crew, and nobody tried to stop us. We took pictures
of the injured, some of them barely conscious, struggling to live. I
didn't want to bother any of them. Just being there meant that we
were increasing their chances of infection. So we just took pictures,
talked with one of the surgeons, then packed up to leave. That's
when a reporter from Channel 11 showed up with his crew and

started interviewing some of the victims, including a guy who was obviously dying. I said to myself: This is an abomination. I am not going to stoop to anything so gross. I'm going to leave.

"Back at the station," Gloria went on, "our executive pro-   4
ducer saw Channel 11's exclusive on the 10 o'clock news. He wanted to know whether I'd interviewed the same guy or even somebody else in critical condition. When I said I had decided not to do it as a matter of decency, he damn near had a fit. He said I should have done it, too. So what finally happened was, our station called Channel 11 and begged a copy of their tape. We ran the interview on our program at 11 with a credit line that said, 'Courtesy of WPIX.' I was so mad I couldn't even cry."

The fact is, you never know which of the many damned-if-   5
you-do, damned-if-you-don't choices you will have to make on a given day.

Once upon a time in the Bronx, police discovered several tons   6
of toxic chemicals illegally dumped on scattered vacant lots—a menace to neighborhood youngsters. An enterprising Channel 2 reporter, poking through an isolated pile of glass and cardboard containers being collected by sanitation trucks, found a ledger. It gave away the manufacturer's name and address, with a catalogue of the lethal compounds in that load.

"After doing my stand-upper with the ledger," the WCBS   7
man said later, "I planned to turn it over to the cops. Then a Channel 7 reporter showed up with his crew. I decided to share the ledger with him. You know, like some day I'll be the guy playing catch-up and maybe he will give me a clue.

"You won't believe this, but he put the ledger back in the pile,   8
hiding it under some boxes. Then, with his camera rolling, he starts prowling through the stuff. All of a sudden he picks it up, turns to the camera and says, 'Look what I've found.'

"I was so mad I could have killed him. No point in trying to   9
talk him out of it. I knew that. So after giving the ledger to the cops, I called his boss [then news director Ron Tindiglia] at Channel 7. Tindiglia thanked me. 'I'll take care of it,' he said. Tindiglia is a gentleman. That crummy bit with the ledger never got on the air."

The line between creative coverage and faking the news is a   10
thin one indeed. The WABC reporter, however, had clearly gone too far.

Conflicts between local newspeople rarely involve questions 11
of that magnitude. A typical hassle developed between Heather
Bernard of Channel 4 and Arnold Diaz of Channel 2 on the hottest
story in New Jersey at that time. The family of Karen Anne Quinlan
was in a legal battle with the state for the right to disconnect the
life-support apparatus that prevented their comatose daughter from
"dying with dignity." When Heather reached the home of the
Quinlan family, several competing camera teams were standing in
line at the front door awaiting their turns to shoot.

"Arnold Diaz was next in line ahead of me," Heather recalled 12
with rancor. "The other crews ahead of us took only fifteen to
twenty minutes each. Arnold was in there for over an hour. I was
furious. Finally, I went inside to see what the heck was taking so
long. I couldn't believe it. His crew was all packed up. He was sitting at the table with the Quinlans, having lunch.

"OK. The family had to eat anyway. No harm done. Then as 13
they finished lunch—Arnold and his crew were starting to leave—I
noticed a stack of letters on a table in the corner. I made the mistake
of asking Mrs. Quinlan about all that mail. She said it was the letters and cards they had received in recent weeks expressing
sympathy for their daughter and the family. Arnold had missed that
angle completely. Now he tells his crew to unpack their gear. He
wants to do another sound bite and shoot the letters. I grab him by
the arm and say, 'Arnold, come on. Enough is enough.'

"We had such a big argument about it that Mrs. Quinlan but- 14
ted in. 'Now, children. No fighting in this house.' Arnold backed off
and I did my piece first.

"The next day he called NBC and told [then news director] 15
Earl Ubell that Heather Bernard had been bitchy and obnoxious,
very unprofessional on the Quinlan story. When I saw Arnold again
a day later, I thanked him. I said: 'NBC had been threatening to fire
me because they said I'm not aggressive enough in the field. You've
saved my job.'"

If your zeal propels you into conflict with another reporter, 16
you can huff and puff with reckless abandon. You know the other
guy does not want to risk damage to his money-in-the-bank profile
or risk a multimillion-dollar lawsuit for damaging yours.

From Square One of my career in the news biz, I had bent my 17
personal rules of good conduct, decency and integrity again and

again to get news stories on the tube. Sure, I worried about it some, but I kept on doing it. One particular incident in the field, though, left me with a churning knot of self-loathing. In Coney Island, covering the suicide leap of a twenty-three-year-old man from the roof of a twenty-one-story apartment building, I flimflammed the dead man's mother into giving me the exclusive sound bite I needed to flesh out my scenario. My excuse was: Who knows what Channel 2 or Channel 7 might have filmed before I reached the scene some three hours later?

After picking the brains of neighbors who had known the victim, I still had no idea why he did it. There was no suicide note. My cameraman suggested that somebody in the family might be able to fill in the blank, and added that they also might have a picture of the guy that we could put on film.   18

I didn't hesitate. Nothing seemed more important than getting those elements.   19

The man's mother, a middle-aged, red-eyed widow in a blue-and-white flower-print kimono, cracked the door only an inch or so when I rang her bell. She did not want to go on television. "Go away," she sobbed. "I'm in mourning."   20

In my best phony sympathetic manner I advised her that neighbors were saying that her son had killed himself because he was heavily into hard drugs. "They're claiming he started selling it, then got hooked on scag himself. I'd hate to put that on the air if it's not true. I'm sure your son was a decent guy. Unless I get the real story from you, I'll have no choice." The truth is, only one person, speculating off-camera, had suggested any such thing. Nevertheless, it worked.   21

While the camera rolled, the woman launched into an anguished tirade against people who will say anything to get on TV. Then she told me that her son had been depressed for several days. His nineteen-year-old girl friend had been devastated by his confession that he also liked to have sex with men occasionally; she had broadcast his shame to their friends.   22

That interview—plus an exclusive snapshot of the dead man—boosted my stock in the trade but not with my girl friend at that time. As the two of us watched that story on the TV set in my pad, she accused me with her eyes and with the question: "Wouldn't it have been better to let the reason for his suicide remain a mystery,   23 to spare his mother that kind of useless humiliation?"

I didn't know the answer at that point. I was trying to come to   24
grips with the problem.

A willingness to defy authorities is one of several personality   25
traits you have to develop to be effective as a streetwalker. In many
instances, the story you're out to cover is not just lying there for the
taking. It is hidden by vested interests and protected by protocols.
To circumvent them and get the story, you may, for example, imply
to a stubborn, tight-lipped district attorney that you already know
more than he has told you—to draw him out at least far enough to
confirm your hunches. You may ignore "No Trespassing" signs and
sneak into a mental hospital where you have reason to believe that
the patients are being mistreated. You may walk into someone's
home or office with a concealed microphone and a camera that appears to be inactive, to catch the person off guard.

Deceitful? Yes, but morally correct in my judgment. Long be-   26
fore my time, society gave journalists the right to play by a slightly
different set of rules. We are not, of course, above the law. On the
other hand, some white lies and deceits can be justified if perpetrated solely for the purpose of digging up the truth and airing it,
but not for the purpose of sensation-mongering as I did with the
poor woman whose son committed suicide. Realizing that, belat-
edly, I never again went that far.

Witnesses on Bleecker Street in Greenwich Village reported   27
that one building superintendent shot his next-door counterpart to
death—the bloody climax of a long-running feud over who had
been putting garbage in front of whose building on the sly. The
dead man left a wife and two preteen-age children.

On this story, I vowed in advance, I was not going to be insen-   28
sitive for a change. Instead, I would show compassion by leaving
the bereaved survivors alone. I would use only sound bites of neighbors and homicide detectives on the case. Which was exactly how I
did it at first. I could afford to on this particular outing; no other
newsreel was present to coerce me into typical gaucheries.

My crew were packing their gear in the trunk, ready to leave   29
Bleecker Street, when two urchins with dirty faces tugged my
elbow. "Put us on TV, mister. We saw the whole thing."

I explained that I already had interviewed witnesses. I didn't   30
need them.

"But it was our father who got killed," one of the boys   31
pleaded.

My professional instincts got the better of me. Since they had   32
volunteered, I could put them on-camera with a relatively clear con-
science. And great God in the foothills, what terrific sound bites
they gave me! In simple, dramatic sentences, they took turns telling
what they heard, what they saw. They could have been talking
about the death of an alien from Mars. "And pow. He shot my father
in the eye."

Again, my crew and I started to leave. An old guy wearing   33
shabby and shapeless clothes tugged by elbow. "She's waiting for
you," he announced. He pointed toward a frail young Puerto Rican
woman in tears. She was wearing what had to be the prettiest dress
she owned.

"The victim's wife?" I inquired.   34

The old man in the baggy suit nodded. "Yes, my granddaugh-   35
ter. She's waiting for you."

Reluctantly, I shoved the microphone under her quivering,   36
freshly painted lips. She wailed about the loss of her husband, wept
without embarrassment. Great TV. Some of her tears fell on my
hand. That's when I got the message; she, as well as her kids,
wanted the whole damn world to share their grief.

Experiences in that vein allowed me to feel more comfortable   37
in my television role. There was a quid pro quo that mitigated my
indiscretions to some degree. Just as I used people to suit my purposes, they used me. Why not? Television belonged to everybody.

Understanding Content

1. What is the selection's main idea? If it is stated directly, locate
the relevant sentence(s). If it is implied, state the main idea in
your own words.

2. How does Teague feel about having tricked the suicide victim's
mother into talking to him? How does Teague's girlfriend feel
about it?

3. Judging from his statements and examples, what are Teague's
standards for being a good television reporter? Which kinds of

behavior does he consider appropriate? Which does he consider inappropriate?

Understanding Technique

1. Reread the essay, noting how many separate examples Teague cites. What do all these examples have in common? Why do you think Teague arranges them in the order he does?

2. Review the incident (paragraphs 17–23) from which Teague derives the title of his essay. What strategies does he use to make the incident dramatic and immediate?

3. Teague uses strong, emotional language to describe TV news reporters. For example, he refers to them as "streetwalkers" (paragraphs 2 and 25). Why do you suppose he uses this word? What is its effect? Find other examples in the essay of emotionally charged language, and explain how these examples help reinforce Teague's main point.

Thinking About Ideas

1. Do you think a news reporter should be permitted to invade the privacy of anyone who is "in the news"—for example, the family member of a victim or a celebrity accused of wrongdoing? Should a reporter have the right to take people's pictures or use what they say without their permission or knowledge? Why or why not?

2. Do you think there are some news stories that should never, under any circumstances, be shown on television? If so, what are some examples, and why shouldn't these stories be shown?

3. Teague's last example illustrates the strong desire that many people have to appear on television news, often at the expense of their privacy and dignity. Where else on television can you find evidence of this pressing desire? Would you want to appear on television if you were experiencing personal difficulty? Why or why not?

Writing About Ideas

⊂⊃ 1. In paragraph 2, Teague says that sometimes a reporter just has "to hang tough and follow through." The same can be said about anyone—athletes, parents, students, employees, for instance. Write a *paragraph* about an incident during which you or someone you know well had to "hang tough and follow through." Be sure to provide vivid details to illustrate the challenge that had to be mastered. Before you write, you might want to read Frank Langella's "The Monsters in My Head" (page 3) and James Lincoln Collier's "Anxiety: Challenge by Another Name" (page 14) for the authors' views on confronting difficulties.

2. Teague points out that intense competition among reporters is responsible for much of the insensitivity of TV news. In an *essay,* explore the consequences of intense competition in another area of life—for example, on the job, in a family, during an athletic contest. Is the competition basically positive or negative? Support your conclusion with specific examples of what can happen when people compete fiercely for the same goal.

3. Teague suggests that some television reporters overstep the boundaries of decency when pursuing news stories. Imagine that you have been asked to prepare a set of guidelines for members of another group of individuals—perhaps college professors, medical doctors, telephone solicitors, or parents of adolescents. Present and defend your guidelines in an *essay.* Consider beginning with a vivid incident dramatizing the overall need for such guidelines. As you present each guideline, explain its importance and how it should be implemented. When discussing the guidelines, present them in order of importance, either from most to least important or vice versa, and explain fully the reasons underlying each guideline.

The Bystander Effect

Dorothy Barkin

A few years ago, thirty-eight people witnessed a brutal attack—and hardly raised a finger to stop it. That kind of unwillingness to get involved is the topic of this article by journalist Dorothy Barkin, who analyzes the confusion and lack of responsibility bystanders often feel when witnessing a crime or medical emergency. She begins by describing four crisis situations—and placing you right there at the scene. How would you react?

Words to Watch

phenomena (4): facts
ambiguity (29): uncertainty
diffuses (32): spreads out

It is a pleasant fall afternoon. The sun is shining. You are   1
heading toward the parking lot after your last class of the day. All
of a sudden, you come across the following situations. What do you
think you'd do in each case?

Situation One: A man in his early twenties dressed in jeans
and a T-shirt is using a coat hanger to pry open a door of a
late-model car. An overcoat and camera are visible on the
back seat of the car. You're the only one who sees this.

Situation Two: A man and woman are fighting physically. The
woman is in tears. Attempting to fight the man off, she

29

screams, "Who are you? Get away from me!" You're the only one who witnesses this.

Situation Three: Imagine the same scenario as in Situation Two except that this time the woman screams, "I don't know why I ever married you! Get away from me!"

Situation Four: Again imagine Situation Three. This time, however, there are a few other people (strangers to you and each other) who also observe the incident.

Many people would choose not to get involved in situations like these. Bystanders are often reluctant to intervene in criminal or medical emergencies for reasons they are well aware of. They fear possible danger to themselves or getting caught up in a situation that could lead to complicated and time-consuming legal proceedings. 2

There are, however, other, less obvious factors which influence the decision to get involved in emergency situations. Complex psychological factors, which many are unaware of, play an important part in the behavior of bystanders; knowing about these factors can help people to act more responsibly when faced with emergencies. 3

To understand these psychological phenomena, it is helpful to look at what researchers have learned about behavior in the situations like the ones mentioned above. 4

Situation One: Research reveals a remarkably low rate of by-stander intervention to protect property. In one study, more than 3,000 people walked past 214 staged car break-ins like the one described in this situation. The vast majority of passers-by completely ignored what appeared to be a crime in progress. Not one of the 3000 bothered to report the incident to the police.

Situation Two: Another experiment involved staging scenarios like this and the next situation. In Situation Two, bystanders offered some sort of assistance to the young woman 65 percent of the time.

Situation Three: Here the rate of bystander assistance dropped down to 19 percent. This demonstrates that bystanders are more reluctant to help a woman when they believe she's fighting with her husband. Not only do they consider a wife in less need of help; they think interfering with a married couple may be more dangerous. The husband, unlike a stranger, will not flee the situation.

Situation Four: The key point in this situation is that there are several bystanders present. In more than fifty studies involving many different conditions, one outcome has been consistent: bystanders are much less likely to get involved when other witnesses are present than when they are alone.

Thus, membership in a group of bystanders lowers the likeli- 5 hood of each member of the group becoming involved. This finding may seem surprising. You might think there would be safety in numbers and that being a member of a group would increase the likelihood of intervention. How can we explain this aspect of group behavior?

A flood of research has tried to answer this and other ques- 6 tions about emergency bystanders ever since the infamous case of the murder of Kitty Genovese.

In 1964 in the borough of Queens in New York City, 7 Catherine "Kitty" Genovese, 28, was brutally murdered in a shocking crime that outraged the nation.

The crime began at 3 a.m. Kitty Genovese was coming home 8 from her job as manager of a bar. After parking her car in a parking lot, she began the hundred-foot walk to the entrance of her apartment. But she soon noticed a man in the lot and decided instead to walk toward a police call box. As she walked by a bookstore on her way there, the man grabbed her. She screamed.

Lights went on and windows opened in the ten-story apart- 9 ment building.

Next, the attacker stabbed Genovese. She shrieked, "Oh, my 10 God, he stabbed me! Please help me! Please help me!"

From an upper window in the apartment house, a man 11 shouted, "Let that girl alone!"

The assailant, alarmed by the man's shout, started toward his 12 car, which was parked nearby. However, the lights in the building soon went out, and the man returned. He found Genovese struggling to reach her apartment—and stabbed her again.

She screamed, "I'm dying! I'm dying!" 13

Once more lights went on and windows opened in the apart-   14
ment building. The attacker then went to his car and drove off.
Struggling, Genovese made her way inside the building.

But the assailant returned to attack Genovese yet a third time.   15
He found her slumped on the floor at the foot of the stairs and
stabbed her again, this time fatally.

The murder took over a half hour, and Kitty Genovese's des-   16
perate cries for help were heard by at least thirty-eight people. Not
a single one of the thirty-eight who later admitted to having witnessed the murder bothered to pick up the phone during the attack
and call the police. One man called after Genovese was dead.

Comments made by bystanders after this murder provide im-   17
portant insight into what group members think when they consider
intervening in an emergency.

These are some of the comments: 18

"I didn't want my husband to get involved."   19

"Frankly, we were afraid."   20

"We thought it was a lovers' quarrel."   21

"I was tired."   22

The Genovese murder sparked a national debate on the ques-   23
tions of public apathy and fear and became the basis for thousands
of sermons, editorials, classroom discussions, and even a made-for-
television movie. The same question was on everybody's
mind—how could thirty-eight people have done so little?

Nine years later, another well-publicized incident provided   24
additional information about the psychology of a group witnessing
a crime.

On a summer afternoon in Trenton, New Jersey, a twenty-   25
year-old woman was brutally raped in a parking lot in full view of
twenty-five employees of a nearby roofing company. Though the
workers witnessed the entire incident and the woman repeatedly
screamed for help, no one came to her assistance.

Comments made by witnesses to the rape were remarkably   26
similar to those made by the bystanders to the Genovese murder.
For example, one witness said, "We thought, well, it might turn out
to be her boyfriend or something like that."

It's not surprising to find similar excuses for not helping in   27
cases involving a group of bystanders. The same psychological
principles apply to each. Research conducted since the Genovese

murder indicates that the failure of bystanders to get involved can't be simply dismissed as a symptom of an uncaring society. Rather, the bystander effect, as it is called by social scientists, is the product of a complex set of psychological factors.

Two factors appear to be most important in understanding the reactions of bystanders to emergencies. 28

First is the level of ambiguity involved in the situation. Bystanders are afraid to endanger themselves or look foolish if they take the wrong action in a situation they're not sure how to interpret. A person lying face down on the floor of a subway train may have just suffered a heart attack and be in need of immediate medical assistance—or he may be a dangerous drunk. 29

Determining what is happening is especially difficult when a man is attacking a woman. Many times lovers do quarrel, sometimes violently. But they may strongly resent an outsider, no matter how well-meaning, intruding into their affairs. 30

When a group of bystanders is around, interpreting an event can be even more difficult than when one is alone. Bystanders look to others for cues as to what is happening. Frequently other witnesses, just as confused, try to look calm. Thus bystanders can mislead each other about the seriousness of an incident. 31

The second factor in determining the reactions of bystanders to emergencies is what psychologists call the principle of moral diffusion. Moral diffusion is the lessening of a sense of individual responsibility when someone is a member of a group. Responsibility to act diffuses throughout the crowd. When a member of the group is able to escape the collective paralysis and take action, others in the group tend to act as well. But the larger the crowd, the greater the diffusion of responsibility, and the less likely someone is to intervene. 32

The more social scientists are able to teach us about how bystanders react to emergencies, the better the chances that we will take appropriate action when faced with one. Knowing about moral diffusion, for example, makes it easier for us to escape it. If you find yourself witnessing an emergency with a group, remember that everybody is waiting for someone else to do something first. If you take action, others may also help. 33

Also realize that any one of us could at some time be in desperate need of help. Imagine what it feels like to need help and have a 34

crowd watching you suffer and doing nothing. Remember Kitty
Genovese.

Understanding Content

1. What is the selection's main idea? If it is stated directly, locate
   the relevant sentence(s). If it is implied, state the main idea in
   your own words.

2. According to Barkin, what two factors explain why bystanders
   fail to get involved in emergencies? How do those factors keep a
   witness from acting?

3. Barkin states, "Bystanders look to others for cues as to what is
   happening. Frequently other witnesses, just as confused, try to
   look calm." Why do you think witnesses would try to look calm
   during an emergency?

Understanding Technique

1. At the beginning of her essay, Barkin writes, "All of a sudden,
   you come across the following situations. What do you think
   you'd do in each case?" Why do you suppose Barkin uses the
   second person ("you") in the essay's opening? Why do you suppose she returns to the second person in the final two
   paragraphs?

2. Why might Barkin have decided to list and label the four situations in the first paragraph? What would have been lost if she
   had presented one situation after another—without labels—in
   conventional paragraph format?

3. Barkin could have summarized the story of the Genovese murder in one or two short paragraphs (as she did with the Trenton
   rape story). Instead, she chose to narrate the Genovese murder
   at some length, using suspense, specific details, the victim's ex-
   clamations, and witnesses' remarks. Why do you think she
   described the event in such detail? What does her detailed narrative add to the essay?

Thinking About Ideas

1. In the last paragraph, Barkin writes, "Imagine what it feels like to need help and have a crowd watching you suffer and doing nothing." Have you ever observed or been in such a situation, or do you know someone who has? What was the situation, and how did witnesses react?

2. How could you use the information Barkin provides to counteract the bystander effect? For instance, if you were in a group of onlookers while a fight was in progress, what might you do to encourage your own—and other people's—intervention?

3. One witness to the Trenton rape said, "We thought, well, it might turn out to be her boyfriend or something like that." If the rapist had been her boyfriend—or her husband—should witnesses have refrained from interfering? Why or why not?

Writing About Ideas

1. Barkin writes about the impact of emergency situations on people's behavior. Selecting a lighter, less serious topic, write a *paragraph* in which you show the effects of some other factor on the way people act. You might, for example, write about the effects of final exams on college students, the impact of football season on family life, or the influence of the remote control on people's television-viewing habits. Discuss at least two effects, illustrating each with lively examples from your own experiences or those of people you know.

2. Despite the reluctance of bystanders, most of us know someone who has gone to great trouble to help others. Write an *essay* showing how a witness to an event went out of his or her way to help someone in need. Explain specifically what the problem was (perhaps it was a crime, a car accident, or a health emergency), what the witness did, and how the situation turned out. Include clear, striking details to help your reader picture the sequence of events. In your conclusion, you may wish to explain how the situation could have turned out if help had not been given.

○○ 3. Select another situation in which people sometimes fail to act responsibly. Then write an *essay* exploring the reasons for this failure. You could, for example, write about why some parents adopt a "hands-off" approach to disciplining their children, why some college students fail to pay back their academic loans, or why some teachers adopt a slap-dash approach to grading student work. Discuss some of the more subtle and complex reasons for people's behavior, and be sure to provide convincing examples to illustrate your points. Speaking to others who share your concern will help you develop insight into the situation. For another perspective on the clash between people's finer impulses and their baser instincts, you might want to read Bob Teague's "To Get a Story, I Flimflammed a Dead Man's Mother" (page 20).

A Crime of Compassion

Barbara Huttmann

The cycle of life sounds simple: We are born, we live, then we die. Only just as "When does life begin?" has become a focus of heated debate, so has the question "When should life end?" In "A Crime of Compassion," nurse Barbara Huttmann tells us about her patient Mac. Mac's case raises an issue that many families, as well as health professionals, will someday confront: Are we morally justified in refusing medical care that would prolong life—our own or that of a loved one? For Huttman, the question found its answer when she faced the decision of whether to resuscitate Mac yet again. "A Crime of Compassion" first appeared on the "My Turn" page of Newsweek magazine.

Words to Watch

resuscitated (3): brought back to life
haggard (5): worn out
IV (6): given by an intravenous injection into a vein
irrigate (7): wash out
lucid (10): clear-minded
infusing (10): filling
impotence (10): powerlessness
imperative (11): requirement
riddled (13): pierced
clutch (15): tight grip
pallor (15): paleness

"Murderer," a man shouted. "God help patients who get   1
you for a nurse."

"What gives you the right to play God?" another one asked.   2

It was the Phil Donahue show where the guest is a fatted calf   3
and the audience a two-hundred-strong flock of vultures hungering
to pick up the bones. I had told them about Mac, one of my favorite
cancer patients. "We resuscitated him fifty-two times in just one
month. I refused to resuscitate him again. I simply sat there and
held his hand while he died."

There wasn't time to explain that Mac was a young, witty,   4
macho cop who walked into the hospital with thirty-two pounds of
attack equipment, looking as if he could single-handedly protect the
whole city, if not the entire state. "Can't get rid of this cough," he
said. Otherwise, he felt great.

Before the day was over, tests confirmed that he had lung can-   5
cer. And before the year was over, I loved him, his wife, Maura, and
their three kids as if they were my own. All the nurses loved him.
And we all battled his disease for six months without ever giving
death a thought. Six months isn't such a long time in the whole
scheme of things, but it was long enough to see him lose his youth,
his wit, his macho, his hair, his bowel and bladder control, his sense
of taste and smell, and his ability to do the slightest thing for himself. It was long enough to watch Maura's transformation from a
young woman into a haggard, beaten old lady.

When Mac had wasted away to a sixty-pound skeleton kept   6
alive by liquid food we poured down a tube, IV solutions we
dripped into his veins, and oxygen we piped to a mask on his face,
he begged us: "Mercy . . . for God's sake, please just let me go."

Miracles: The first time he stopped breathing, the nurse   7
pushed the button that calls a "code blue" throughout the hospital
and sends a team rushing to resuscitate the patient. Each time he
stopped breathing, sometimes two or three times in one day, the
code team came again. The doctors and technicians worked their
miracles and walked away. The nurses stayed to wipe the saliva that
drooled from his mouth, irrigate the big craters of bedsores that covered his hips, suction the lung fluids that threatened to drown him,
clean the feces that burned his skin like lye, pour the liquid food
down the tube attached to his stomach, put pillows between his

knees to ease the bone-on-bone pain, turn him every hour to keep the bedsores from getting worse, and change his gown and linen every two hours to keep him from being soaked in perspiration.

At night I went home and tried to scrub away the smell of de-   8 caying flesh that seemed woven into the fabric of my uniform. It was in my hair, the upholstery of my car—there was no washing it away. And every night I prayed that his agonized eyes would never again plead with me to let him die.

Every morning I asked the doctor for a "no code" order.   9 Without that order, we had to resuscitate every patient who stopped breathing. His doctor was one of the several who believe we must extend life as long as we have the means and knowledge to do it. To not do it is to be liable for negligence, at least in the eyes of many people, including some nurses. I thought about what it would be like to stand before a judge, accused of murder, if Mac stopped breathing and I didn't call a code.

And after the fifty-second code, when Mac was still lucid   10 enough to beg for death again, and Maura was crumbled in my arms again, and when no amount of pain medication stilled his moaning and agony, I wondered about a spiritual judge. Was all this misery and suffering supposed to be building character or infusing us all with the sense of humility that comes from impotence?

Had we, the whole medical community, become so arrogant   11 that we believed in the illusion of salvation through science? Had we become so self-righteous that we thought meddling in God's work was our duty, our moral imperative, and our legal obligation? Did we really believe that we had the right to force "life" on a suffering man who had begged for the right to die?

Such questions haunted me more than ever early one morning   12 when Maura went home to change her clothes and I was bathing Mac. He had been still for so long, I thought he at last had the blessed relief of coma. Then he opened his eyes and moaned, "Pain . . . no more . . . Barbara . . . do something . . . God, let me go."

Death: The desperation in the eyes and voice riddled me with   13 guilt. "I'll stop," I told him as I injected the pain medication.

I sat on the bed and held Mac's hands in mine. He pressed his   14 bony fingers against my hand and muttered, "Thanks." Then there was the one soft sigh and I felt his hands go cold in mine. "Mac?" I whispered, as I waited for his chest to rise and fall again.

A clutch of panic banded my chest, drew my finger to the   15
code button, urged me to do something, anything . . . but sit there
alone with death. I kept one finger on the button, without pressing
it, as a waxen pallor slowly transformed his face from person to
empty shell. Nothing I've ever done in my forty-seven years has
taken so much effort as it took not to press that code button.

Eventually, when I was as sure as I could be that the code   16
team would fail to bring him back, I entered the legal twilight zone
and pushed the button. The team tried. And while they were trying,
Maura walked in the room and shrieked, "No . . . don't let them do
this to him . . . for God's sake . . . please, no more."

Cradling her in my arms was like cradling myself, Mac, and   17
all those patients and nurses who had been in this place before who
do the best they can in a death-denying society.

So a TV audience accused me of murder. Perhaps I am guilty.   18
If a doctor had written a no-code order, which is the only legal alternative, would he have felt any less guilty? Until there is
legislation making it a criminal act to code a patient who has requested the right to die, we will all of us risk the same fate as Mac.
For whatever reason, we developed the means to prolong life, and
now we are forced to use it. We do not have the right to die.

Understanding Content

1. What is the selection's main idea? If it is stated directly, locate
   the relevant sentence(s). If it is implied, state the main idea in
   your own words.

2. What is a "code blue"? Why was it used so often for Mac during his stay in the hospital? Why, finally, did it not work?

3. How did Mac feel about continuing to live? Why did he feel this
   way? Compare his attitude with the attitudes of his wife, his
   doctor, and his nurse (Huttmann).

Understanding Technique

1. Why do you think Huttmann begins her story by quoting audience members of the *Donahue* show? Why do you suppose she comes back to that TV audience in her last paragraph? Does she agree with their "verdict" on her? How can you tell?

2. Huttmann describes Mac both before and after his illness. Contrast the two descriptions. Which Mac does Huttmann spend more words describing? Why do you think she proceeds in this manner?

3. Although she begins by quoting members of the *Donahue* audience, after that, Huttmann tells almost all her story in her own words, only rarely citing what other people say. Who else does she quote? What do these direct quotations add to her narrative?

Thinking About Ideas

1. Huttmann titled her essay "A Crime of Compassion." Do you think Huttmann is guilty of a crime? If so, what crime? Which do you think is more important, her crime or her compassion?

2. Who do you think should decide whether an incurably ill patient should be allowed to die—the patient, the doctor, or someone else? What should happen when patients are too ill to decide for themselves?

3. Huttmann asks about Mac and Maura, "Was all this misery and suffering supposed to be building character . . . ?" Do you think suffering can make people stronger? If so, how? Do you know of situations where suffering seemed to serve no redeeming value? Explain.

Writing About Ideas

1. Write a *paragraph* about a time that you performed a compassionate act. Perhaps you were kind to an injured person, helped a lost stranger, came to the rescue of someone who was being

teased. Provide vivid details to show what happened and how you felt about the experience.

2. Write an *essay* giving your reasons for thinking that Huttmann is either guilty or innocent of committing murder. Your main idea might be "I think Barbara Huttmann is guilty of murder" or "Finding Barbara Huttmann guilty of murder would be a terrible injustice." No matter which position you take, be sure to take into account the viewpoints of Mac's doctors, his wife, and people like those on the Donahue show.

3. Write an *essay* about a time that you, like Huttmann, had to make a difficult decision—one that required you to sort out conflicting values. Perhaps the decision involved "putting to sleep" a beloved pet, standing up for an unpopular position, resisting peer pressure to do something you weren't comfortable doing. Explain the circumstances leading to the moment of decision, the decision you finally made, and the consequences of that decision. To see how another writer has explored conflicting values, read Bob Teague's "To Get a Story, I Flimflammed a Dead Man's Mother" (page 20).

2

Education
and Learning

Do It Better!

Ben Carson, M.D., with Cecil Murphey

Educators have been debating for decades about how to put American students on a sure and fast track to success. Shall we buy more computers? Build new schools? Institute year-round schooling? In the midst of this confusion, a single mother—a household domestic with a third-grade education—found her own answers to the academic failure of her two young sons. The following excerpt from the book Think Big *by Ben Carson and Cecil Murphey tells how Carson's mother turned his life around from being "the dumbest kid in the class" and from a sure path of failure. Today he is a world-famous neurosurgeon at Johns Hopkins University Hospital in Baltimore.*

Words to Watch

indifferent (58): uninterested
acknowledged (67): recognized

"Benjamin, is this your report card?" my mother asked as   1
she picked up the folded white card from the table.

"Uh, yeah," I said, trying to sound casual. Too ashamed to   2
hand it to her, I had dropped it on the table, hoping that she
wouldn't notice until after I went to bed.

It was the first report card I had received from Higgins   3
Elementary School since we had moved back from Boston to
Detroit, only a few months earlier.

45

I had been in the fifth grade not even two weeks before every-   4
one considered me the dumbest kid in the class and frequently
made jokes about me. Before long I too began to feel as though I
really was the most stupid kid in fifth grade. Despite Mother's frequently saying, "You're smart, Bennie. You can do anything you
want to do," I did not believe her.

No one else in school thought I was smart, either.   5

Now, as Mother examined my report card, she asked, "What's   6
this grade in reading?" (Her tone of voice told me that I was in trouble.) Although I was embarrassed, I did not think too much about it.
Mother knew that I wasn't doing well in math, but she did not know
I was doing so poorly in every subject.

While she slowly read my report card, reading everything one   7
word at a time, I hurried into my room and started to get ready for
bed. A few minutes later, Mother came into my bedroom.

"Benjamin," she said, "are these your grades?" She held the   8
card in front of me as if I hadn't seen it before.

"Oh, yeah, but you know, it doesn't mean much."   9

"No, that's not true, Bennie. It means a lot."   10

"Just a report card."   11

"But it's more than that."   12

Knowing I was in for it now, I prepared to listen, yet I was not   13
all that interested. I did not like school very much and there was no
reason why I should. Inasmuch as I was the dumbest kid in the
class, what did I have to look forward to? The others laughed at me
and made jokes about me every day.

"Education is the only way you're ever going to escape   14
poverty," she said. "It's the only way you're ever going to get ahead
in life and be successful. Do you understand that?"

"Yes, Mother," I mumbled.   15

"If you keep on getting these kinds of grades you're going to   16
spend the rest of your life on skid row, or at best sweeping floors in
a factory. That's not the kind of life that I want for you. That's not
the kind of life that God wants for you."

I hung my head, genuinely ashamed. My mother had been   17
raising me and my older brother, Curtis, by herself. Having only a
third-grade education herself, she knew the value of what she did
not have. Daily she drummed into Curtis and me that we had to do
our best in school.

"You're just not living up to your potential," she said. "I've   18
got two mighty smart boys and I know they can do better."

I had done my best—at least I had when I first started at   19
Higgins Elementary School. How could I do much when I did not
understand anything going on in our class?

In Boston we had attended a parochial school, but I hadn't   20
learned much because of a teacher who seemed more interested in
talking to another female teacher than in teaching us. Possibly, this
teacher was not solely to blame—perhaps I wasn't emotionally able
to learn much. My parents had separated just before we went to
Boston, when I was eight years old. I loved both my mother and father and went through considerable trauma over their separating. For
months afterward, I kept thinking that my parents would get back together, that my daddy would come home again the way he used to,
and that we could be the same old family again—but he never came
back. Consequently, we moved to Boston and lived with Aunt Jean
and Uncle William Avery in a tenement building for two years until
Mother had saved enough money to bring us back to Detroit.

Mother kept shaking the report card at me as she sat on the   21
side of my bed. "You have to work harder. You have to use that
good brain that God gave you, Bennie. Do you understand that?"

"Yes, Mother." Each time she paused, I would dutifully say   22
those words.

"I work among rich people, people who are educated," she said.   23
"I watch how they act, and I know they can do anything they want to
do. And so can you." She put her arm on my shoulder. "Bennie, you
can do anything they can do—only you can do it better!"

Mother had said those words before. Often. At the time, they   24
did not mean much to me. Why should they? I really believed that I
was the dumbest kid in fifth grade, but of course, I never told her
that.

"I just don't know what to do about you boys," she said. "I'm   25
going to talk to God about you and Curtis." She paused, stared into
space, then said (more to herself than to me), "I need the Lord's
guidance on what to do. You just can't bring in any more report
cards like this."

As far as I was concerned, the report card matter was over.   26

The next day was like the previous ones—just another bad   27
day in school, another day of being laughed at because I did not get

a single problem right in arithmetic and couldn't get any words right on the spelling test. As soon as I came home from school, I changed into play clothes and ran outside. Most of the boys my age played softball, or the game I liked best, "Tip the Top."

We played Tip the Top by placing a bottle cap on one of the   28
sidewalk cracks. Then taking a ball—any kind that bounced—we'd stand on a line and take turns throwing the ball at the bottle top, trying to flip it over. Whoever succeeded got two points. If anyone actually moved the cap more than a few inches, he won five points. Ten points came if he flipped it into the air and it landed on the other side.

When it grew dark or we got tired, Curtis and I would finally   29
go inside and watch TV. The set stayed on until we went to bed. Because Mother worked long hours, she was never home until just before we went to bed. Sometimes I would awaken when I heard her unlocking the door.

Two evenings after the incident with the report card, Mother   30
came home about an hour before our bedtime. Curtis and I were sprawled out, watching TV. She walked across the room, snapped off the set, and faced both of us. "Boys," she said, "you're wasting too much of your time in front of that television. You don't get an education from staring at television all the time."

Before either of us could make a protest, she told us that she   31
had been praying for wisdom. "The Lord's told me what to do," she said. "So from now on, you will not watch television, except for two preselected programs each week."

"Just *two* programs?" I could hardly believe she would say   32
such a terrible thing. "That's not—"

"And *only* after you've done your homework. Furthermore,   33
you don't play outside after school, either, until you've done all your homework."

"Everybody else plays outside right after school," I said, un-   34
able to think of anything except how bad it would be if I couldn't play with my friends. "I won't have any friends if I stay in the house all the time—"

"That may be," Mother said, "but everybody else is not going   35
to be as successful as you are—"

"But, Mother—"   36

"This is what we're going to do. I asked God for wisdom, and 37
this is the answer I got."

I tried to offer several other arguments, but Mother was firm. I 38
glanced at Curtis, expecting him to speak up, but he did not say
anything. He lay on the floor, staring at his feet.

"Don't worry about everybody else. The whole world is full 39
of 'everybody else,' you know that? But only a few make a significant achievement."

The loss of TV and play time was bad enough. I got up off the 40
floor, feeling as if everything was against me. Mother wasn't going
to let me play with my friends, and there would be no more television—almost none, anyway. She was stopping me from having any
fun in life.

"And that isn't all," she said. "Come back, Bennie." 41

I turned around, wondering what else there could be. 42

"In addition," she said, "to doing your homework, you have to 43
read two books from the library each week. Every single week."

"Two books? Two?" Even though I was in fifth grade, I had 44
never read a whole book in my life.

"Yes, two. When you finish reading them, you must write me 45
a book report just like you do at school. You're not living up to your
potential, so I'm going to see that you do."

Usually Curtis, who was two years older, was the more rebel- 46
lious. But this time he seemed to grasp the wisdom of what Mother
said. He did not say one word.

She stared at Curtis. "You understand?" 47

He nodded. 48

"Bennie, is it clear?" 49

"Yes, Mother." I agreed to do what Mother told me—it wouldn't 50
have occurred to me not to obey—but I did not like it. Mother was
being unfair and demanding more of us than other parents did.

The following day was Thursday. After school, Curtis and I 51
walked to the local branch of the library. I did not like it much, but
then I had not spent that much time in any library.

We both wandered around a little in the children's section, not 52
having any idea about how to select books or which books we
wanted to check out.

The librarian came over to us and asked if she could help. We   53
explained that both of us wanted to check out two books.

"What kind of books would you like to read?" the librarian   54
asked.

"Animals," I said after thinking about it. "Something about   55
animals."

"I'm sure we have several that you'd like." She led me over to   56
a section of books. She left me and guided Curtis to another section
of the room. I flipped through the row of books until I found two
that looked easy enough for me to read. One of them, *Chip, the
Dam Builder*—about a beaver—was the first one I had ever
checked out. As soon as I got home, I started to read it. It was the
first book I ever read all the way through even though it took me
two nights. Reluctantly I admitted afterward to Mother that I really
had liked reading about Chip.

Within a month I could find my way around the children's   57
section like someone who had gone there all his life. By then the library staff knew Curtis and me and the kind of books we chose.
They often made suggestions. "Here's a delightful book about a
squirrel," I remember one of them telling me.

As she told me part of the story, I tried to appear indifferent,   58
but as soon as she handed it to me, I opened the book and started to
read.

Best of all, we became favorites of the librarians. When new   59
books came in that they thought either of us would enjoy, they held
them for us. Soon I became fascinated as I realized that the library
had so many books—and about so many different subjects.

After the book about the beaver, I chose others about ani-   60
mals—all types of animals. I read every animal story I could get my
hands on. I read books about wolves, wild dogs, several about
squirrels, and a variety of animals that lived in other countries.
Once I had gone through the animal books, I started reading about
plants, then minerals, and finally rocks.

My reading books about rocks was the first time the informa-   61
tion ever became practical to me. We lived near the railroad tracks,
and when Curtis and I took the route to school that crossed by the
tracks, I began paying attention to the crushed rock that I noticed
between the ties.

As I continued to read more about rocks, I would walk along 62
the tracks, searching for different kinds of stones, and then see if I
could identify them.

Often I would take a book with me to make sure that I had la- 63
beled each stone correctly.

"Agate," I said as I threw the stone. Curtis got tired of my 64
picking up stones and identifying them, but I did not care because I
kept finding new stones all the time. Soon it became my favorite
game to walk along the tracks and identify the varieties of stones.
Although I did not realize it, within a very short period of time, I
was actually becoming an expert on rocks.

Two things happened in the second half of fifth grade that 65
convinced me of the importance of reading books.

First, our teacher, Mrs. Williamson, had a spelling bee every 66
Friday afternoon. We'd go through all the words we'd had so far
that year. Sometimes she also called out words that we were supposed to have learned in fourth grade. Without fail, I always went
down on the first word.

One Friday, though, Bobby Farmer, whom everyone acknowl- 67
edged as the smartest kid in our class, had to spell "agriculture" as
his final word. As soon as the teacher pronounced his word, I
thought, I can spell that word. Just the day before, I had learned it
from reading one of my library books. I spelled it under my breath,
and it was just the way Bobby spelled it.

If I can spell "agriculture," I'll bet I can learn to spell any 68
other word in the world. I'll bet I can learn to spell better than
Bobby Farmer.

Just that single word, "agriculture," was enough to give me 69
hope.

The following week, a second thing happened that forever 70
changed my life. When Mr. Jaeck, the science teacher, was teaching
us about volcanoes, he held up an object that looked like a piece of
black, glass-like rock. "Does anybody know what this is? What
does it have to do with volcanoes?"

Immediately, because of my reading, I recognized the stone. I 71
waited, but none of my classmates raised their hands. I thought,
This is strange. Not even the smart kids are raising their hands. I
raised my hand.

"Yes, Benjamin," he said.   72

I heard snickers around me. The other kids probably thought   73
it was a joke, or that I was going to say something stupid.

"Obsidian," I said.   74

"That's right!" He tried not to look startled, but it was obvious   75
he hadn't expected me to give the correct answer.

"That's obsidian," I said, "and it's formed by the supercooling   76
of lava when it hits the water." Once I had their attention and realized I knew information no other student had learned, I began to tell
them everything I knew about the subject of obsidian, lava, lava
flow, super- cooling, and compacting of the elements.

When I finally paused, a voice behind me whispered, "Is that   77
Bennie Carson?"

"You're absolutely correct," Mr. Jaeck said and he smiled at   78
me. If he had announced that I'd won a million-dollar lottery, I
couldn't have been more pleased and excited.

"Benjamin, that's absolutely, absolutely right," he repeated   79
with enthusiasm in his voice. He turned to the others and said,
"That is wonderful! Class, this is a tremendous piece of information
Benjamin has just given us. I'm very proud to hear him say this."

For a few moments, I tasted the thrill of achievement. I recall   80
thinking, *Wow, look at them. They're all looking at me with admiration. Me, the dummy! The one everybody thinks is stupid. They're
looking at me to see if this is really me speaking.*

Maybe, though, it was I who was the most astonished one in   81
the class. Although I had been reading two books a week because
Mother told me to, I had not realized how much knowledge I was
accumulating. True, I had learned to enjoy reading, but until then I
hadn't realized how it connected with my schoolwork. That day—
for the first time—I realized that Mother had been right. Reading is
the way out of ignorance, and the road to achievement. I did not
have to be the class dummy anymore.

For the next few days, I felt like a hero at school. The jokes   82
about me stopped. The kids started to listen to me. *I'm starting to
have fun with this stuff.*

As my grades improved in every subject, I asked myself,   83
"Ben, is there any reason you can't be the smartest kid in the class?
If you can learn about obsidian, you can learn about social studies
and geography and math and science and everything."

That single moment of triumph pushed me to want to read   84
more. From then on, it was as though I could not read enough
books. Whenever anyone looked for me after school, they could
usually find me in my bedroom—curled up, reading a library
book—for a long time, the only thing I wanted to do. I had stopped
caring about the TV programs I was missing; I no longer cared
about playing Tip the Top or baseball anymore. I just wanted to
read.

In a year and a half—by the middle of sixth grade—I had   85
moved to the top of the class.

Understanding Content

1. What is the selection's main idea? If it is stated directly, locate
   the relevant sentence(s). If it is implied, state the main idea in
   your own words.

2. Why did Bennie consider himself "the dumbest kid in the
   class"? How did this perception of himself affect his schoolwork?

3. How did Mrs. Carson encourage Bennie to make school—particularly reading—a priority in his life? What effect did her
   efforts have on Bennie's academic performance and self-esteem?

Understanding Technique

1. Carson reveals his mother's character through her words and actions. What, for example, does paragraph 25 convey about Mrs.
   Carson?

2. In paragraph 65, Carson states, "Two things happened in the
   second half of fifth grade that convinced me of the importance
   of reading books." What words does Carson use in later paragraphs to help readers recognize those two events? Does Carson
   present the events in the order they occurred, in order of their
   importance, or both?

3. Why do you suppose Carson italicizes sentences in paragraphs 68, 71, 80, and 82? What purpose do the italicized sentences serve?

Thinking About Ideas

1. Mrs. Carson limited her sons to two television programs a week. Do you agree with her that unrestricted television watching is harmful to children? If you have children, what rules about watching TV have you established in your home? What has been the effect of the rules?

2. Carson explains that the trauma he suffered because of his parents' separation may have interfered with his ability to learn. How might schools and parents help students get through such traumatic times?

3. As a child, Carson began to feel confident about his own abilities when he followed his mother's guidelines. How might Mrs. Carson's methods help *adult* students build up their own self-confidence and motivation?

Writing About Ideas

1. Mrs. Carson discovered an effective way to boost her children's achievement and self-confidence. But not all parents are as well-informed. To help them, write a *paragraph* beginning "There are several ways parents can help their children live up to their potential." Then explain and illustrate two or three methods parents can use. Draw upon examples from your own experiences or from someone else's—including those of Bennie Carson, if you like.

2. What would your life be like if you watched less television, or none at all? To get an idea of how it would be, spend several days without watching television. In a journal, record your reaction to the experiment. What is it like to be suddenly without TV, what do you miss most about TV, what do you do instead of watching TV, and what surprises you about the experience?

Using your journal notes, write an *essay* on the effects of eliminating TV from your life.

CO 3. Bennie's teacher in Boston seemed ineffective, while his science teacher in Detroit was enthusiastic and encouraging. In an *essay,* contrast your best and worst teacher. Before starting to write, list the two teachers' qualities; then select two or more that make for clear-cut, interesting contrasts. In the paper, you may discuss one teacher fully before going on to the other. Alternatively, you may focus on one quality at a time. For instance, you might contrast the two teachers' knowledge of their subjects, then their approaches to discipline, then their levels of enthusiasm. No matter how you organize the paper, provide lively details that emphasize the teachers' differences. Maya Angelou's "Sister Flowers" (page 56) and Dick Gregory's "Shame" (page 79), which present portraits of two very different kinds of teachers, might give you some ideas for your paper.

Sister Flowers

Maya Angelou

Few people have overcome more to rise as high as Maya Angelou, the acclaimed author, actress, and singer who delivered a poem at the inauguration of President Bill Clinton. Born Marguerite Johnson in 1928, Angelou was shuttled between the worlds of her mother in St. Louis and of her grandmother (whom Angelou called "Momma") in Stamps, Arkansas. Angelou writes about her life in a series of autobiographical books, beginning with I Know Why the Caged Bird Sings, *from which "Sister Flowers" is taken. Raped at the age of eight in St. Louis, Angelou responded by ceasing to speak to anyone but her beloved brother Bailey. She and Bailey were soon sent back to Stamps to live with Momma, at which point this excerpt begins.*

Words to Watch

benign (4): kind
familiar (7): close friend
unceremonious (8): not formal enough
gait (8): manner of walking
moors (11): the broad stretches of open, rolling land which were often part of the setting of nineteenth-century English novels
incessantly (11): continually
scones (11): a biscuitlike pastry
crumpets (11): a small, flat bread

chifforobe (17): a piece of furniture that usually has
drawers and a place to hang clothes
sacrilegious (17): disrespectful of something sacred
infuse (24): fill
homely (35): simple
couched (35): stated

For nearly a year [after the rape], I sopped around the house,   1
the Store, the school and the church, like an old biscuit, dirty and
inedible. Then I met, or rather got to know, the lady who threw me
my first life line.

Mrs. Bertha Flowers was the aristocrat of Black Stamps. She   2
had the grace of control to appear warm in the coldest weather, and
on the Arkansas summer days it seemed she had a private breeze
which swirled around, cooling her. She was thin without the taut
look of wiry people, and her printed voile dresses and flowered hats
were as right for her as denim overalls for a farmer. She was our
side's answer to the richest white woman in town.

Her skin was a rich black that would have peeled like a plum   3
if snagged, but then no one would have thought of getting close
enough to Mrs. Flowers to ruffle her dress, let alone snag her skin.
She didn't encourage familiarity. She wore gloves too.

I don't think I ever saw Mrs. Flowers laugh, but she smiled   4
often. A slow widening of her thin black lips to show even, small
white teeth, then the slow effortless closing. When she chose to
smile on me, I always wanted to thank her. The action was so
graceful and inclusively benign.

She was one of the few gentlewomen I have ever known, and   5
has remained throughout my life the measure of what a human
being can be.

Momma had a strange relationship with her. Most often when   6
she passed on the road in front of the Store, she spoke to Momma in
that soft yet carrying voice, "Good day, Mrs. Henderson." Momma
responded with "How you, Sister Flowers?"

Mrs. Flowers didn't belong to our church, nor was she   7
Momma's familiar. Why on earth did she insist on calling her Sister
Flowers? Shame made me want to hide my face. Mrs. Flowers

deserved better than to be called Sister. Then, Momma left out the verb. Why not ask, "How *are* you, *Mrs.* Flowers?" With the unbalanced passion of the young, I hated her for showing her ignorance to Mrs. Flowers. It didn't occur to me for many years that they were as alike as sisters, separated only by formal education.

Although I was upset, neither of the women was in the least 8 shaken by what I thought an unceremonious greeting. Mrs. Flowers would continue her easy gait up the hill to her little bungalow, and Momma kept on shelling peas or doing whatever had brought her to the front porch.

Occasionally, though, Mrs. Flowers would drift off the road 9 and down to the Store and Momma would say to me, "Sister, you go on and play." As she left I would hear the beginning of an intimate conversation. Momma persistently using the wrong verb, or none at all.

"Brother and Sister Wilcox is sho'ly the meanest—" "Is," 10 Momma? "Is"? Oh, please, not "is," Momma, for two or more. But they talked, and from the side of the building where I waited for the ground to open up and swallow me, I heard the soft-voiced Mrs. Flowers and the textured voice of my grandmother merging and melting. They were interrupted from time to time by giggles that must have come from Mrs. Flowers (Momma never giggled in her life). Then she was gone.

She appealed to me because she was like people I had never 11 met personally. Like women in English novels who walked the moors (whatever they were) with their loyal dogs racing at a respectful distance. Like the women who sat in front of roaring fireplaces, drinking tea incessantly from silver trays full of scones and crumpets. Women who walked over the "heath" and read morocco-bound books and had two last names divided by a hyphen. It would be safe to say that she made me proud to be Negro, just by being herself.

She acted just as refined as whitefolks in the movies and 12 books and she was more beautiful, for none of them could have come near that warm color without looking gray by comparison.

It was fortunate that I never saw her in the company of 13 powhitefolks. For since they tend to think of their whiteness as an evenizer, I'm certain that I would have had to hear her spoken to commonly as Bertha, and my image of her would have been shattered like the unmendable Humpty-Dumpty.

One summer afternoon, sweet-milk fresh in my memory, she   14
stopped at the Store to buy provisions. Another Negro woman of
her health and age would have been expected to carry the paper
sacks home in one hand, but Momma said, "Sister Flowers, I'll
send Bailey up to your house with these things."

She smiled that slow dragging smile, "Thank you, Mrs.   15
Henderson. I'd prefer Marguerite, though." My name was beautiful
when she said it. "I've been meaning to talk to her, anyway." They
gave each other age-group looks.

Momma said, "Well, that's all right then. Sister, go and   16
change your dress. You going to Sister Flowers's."

The chifforobe was a maze. What on earth did one put on to   17
go to Mrs. Flowers's house? I knew I shouldn't put on a Sunday
dress. It might be sacrilegious. Certainly not a house dress, since I
was already wearing a fresh one. I chose a school dress, naturally. It
was formal without suggesting that going to Mrs. Flowers's house
was equivalent to attending church.

I trusted myself back into the Store.   18

"Now, don't you look nice." I had chosen the right thing, for   19
once. . . .

There was a little path beside the rocky road, and Mrs.   20
Flowers walked in front swinging her arms and picking her way
over the stones.

She said, without turning her head, to me, "I hear you're   21
doing very good school work, Marguerite, but that it's all written.
The teachers report that they have trouble getting you to talk in
class." We passed the triangular farm on our left and the path
widened to allow us to walk together. I hung back in the separate
unasked and unanswerable questions.

"Come and walk along with me, Marguerite." I couldn't have   22
refused even if I wanted to. She pronounced my name so nicely. Or
more correctly, she spoke each word with such clarity that I was
certain a foreigner who didn't understand English could have understood her.

"Now no one is going to make you talk—possibly no one can.   23
But bear in mind, language is man's way of communicating with
his fellow man and it is language alone which separates him from
the lower animals." That was a totally new idea to me, and I would
need time to think about it.

"Your grandmother says you read a lot. Every chance you get. 24
That's good, but not good enough. Words mean more than what is
set down on paper. It takes the human voice to infuse them with the
shades of deeper meaning."

I memorized the part about the human voice infusing words. 25
It seemed so valid and poetic.

She said she was going to give me some books and that I not 26
only must read them, I must read them aloud. She suggested that I
try to make a sentence sound in as many different ways as possible.

"I'll accept no excuse if you return a book to me that has been 27
badly handled." My imagination boggled at the punishment I would
deserve if in fact I did abuse a book of Mrs. Flowers's. Death would
be too kind and brief.

The odors in the house surprised me. Somehow I had never 28
connected Mrs. Flowers with food or eating or any other common
experience of common people. There must have been an outhouse,
too, but my mind never recorded it.

The sweet scent of vanilla had met us as she opened the door. 29

"I made tea cookies this morning. You see, I had planned to 30
invite you for cookies and lemonade so we could have this little
chat. The lemonade is in the icebox."

It followed that Mrs. Flowers would have ice on an ordinary 31
day, when most families in our town bought ice late on Saturdays
only a few times during the summer to be used in the wooden ice-
cream freezers.

She took the bags from me and disappeared through the 32
kitchen door. I looked around the room that I had never in my
wildest fantasies imagined I would see. Browned photographs
leered or threatened from the walls and the white, freshly done curtains pushed against themselves and against the wind. I wanted to
gobble up the room entire and take it to Bailey, who would help me
analyze and enjoy it.

"Have a seat, Marguerite. Over there by the table." She carried 33
a platter covered with a tea towel. Although she warned that she
hadn't tried her hand at baking sweets for some time, I was certain
that like everything else about her the cookies would be perfect.

They were flat round wafers, slightly browned on the edges 34
and butter-yellow in the center. With the cold lemonade they were

sufficient for childhood's lifelong diet. Remembering my manners, I took nice little lady-like bites off the edges. She said she had made them expressly for me and that she had a few in the kitchen that I could take home to my brother. So I jammed one whole cake in my mouth and the rough crumbs scratched the insides of my jaws, and if I hadn't had to swallow, it would have been a dream come true.

As I ate she began the first of what we later called "my lessons in living." She said that I must always be intolerant of ignorance but understanding of illiteracy. That some people, unable to go to school, were more educated and even more intelligent than college professors. She encouraged me to listen carefully to what country people called mother wit. That in those homely sayings was couched the collective wisdom of generations. 35

When I finished the cookies she brushed off the table and brought a thick, small book from the bookcase. I had read *A Tale of Two Cities* and found it up to my standards as a romantic novel. She opened the first page and I heard poetry for the first time in my life. 36

"It was the best of times and the worst of times . . ." Her voice slid in and curved down through and over the words. She was nearly singing. I wanted to look at the pages. Were they the same that I had read? Or were there notes, music, lined on the pages, as in a hymn book? Her sounds began cascading gently. I knew from listening to a thousand preachers that she was nearing the end of her reading, and I hadn't really heard, heard to understand, a single word. 37

"How do you like that?" 38

It occurred to me that she expected a response. The sweet vanilla flavor was still on my tongue and her reading was a wonder in my ears. I had to speak. 39

I said, "Yes, ma'am." It was the least I could do, but it was the most also. 40

"There's one more thing. Take this book of poems and memorize one for me. Next time you pay me a visit, I want you to recite." 41

I have tried often to search behind the sophistication of years for the enchantment I so easily found in those gifts. The essence escapes but its aura remains. To be allowed, no, invited, into the private lives of strangers, and to share their joys and fears, was a chance to exchange the Southern bitter wormwood for a cup of 42 mead with Beowulf[1] or a hot cup of tea and milk with Oliver Twist[2]. When I said aloud, "It is a far, far better thing that I do, than I have ever done . . ."[3] tears of love filled my eyes at my selflessness.

On that first day, I ran down the hill and into the road (few   43
cars ever came along it) and had the good sense to stop running before I reached the Store.

I was liked, and what a difference it made. I was respected not   44
as Mrs. Henderson's grandchild or Bailey's sister but for just being
Marguerite Johnson.

Childhood's logic never asks to be proved (all conclusions are   45
absolute). I didn't question why Mrs. Flowers had singled me out
for attention, nor did it occur to me that Momma might have asked
her to give me a little talking to. All I cared about was that she had
made tea cookies for *me* and read to *me* from her favorite book. It
was enough to prove that she liked me.

Understanding Content

1. What is the selection's main idea? If it is stated directly, locate
   the relevant sentence(s). If it is implied, state the main idea in
   your own words.

2. What does Angelou mean when she writes that Mrs. Flowers
   was "our side's answer to the richest white woman in town"
   (paragraph 2)?

3. What does Mrs. Flowers do to make Marguerite feel special and
   encourage her to talk?

---

[1]The hero of an Old English epic poem dating from the eighth century.

[2]The main character in Charles Dickens's novel *Oliver Twist* (1837).

[3]The last words of Sydney Carton, the selfless hero of Charles Dickens's
novel *A Tale of Two Cities* (1859).

Understanding Technique

1. Angelou's writing is full of vivid words and images. Look, for example, at the selection's first paragraph. How does the vigorous language there help the reader understand Marguerite's state of mind following the rape?

2. One way writers reveal character is by showing how an individual reacts to a specific situation. Consider the way Angelou depicts her reaction, as a child, to Momma's and Mrs. Flowers's conversation (paragraphs 6–10). What does this reaction convey about Angelou as a young girl?

3. Look carefully at Angelou's description of Mrs. Flowers's home and belongings. What does this description suggest about Mrs. Flowers and her values?

Thinking About Ideas

1. What traits of Mrs. Flowers does Marguerite admire? Why does Mrs. Flowers provide a better model for Marguerite than the heroines of the English novels she reads?

2. Marguerite seems embarrassed by her grandmother's use of English. Do you understand her feelings? Do you think she was wrong to feel this way? Why or why not? How do you think you would have felt?

3. What does this selection suggest about the connection between generations? What lessons about life might the selection teach you, both now and years from now?

Writing About Ideas

∞ 1. Angelou calls Mrs. Flowers "the measure of what a human being can be." Write a *paragraph* about someone you admire greatly. Focus on one of the person's outstanding qualities, and recount a single dramatic incident that illustrates this quality. Use vivid specifics to convey why this person is so worthy of admiration. Before planning your paper, you might want to read

"Do It Better!" (page 45), in which Ben Carson gives a glowing depiction of his mother.

2. Mrs. Flowers threw Marguerite a "lifeline" during a difficult time in her life. Who has reached out to you at a troubling time? Write an *essay* showing how someone offered you significant help when you needed it. Start by explaining the difficulty you faced (perhaps you were depressed, physically ill, unsure of your options, afraid of your future). Then provide plentiful specifics to illustrate how the person came through for you. End, as Angelou does, by explaining the person's influence on your life.

3. Mrs. Flowers gives Marguerite gentle "lessons in life"—for example, teaching her the difference between illiteracy and ignorance. Write an *essay* about an incident in your life that helped you realize that your previous understanding of someone or something was erroneous or incomplete. Be sure to show clearly what it was about the experience that deepened your understanding.

A Love Affair with Books

Bernadete Piassa

---

*Although Bernadete Piassa loved to read as a child, she
was discouraged from doing so. In this prize-winning
essay in a national writing contest, Piassa tells how she
managed to remain a devoted reader and how books have
repaid her well for that devotion. For her, books are not
just a bookshelf decoration, an occasional light pastime, or
a homework assignment. Throughout her life they have
been her "friends," "guides," and "most faithful lovers."*

Words to Watch

illicit (9): forbidden
ardor (9): love and passion
exult (9): rejoice
infatuated (13): passionately fascinated
subversive (15): turning people against something
lackluster (15): dull

When I was young, I thought that reading was like a drug   1
which I was allowed to take only a teaspoon at a time, but which,
nevertheless, had the effect of carrying me away to an enchanted
world where I experienced strange and forbidden emotions. As time
went by and I took that drug again and again, I became addicted to
it. I could no longer live without reading. Books became an intrin-
sic part of my life. They became my friends, my guides, my lovers.
My most faithful lovers.

I didn't know I would fall in love with books when I was   2
young and started to read. I don't even recall when I started to read
and how. I just remember that my mother didn't like me to read. In
spite of this, every time I had an opportunity I would sneak somewhere with a book and read one page, two pages, three, if I were
lucky enough, always feeling my heart beating fast, always hoping
that my mother wouldn't find me, wouldn't shout as always:
"Bernadete, don't you have anything to do?" For her, books were
nothing. For me, they were everything.

In my childhood I didn't have a big choice of books. I lived in   3
a small town in Brazil, surrounded by swamp and farms. It was impossible to get out of town by car; there weren't roads. By train it
took eight hours to reach the next village. There were airplanes,
small airplanes, only twice a week. Books couldn't get to my town
very easily. There wasn't a library there, either. However, I was
lucky: My uncle was a pilot.

My uncle, who owned a big farm and also worked flying peo-   4
ple from place to place in his small airplane, had learned to fly, in
addition, with his imagination. At home, he loved to sit in his ham-
mock on his patio and travel away in his fantasy with all kinds of
books. If he happened to read a bestseller or a romance, when he was
done he would give it to my mother, who also liked to read although
she didn't like me to. But I would get to read the precious book anyway, even if I needed to do this in a hiding place, little by little.

I remember very well one series of small books. Each had a   5
green cover with a drawing of a couple kissing on it. I think the series had been given to my mother when she was a teenager because
all the pages were already yellow and almost worn-out. But although
the books were old, for me they seemed alive, and for a long time I
devoured them, one by one, pretending that I was the heroine and
my lover would soon come to rescue me. He didn't come, of course.
And I was the one who left my town to study and live in Rio de
Janeiro, taking only my clothes with me. But inside myself I was
taking my passion for books that would never abandon me.

I had been sent to study in a boarding school, and I was soon   6
appalled to discover that the expensive all-girls school had even
fewer books than my house. In my class there was a bookshelf with
maybe fifty books, and almost all of them were about the lives of

saints and the miracles of Christ. I had almost given up the hope of finding something to read when I spotted, tucked away at the very end of the shelf, a small book already covered by dust. It didn't seem to be about religion because it had a more intriguing title, *The Old Man and the Sea.* It was written by an author that I had never heard of before: Ernest Hemingway. Curious, I started to read the book and a few minutes later was already fascinated by Santiago, the fisherman.

I loved that book so much that when I went to my aunt's   7
house to spend the weekend, I asked her if she had any books by the man who had written it. She lent me *For Whom the Bell Tolls,* and I read it every Sunday I could get out of school, only a little bit at a time, only one teaspoon at a time. I started to wait anxiously for those Sundays. At the age of thirteen I was deeply in love with Ernest Hemingway.

When I finished with all his books I could find, I discovered   8
Herman Hesse, Graham Greene, Aldous Huxley, Edgar Allan Poe. I could read them only on Sundays, so, during the week, I would dream or think about the world I had discovered in their books.

At that time I thought that my relationship with books was   9
kind of odd, something that set me apart from the world. Only when I read the short story "Illicit Happiness," by Clarice Lispector, a Brazilian author, did I discover that other people could enjoy books as much as I did. The story is about an ugly, fat girl who still manages to torture one of the beautiful girls in her town only because the unattractive girl's father is the owner of a bookstore, and she can have all the books she wants. With sadistic refinement, day after day she promises to give to the beautiful girl the book the girl dearly wants, but never fulfills her promise. When her mother finds out what is going on, she gives the book to the beautiful girl, who then runs through the streets hugging it and, at home, pretends to have lost it only to find it again, showing an ardor for books that made me exult. For the first time I wasn't alone. I knew that someone else also loved books as much as I did.

My passion for books continued through my life, and it had to   10
surmount another big challenge when, at the age of thirty-one, I moved to New York. Because I had almost no money, I was forced to leave all my books in Brazil. Besides, I didn't know enough

English to read in this language. For some years I was condemned again to the darkness; condemned to live without books, my friends, my guides, my lovers.

But my love for books was so strong that I overcame even this   11
obstacle. I learned to read in English, and was finally able to enjoy my favorite authors again.

Although books have always been part of my life, they still   12
hold a mystery for me, and every time I open a new one, I ask myself which pleasures I am about to discover, which routes I am about to travel, which emotions I am about to sink in. Will this new book touch me as a woman, as a foreigner, as a romantic soul, as a curious person? Which horizon is it about to unfold to me, which string of my soul is it bound to touch, which secret is it about to unveil for me?

Sometimes, the book seduces me not only for the story it tells,   13
but also because of the words the author uses in it. Reading Gabriel Garcia Marquez's short story "The Handsomest Drowned Man in the World," I feel dazzled when he writes that it took "the fraction of centuries for the body to fall into the abyss." The fraction of centuries! I read those words again and again, infatuated by them, by their precision, by their hidden meaning. I try to keep them in my mind, even knowing that they are already part of my soul.

After reading so many books that touch me deeply, each one   14
in its special way, I understand now that my mother had a point when she tried to keep me away from books in my childhood. She wanted me to stay in my little town, to marry a rich and tiresome man, to keep up with the traditions. But the books carried me away; they gave me wings to fly, to discover new places. They made me dare to live another kind of life. They made me wish for more, and when I couldn't have all I wished for, they were still there to comfort me, to show me new options.

Yes, my mother was right. Books are dangerous; books are   15
subversive. Because of them I left a predictable future for an unforeseeable one. However, if I had to choose again, I would always choose the books instead of the lackluster life I could have had. After all, what joy would I find in my heart without my books, my most faithful lovers?

Understanding Content

1. What is the selection's main idea? If it is stated directly, locate the relevant sentence(s). If it is implied, state the main idea in your own words.

2. What does Piassa mean when she writes (in paragraph 1) that reading "was like a drug" for her and that she "became addicted" to it?

3. Piassa writes in paragraph 14 that books made her "dare to live another kind of life" from the one her mother wanted for her. In what ways has Piassa's life differed from her mother's plan for her? How did books contribute to those differences?

Understanding Technique

1. When writing about books, Piassa draws upon language typically used to describe romance. Identify places in the essay where Piassa uses "romantic" words. What does she achieve by using this language?

2. In her essay, Piassa mentions a number of books and short stories that were important to her, yet she describes in considerable detail only one of these. Which one? Why might she have selected this particular item to describe so specifically?

3. Why do you think Piassa returns to the topic of her mother in her essay's conclusion (paragraphs 14–15)?

Thinking About Ideas

1. As a child, Piassa found that books carried her away to "an enchanted world." Did you have any special reading experiences in your childhood? If so, describe them, and explain what made them so special.

2. Piassa's mother discouraged her from reading. Often, though, parents would like their children to read more. What are some ways that parents can encourage children to read?

3. Piassa states that her life has turned out very differently from the way her mother would have liked it to be. Discuss the similarities and differences between your goals for yourself and your parents' goals for you. For example, do you share similar ideas about education, career, marriage, and other matters? Explain.

Writing About Ideas

1. When Piassa was young, she "would sneak somewhere with a book" whenever she could. What did you do as a child that you didn't want adults to know about? Perhaps you skipped school now and then to go to the movies or spent time with a friend your parents didn't approve of. Write a *paragraph* about a childhood experience you wanted to keep secret from adults. Use vivid details to describe what you did and how you tried to hide the activity. If you were eventually found out, you might end the paragraph by briefly dramatizing that moment of discovery.

2. For what activity do you feel the kind of passion that Piassa feels for reading? Perhaps you love jogging, movies, or cooking. Select one of your interests, and write an *essay* explaining what it means to you. Be sure to provide colorful and detailed examples so readers will be able to understand your enthusiasm for your special interest. To see how Mortimer Adler expresses enthusiasm for a special interest, read "How to Mark a Book" (page 71).

3. Piassa and her mother obviously do not see eye to eye. Write an *essay* explaining how to resolve disagreements between individuals often entangled in conflict—for example, roommates, coworkers, parents and teenagers, or husbands and wives. To gather material for your paper, talk to people who have been involved in the kind of conflict you plan to write about. Taking notes, ask them what specific problems they faced and how the problems were resolved. In your essay, describe fully the problems typically encountered, and offer advice on how to handle each one.

How to Mark a Book

Mortimer Adler

Mortimer J. Adler has made a career of books—as associate editor of the series Great Books of the Western World, *editor-in-chief of* The Great Ideas of Today *series, and author of a popular guide called* How to Read a Book. *Considering the high regard in which Adler obviously holds books, you might expect him to take a reverential attitude toward the volumes themselves—preferring to see them kept in neat dusted rows on handsome bookshelves. But, as this essay from* Saturday Review *reveals, you would be wrong. You may be surprised by what Adler considers the sign of a true book lover.*

Words to Watch

mutilation (2): destruction
prelude (4): introductory event
deluded (6): deceived
dog-eared (6): having corners of the pages turned down
dilapidated (6): deteriorated
intact (7): uninjured
score (8): written form of a musical piece
integral (13): necessary for completeness
receptacle (14): container

You know you have to read "between the lines" to get the   1
most out of anything. I want to persuade you to do something

equally important in the course of your reading. I want to persuade you to "write between the lines." Unless you do, you are not likely to do the most efficient kind of reading.

I contend, quite bluntly, that marking up a book is not an act   2
of mutilation but of love.

You shouldn't mark up a book which isn't yours. Librarians   3
[or your friends] who lend you books expect you to keep them clean, and you should. If you decide that I am right about the usefulness of marking books, you will have to buy them. Most of the world's great books are available today, in reprint editions, at less than a dollar[1].

There are two ways in which one can own a book. The first is   4
the property right you establish by paying for it, just as you pay for clothes and furniture. But this act of purchase is only the prelude to possession. Full ownership comes only when you have made it a part of yourself, and the best way to make yourself a part of it is by writing in it. An illustration may make the point clear. You buy a beefsteak and transfer it from the butcher's ice-box to your own. But you do not own the beefsteak in the most important sense until you consume it and get it into your bloodstream. I am arguing that books, too, must be absorbed in your bloodstream to do you any good.

Confusion about what it means to *own* a book leads people to   5
a false reverence for paper, binding, and type—a respect for the physical thing—the craft of the printer rather than the genius of the author. They forget that it is possible for a man to acquire the idea, to possess the beauty, which a great book contains, without staking his claim by pasting his bookplate inside the cover. Having a fine library doesn't prove that its owner has a mind enriched by books; it proves nothing more than that he, his father, or his wife, was rich enough to buy them.

There are three kinds of book owners. The first has all the   6
standard sets and bestsellers—unread, untouched. (This deluded individual owns woodpulp and ink, not books.) The second has a great many books—a few of them read through, most of them dipped into, but all of them as clean and shiny as the day they were bought. (This person would probably like to make books his own,

[1]In 1940, when this essay first appeared.

but is restrained by a false respect for their physical appearance.) The third has a few books or many—every one of them dog-eared and dilapidated, shaken and loosened by continual use, marked and scribbled in from front to back. (This man owns books.)

Is it false respect, you may ask, to preserve intact and unblem- 7 ished a beautifully printed book, an elegantly bound edition? Of course not. I'd no more scribble all over the first edition of *Paradise Lost*[1] than I'd give my baby a set of crayons and an original Rembrandt[2]! I wouldn't mark up a painting or a statue. Its soul, so to speak, is inseparable from its body. And the beauty of a rare edition or of a richly manufactured volume is like that of a painting or a statue.

But the soul of a book can be separated from its body. A book 8 is more like the score of a piece of music than it is like a painting. No great musician confuses a symphony with the printed sheets of music. Arturo Toscanini[3] reveres Brahms[4], but Toscanini's score of the C-minor Symphony is so thoroughly marked up that no one but the maestro himself can read it. The reason why a great conductor makes notations on his musical scores—marks them up again and again each time he returns to study them—is the reason why you should mark up your books. If your respect for magnificent binding or typography gets in the way, buy yourself a cheap edition and pay your respects to the author.

Why is marking up a book indispensable to reading it? First, 9 it keeps you awake. (And I don't mean merely conscious; I mean wide awake.) In the second place, reading, if it is active, is thinking, and thinking tends to express itself in words, spoken or written. The marked book is usually the thought-through book. Finally, writing helps you remember the thoughts you had, or the thoughts the author expressed. Let me develop these three points.

---

[1]An epic poem by John Milton, published in 1667, whose subject is humanity's fall from grace.

[2]An oil painting by the Dutch artist Rembrandt van Rijn (1606–1669).

[3]A famous orchestral conductor (1867–1957) of the Metropolitan Opera and the New York Philharmonic, among others.

[4]A world-famous composer (1833–1897).

If reading is to accomplish anything more than passing time, it   10
must be active. You can't let your eyes glide across the lines of a
book and come up with an understanding of what you have read.
Now an ordinary piece of light fiction, like say, *Gone with the Wind*,
doesn't require the most active kind of reading. The books you read
for pleasure can be read in a state of relaxation, and nothing is lost.
But a great book, rich in ideas and beauty, a book that raises and tries
to answer great fundamental questions, demands the most active
reading of which you are capable. You don't absorb the ideas of John
Dewey[1] the way you absorb the crooning of Mr. Vallee[2]. You have to
reach for them. That you cannot do while you're asleep.

If, when you've finished reading a book, the pages are filled   11
with your notes, you know that you read actively. The most famous
active reader of great books I know is President Hutchins, of the
University of Chicago. He also has the hardest schedule of business
activities of any man I know. He invariably reads with a pencil, and
sometimes, when he picks up a book and pencil in the evening, he
finds himself, instead of making intelligent notes, drawing what he
calls "caviar factories" on the margins. When that happens, he puts
the book down. He knows he's too tired to read, and he's just
wasting time.

But, you may ask, why is writing necessary? Well, the physi-   12
cal act of writing, with your own hand, brings words and sentences
more sharply before your mind and preserves them better in your
memory. To set down your reaction to important words and sentences you have read, and the questions they have raised in your
mind, is to preserve those reactions and sharpen those questions.

Even if you wrote on a scratch pad, and threw the paper away   13
when you had finished writing, your grasp of the book would be
surer. But you don't have to throw the paper away. The margins
(top and bottom, as well as side), the endpapers, the very space between the lines, are all available. They aren't sacred. And, best of
all, your marks and notes become an integral part of the book and
stay there forever. You can pick up the book the following week or

[1]John Dewey: an American philosopher and educator (1859–1952)
known for his belief in practical education.

[2]Rudy Vallee: an American popular singer of the 1940s.

year, and there are all your points of agreement, disagreement, doubt, and inquiry. It's like resuming an interrupted conversation with the advantage of being able to pick up where you left off.

And that is exactly what reading a book should be: a conversa- 14 tion between you and the author. Presumably he knows more about the subject than you do; naturally, you'll have the proper humility as you approach him. But don't let anybody tell you that a reader is supposed to be solely on the receiving end. Understanding is a two-way operation; learning doesn't consist in being an empty receptacle. The learner has to question himself and question the teacher. He even has to argue with the teacher, once he understands what the teacher is saying. And marking a book is literally an expression of your differences, or agreements of opinion, with the author.

There are all kinds of devices for marking a book intelligently 15 and fruitfully. Here's the way I do it:

1. *Underlining:* Of major points, of important or forceful statements.

2. *Vertical lines at the margin:* To emphasize a statement already underlined.

3. *Star, asterisk, or other doodad at the margin:* To be used sparingly, to emphasize the ten or twenty most important statements in the book. (You may want to fold the bottom corner of each page on which you use such marks. It won't hurt the sturdy paper on which most modern books are printed, and you will be able to take the book off the shelf at any time and, by opening it at the folded-corner page, refresh your recollection of the book.)

4. *Numbers in the margin:* To indicate the sequence of points the author makes in developing a single argument.

5. *Numbers of other pages in the margin:* To indicate where else in the book the author makes points relevant to the point marked; to tie up the ideas in a book, which, though they may be separated by many pages, belong together.

6. *Circling of key words or phrases.*

7. *Writing in the margin, or at the top or bottom of the page,*

for the sake of: Recording questions (and perhaps answers) which a passage raised in your mind; reducing a complicated discussion to a simple statement; recording the sequence of major points right through the book. I use the endpapers at the back of the book to make a personal index of the author's points in the order of their appearance.

The front endpapers are, to me, the most important. Some 16 people reserve them for a fancy bookplate. I reserve them for fancy thinking. After I have finished reading the book and making my personal index on the back endpapers, I turn to the front and try to outline the book, not page by page, or point by point (I've already done that at the back), but as an integrated structure, with a basic unity and an order of parts. This outline is, to me, the measure of my understanding of the work.

If you're a die-hard anti-book-marker, you may object that the 17 margins, the space between the lines, and the endpapers don't give you room enough. All right. How about using a scratch pad slightly smaller than the page-size of the book—so that the edges of the sheets won't protrude? Make your index, outlines, and even your notes on the pad, and then insert these sheets permanently inside the front and back covers of the book.

Or, you may say that this business of marking books is going to 18 slow up your reading. It probably will. That's one of the reasons for doing it. Most of us have been taken in by the notion that speed of reading is a measure of our intelligence. There is no such thing as the right speed for intelligent reading. Some things should be read quickly and effortlessly, and some should be read slowly and even laboriously. The sign of intelligence in reading is the ability to read different things differently according to their worth. In the case of good books, the point is not to see how many of them you can get through, but rather how many can get through you—how many you can make your own. A few friends are better than a thousand acquaintances. If this be your aim, as it should be, you will not be impatient if it takes more time and effort to read a great book than it does a newspaper.

You may have one final objection to marking books. You 19 can't lend them to your friends because nobody else can read them without being distracted by your notes. Furthermore, you won't want to lend them because a marked copy is a kind of intellectual diary, and lending it is almost like giving your mind away.

If your friend wishes to read your *Plutarch's Lives*[1], 20
Shakespeare, or *The Federalist Papers*[2], tell him, gently but firmly,
to buy a copy. You will lend him your car or your coat—but your
books are as much a part of you as your head or your heart.

Understanding Content

1. What is the selection's main idea? If it is stated directly, locate
   the relevant sentence(s). If it is implied, state the main idea in
   your own words.

2. Why does Adler insist that marking up a book is an essential
   part of reading?

3. What objections to his ideas about marking books does Adler assume readers will have? How does he dismantle these objections?

Understanding Technique

1. What is Adler's purpose for writing this essay? Where does he
   state this purpose? Why do you think he states this purpose
   where he does?

2. What indications are there that Adler wants to establish a personal connection with his readers? How does he show
   sensitivity to their needs and concerns?

3. Adler uses comparison-contrast (showing how things are similar
   or different) a number of times in his essay. Examples occur in
   paragraphs 7, 8, and 10. What does Adler compare and contrast
   in these paragraphs? What points is he making through these
   comparisons and contrasts?

---

[1] A set of biographies of famous Greeks and Romans written by the Greek
author Plutarch during the second century A.D.

[2] A collection of eighty-five essays on the U. S. Constitution written by
Alexander Hamilton, James Madison, and John Jay and published in
1787–1788.

Thinking About Ideas

1. Are you, according to Adler's definition, an active reader? Do you mark your books? Why or why not? When you read, do you have "a conversation with the author"? Explain.

2. In what ways has reading enriched your life? What kinds of reading do you like best? Why?

3. Are there particular kinds of reading material that you avoid? What are they? Why do you avoid them? Do you feel you are missing out on something by avoiding them? Explain.

Writing About Ideas

1. In "How to Mark a Book," Adler explains the process for doing something serious. Write a *paragraph* showing how to do something more lighthearted. Your paragraph might take the form of a step-by-step "how to" guide: how to survive a blind date, how to avoid studying for exams, how to become a couch potato, how to make a gourmet meal out of leftovers. Before writing the paragraph, take some time to list in order the steps you plan to describe.

2. Some people do as little reading as they can. Focus on a particular group (for example, elementary school children, adolescents, college students), and write an *essay* explaining the steps that could be taken to encourage reading in this segment of the population. Consider opening the essay with a vivid example dramatizing that the people under discussion are indeed reluctant readers. For inspiration, you might want to read Bernadete Piassa's "A Love Affair with Books" (page 65), an essay which focuses on the special joys of reading.

3. Adler's purpose is to convince his audience to read actively. Select an activity that you consider equally important, and write an *essay* persuading readers of the activity's value. You might, for example, try to persuade readers to take up a sport, learn a musical instrument, join a campus organization, study a second language, or obey traffic laws. To win over your readers, use, as Adler does, a friendly tone and plenty of lively examples.

Shame

Dick Gregory

Upon receiving help, most of us feel grateful. But what if the help is given in an inconsiderate way? In this piece from Nigger: An Autobiography, *comedian and social activist Dick Gregory shows that the good intentions of a giver are not enough if they don't take the recipient's pride into account. He first recalls a time when an uncaring teacher imparted to Gregory the type of lesson for which no teaching certificate is required, a lesson of hate and shame. He then goes on to describe a parallel incident in which he learns that same lesson from a very different perspective.*

Words to Watch

complected (1): complexioned
stoop (2): an outside stairway, porch, or platform at the entrance to a house
mackinaw (28): a short, plaid coat or jacket
hustling (29): working energetically
googobs (29): Gregory's slang for *gobs,* a large amount

I never learned hate at home, or shame. I had to go to school   1
for that. I was about seven years old when I got my first big lesson.
I was in love with a little girl named Helene Tucker, a light-complected little girl with pigtails and nice manners. She was always
clean and she was smart in school. I think I went to school then

mostly to look at her. I brushed my hair and even got me a little old handkerchief. It was a lady's handkerchief, but I didn't want Helene to see me wipe my nose on my hand. The pipes were frozen again, there was no water in the house, but I washed my socks and shirt every night. I'd get a pot, and go over to Mister Ben's grocery store, and stick my pot down into his soda machine. Scoop out some chopped ice. By evening the ice melted to water for washing. I got sick a lot that winter because the fire would go out at night before the clothes were dry. In the morning I'd put them on, wet or dry, because they were the only clothes I had.

Everybody's got a Helene Tucker, a symbol of everything you   2
want. I loved her for her goodness, her cleanness, her popularity. She'd walk down my street and my brothers and sisters would yell, "Here comes Helene," and I'd rub my tennis sneakers on the back of my pants and wish my hair wasn't so nappy and the white folks' shirt fit me better. I'd run out on the street. If I knew my place and didn't come too close, she'd wink at me and say hello. That was a good feeling. Sometimes I'd follow her all the way home, and shovel the snow off her walk and try to make friends with her Momma and her aunts. I'd drop money on her stoop late at night on my way back from shining shoes in the taverns. And she had a Daddy, and he had a good job. He was a paper hanger.

I guess I would have gotten over Helene by summertime, but   3
something happened in that classroom that made her face hang in front of me for the next twenty-two years. When I played the drums in high school it was for Helene and when I broke track records in college it was for Helene and when I started standing behind microphones and heard applause I wished Helene could hear it, too. It wasn't until I was twenty-nine years old and married and making money that I finally got her out of my system. Helene was sitting in that classroom when I learned to be ashamed of myself.

It was on a Thursday. I was sitting in the back of the room, in   4
a seat with a chalk circle drawn around it. The idiot's seat, the troublemaker's seat.

The teacher thought I was stupid. Couldn't spell, couldn't   5
read, couldn't do arithmetic. Just stupid. Teachers were never interested in finding out that you couldn't concentrate because you were so hungry, because you hadn't had any breakfast. All you could

think about was noontime, would it ever come? Maybe you could sneak into the cloakroom and steal a bite of some kid's lunch out of a coat pocket. A bite of something. Paste. You can't really make a meal of paste, or put it on bread for a sandwich, but sometimes I'd scoop a few spoonfuls out of the big paste jar in the back of the room. Pregnant people get strange tastes. I was pregnant with poverty. Pregnant with dirt and pregnant with smells that made people turn away, pregnant with cold and pregnant with shoes that were never bought for me, pregnant with five other people in my bed and no Daddy in the next room, and pregnant with hunger. Paste doesn't taste too bad when you're hungry.

The teacher thought I was a troublemaker. All she saw from 6 the front of the room was a little black boy who squirmed in his idiot's seat and made noises and poked the kids around him. I guess she couldn't see a kid who made noises because he wanted someone to know he was there.

It was on a Thursday, the day before the Negro payday. The 7 eagle always flew on Friday. The teacher was asking each student how much his father would give to the Community Chest. On Friday night, each kid would get the money from his father, and on Monday he would bring it to the school. I decided I was going to buy a Daddy right then. I had money in my pocket from shining shoes and selling papers, and whatever Helene Tucker pledged for her Daddy I was going to top it. And I'd hand the money right in. I wasn't going to wait until Monday to buy me a Daddy.

I was shaking, scared to death. The teacher opened her book 8 and started calling out names alphabetically.

"Helene Tucker?" 9

"My Daddy said he'd give two dollars and fifty cents." 10

"That's very nice, Helene. Very, very nice indeed." 11

That made me feel pretty good. It wouldn't take too much to 12 top that. I had almost three dollars in dimes and quarters in my pocket. I stuck my hand in my pocket and held onto the money, waiting for her to call my name. But the teacher closed her book after she called everybody else in the class.

I stood up and raised my hand. 13

"What is it now?" 14

"You forgot me." 15

She turned toward the blackboard. "I don't have time to be   16
playing with you, Richard."

"My Daddy said he'd . . ."   17

"Sit down, Richard, you're disturbing the class."   18

"My Daddy said he'd give . . . fifteen dollars."   19

She turned around and looked mad. "We are collecting this   20
money for you and your kind, Richard Gregory. If your Daddy can
give fifteen dollars you have no business being on relief."

"I got it right now, I got it right now, my Daddy gave it to me   21
to turn in today, my Daddy said . . ."

"And furthermore," she said, looking right at me, her nostrils   22
getting big and her lips getting thin and her eyes opening wide, "we
know you don't have a Daddy."

Helene Tucker turned around, her eyes full of tears. She felt   23
sorry for me. Then I couldn't see her too well because I was crying,
too.

"Sit down, Richard."   24

And I always thought the teacher kind of liked me. She al-   25
ways picked me to wash the blackboard on Friday, after school.
That was a big thrill, it made me feel important. If I didn't wash it,
come Monday the school might not function right.

"Where are you going, Richard!"   26

I walked out of school that day, and for a long time I didn't go   27
back very often. There was shame there.

Now there was shame everywhere. It seemed like the whole   28
world had been inside that classroom, everyone had heard what the
teacher had said, everyone had turned around and felt sorry for me.
There was shame in going to the Worthy Boys Annual Christmas
Dinner for you and your kind, because everybody knew what a
worthy boy was. Why couldn't they just call it the Boys Annual
Dinner, why'd they have to give it a name? There was shame in
wearing the brown and orange and white plaid mackinaw the welfare gave to three thousand boys. Why'd it have to be the same for
everybody so when you walked down the street the people could
see you were on relief? It was a nice warm mackinaw and it had a
hood, and my Momma beat me and called me a little rat when she
found out I stuffed it in the bottom of a pail full of garbage way
over on Cottage Street. There was shame in running over to Mister
Ben's at the end of the day and asking for his rotten peaches, there

was shame in asking Mrs. Simmons for a spoonful of sugar, there was shame in running out to meet the relief truck. I hated that truck, full of food for you and your kind. I ran into the house and hid when it came. And then I started to sneak through alleys, to take the long way home so the people going into White's Eat Shop wouldn't see me. Yeah, the whole world heard the teacher that day, we all know you don't have a Daddy.

It lasted for a while, this kind of numbness. I spent a lot of   29
time feeling sorry for myself. And then one day I met this wino in a restaurant. I'd been out hustling all day, shining shoes, selling newspapers, and I had googobs of money in my pocket. Bought me a bowl of chili for fifteen cents, and a cheeseburger for fifteen cents, and a Pepsi for five cents, and a piece of chocolate cake for ten cents. That was a good meal. I was eating when this old wino came in. I love winos because they never hurt anyone but themselves.

The old wino sat down at the counter and ordered twenty-six   30
cents worth of food. He ate it like he really enjoyed it. When the owner, Mister Williams, asked him to pay the check, the old wino didn't lie or go through his pocket like he suddenly found a hole.

He just said: "Don't have no money."   31

The owner yelled: "Why in hell you come in here and eat my   32
food if you don't have no money? That food cost me money."

Mister Williams jumped over the counter and knocked the   33
wino off his stool and beat him over the head with a pop bottle. Then he stepped back and watched the wino bleed. Then he kicked him. And he kicked him again.

I looked at the wino with blood all over his face and I went   34
over. "Leave him alone, Mister Williams. I'll pay the twenty-six cents."

The wino got up, slowly, pulling himself up to the stool, then   35
up to the counter, holding on for a minute until his legs stopped shaking so bad. He looked at me with pure hate. "Keep your twenty-six cents. You don't have to pay, not now. I just finished paying for it."

He started to walk out, and as he passed me, he reached down   36
and touched my shoulder. "Thanks, sonny, but it's too late now. Why didn't you pay it before?"

I was pretty sick about that. I waited too long to help another 37
man.

Understanding Content

1. What is the selection's main idea? If it is stated directly, locate the relevant sentence(s). If it is implied, state the main idea in your own words.

2. Exactly what made Gregory feel such shame that he stayed away from school? Was it being treated as if he were "stupid" and a "troublemaker"—or was it something else? Explain.

3. Although Gregory had a negative self-image as a child, there was much that was admirable about him. Which of Gregory's positive characteristics emerge from this selection?

Understanding Technique

1. The Community Chest anecdote (paragraphs 7–27) is central to Gregory's essay. What would have been lost if Gregory had briefly summarized the event instead of dramatizing it as he did with description and dialogue? Why do you suppose he tells readers about Helene and the teacher before presenting the anecdote?

2. Why do you think Gregory uses the word "pregnant" in paragraph 5? Why does he use it repeatedly? Where else does he use repetition? What effect do you think Gregory intended these repetitions to have?

3. Why might Gregory have decided to follow the Community Chest episode with the wino incident? What is the connection between the two incidents? How do the two reinforce each other?

Thinking About Ideas

1. The Community Chest incident could have had very different results if Gregory's teacher had handled the situation differently. What do you think she should have done when Gregory said, "You forgot me"? Could she have used a better method of collecting money from students? Explain.

2. Gregory writes that he didn't get over Helene until he was 29. Why do you think it took him so long to get Helene out of his mind? What are some ways we can overcome negative feelings and experiences from our own pasts?

3. Gregory states that he learned about shame at school. What other unintended lessons do you think are sometimes "taught" at schools?

Writing About Ideas

1. Like Gregory, you have probably regretted, at one time or another, the way you acted in a particular situation. Perhaps you didn't stop someone from being teased or spoke harshly to someone who needed kindness. Using vivid description and dramatic dialogue, write a *paragraph* about a time you wished you had acted differently. End, as Gregory does, with one or two brief sentences expressing regret about your response to the incident.

2. Gregory illustrates the word "shame" by narrating an event in which shame played a central part. Write an *essay* about a single event that shed light on another equally powerful word. For example, you could make the point that "My family didn't understand the meaning of 'fear' until a tornado struck the neighborhood." Focus on those aspects of the event that illustrate the meaning of the word you are writing about. Like Gregory, present revealing descriptions and dialogue in your account. Possible words to write about include "pride," "disappointment," "joy," and "relief."

∞ 3. Gregory's teacher obviously gives little thought to Gregory's self-esteem. Many would argue, however, that encouraging students is a key part of a teacher's job. Write an *essay* supporting the point that there are various strategies teachers can use to help students feel good about themselves. Drawing upon your own experiences and those of friends and relatives, include specific suggestions and detailed anecdotes for every method you list. For instance, if you state that teachers should give students opportunities to succeed, you could develop that point by showing how a shy but artistically gifted child gained self-confidence when asked to help the teacher decorate the bulletin board. Ben Carson's "Do It Better!" (page 45) and Mary Sherry's "In Praise of the F Word" (page 87) offer perspectives on ways to encourage students to do their best.

In Praise of the F Word

Mary Sherry

Once upon a time, a high-school diploma was a meaning-ful document. It guaranteed that the holder possessed certain basic abilities and was ready to take on an adult's role in the working world. That is not the case today. High schools which function as "diploma mills" have created a need for a whole new category of adult educators like Mary Sherry. Her observations on why students are passed along in school and her recommended alternative were first printed in the "My Turn" column of Newsweek *magazine.*

Words to Watch

validity (1) soundness
impediments (4) obstacles
composure (6): calmness and self-control
conspiracy (11): plot

Tens of thousands of eighteen-year-olds will graduate this   1
year and be handed meaningless diplomas. These diplomas won't
look any different from those awarded their luckier classmates.
Their validity will be questioned only when their employers discover that these graduates are semiliterate.

Eventually a fortunate few will find their way into educational-   2
repair shops—adult-literacy programs, such as the one where I teach
basic grammar and writing. There, high-school graduates and high-

school dropouts pursuing graduate-equivalency certificates will learn the skills they should have learned in school. They will also discover they have been cheated by our educational system.

As I teach, I learn a lot about our schools. Early in each ses-   3
sion I ask my students to write about an unpleasant experience they had in school. No writers' block here! "I wish someone would have had made me stop doing drugs and made me study." "I liked to party and no one seemed to care." "I was a good kid and didn't cause any trouble, so they just passed me along even though I didn't read well and couldn't write." And so on.

I am your basic do-gooder, and prior to teaching this class I   4
blamed the poor academic skills our kids have today on drugs, divorce and other impediments to concentration necessary for doing well in school. But, as I rediscover each time I walk into the classroom, before a teacher can expect students to concentrate, he has to get their attention, no matter what distractions may be at hand. There are many ways to do this, and they have much to do with teaching style. However, if style alone won't do it, there is another way to show who holds the winning hand in the classroom. That is to reveal the trump card[1] of failure.

I will never forget a teacher who played that card to get the at-   5
tention of one of my children. Our youngest, a world-class charmer, did little to develop his intellectual talents but always got by. Until Mrs. Stifter.

Our son was a high-school senior when he had her for   6
English. "He sits in the back of the room talking to his friends," she told me. "Why don't you move him to the front row?" I urged, believing the embarrassment would get him to settle down. Mrs. Stifter looked at me steely-eyed over her glasses. "I don't move seniors," she said. "I flunk them." I was flustered. Our son's academic life flashed before my eyes. No teacher had ever threatened him with that before. I regained my composure and managed to say that I thought she was right. By the time I got home I was feeling pretty good about this. It was a radical approach for these times, but, well, why not? "She's going to flunk you," I told my son. I did not dis-

---

[1]In cards, an advantage held in reserve until it's needed.

cuss it any further. Suddenly English became a priority in his life. He finished out the semester with an A.

I know one example doesn't make a case, but at night I see a parade of students who are angry and resentful for having been passed along until they could no longer even pretend to keep up. Of average intelligence or better, they eventually quit school, concluding they were too dumb to finish. "I should have been held back," is a comment I hear frequently. Even sadder are those students who are high-school graduates who say to me after a few weeks of class, "I don't know how I ever got a high-school diploma."

Passing students who have not mastered the work cheats them and the employers who expect graduates to have basic skills. We excuse this dishonest behavior by saying kids can't learn if they come from terrible environments. No one seems to stop to think that—no matter what environments they come from—most kids don't put school first on their list unless they perceive something is at stake. They'd rather be sailing.

Many students I see at night could give expert testimony on unemployment, chemical dependency, abusive relationships. In spite of these difficulties, they have decided to make education a priority. They are motivated by the desire for a better job or the need to hang on to the one they've got. They have a healthy fear of failure.

People of all ages can rise above their problems, but they need to have a reason to do so. Young people generally don't have the maturity to value education in the same way my adult students value it. But fear of failure, whether economic or academic, can motivate both.

Flunking as a regular policy has just as much merit today as it did two generations ago. We must review the threat of flunking and see it as it really is—a positive teaching tool. It is an expression of confidence by both teachers and parents that the students have the ability to learn the material presented to them. However, making it work again would take a dedicated, caring conspiracy between teachers and parents. It would mean facing the tough reality that passing kids who haven't learned the material—while it might save them grief for the short term—dooms them to long-term illiteracy. It would mean that teachers would have to follow through on their

threats, and parents would have to stand behind them, knowing
their children's best interests are indeed at stake. This means no
more doing Scott's assignments for him because he might fail. No
more passing Jodi because she's such a nice kid.

This is a policy that worked in the past and can work today. A   12
wise teacher . . . gave our son the opportunity to succeed—or fail.
It's time we return this choice to all students.

Understanding Content

1. What is the selection's main idea? If it is stated directly, locate
   the relevant sentence(s). If it is implied, state the main idea in
   your own words.

2. Sherry begins her essay with the words "Tens of thousands of
   eighteen-year-olds will graduate this year and be handed meaningless diplomas." Why does she call these diplomas
   "meaningless"? What happens to these graduates after high
   school?

3. Most people think of flunking a course as a negative experience.
   Why, then, does Sherry call it a positive teaching tool? In what
   way can the threat of flunking be positive for students?

Understanding Technique

1. Sherry introduces the specific example about her son (paragraphs 5–6) at roughly the mid-point in the essay. Why do you
   think she places this example where she does? What would have
   been lost had she placed the example earlier?

2. Why do you think Sherry uses especially short, crisp sentences
   in the second half of paragraph 6? What is the effect of these
   clipped sentences? How does this effect reinforce Sherry's main
   point?

3. Why do you think Sherry chose the title she did? What is its effect on the reader?

Thinking About Ideas

1. Sherry writes that the threat of flunking can be a positive learning tool. Do you agree with her? What effect, if any, did this threat have on you and your friends?

2. Besides the threat of flunking, what are some tools and strategies instructors can use to improve their students' understanding of material?

3. Although Sherry acknowledges that students "have been cheated by our educational system," she also emphasizes that students need to take responsibility for their education. In what ways can you, as a student, take responsibility for your education? What motivates you to do well in your courses? What can you do if you find you are not motivated?

Writing About Ideas

1. Most everyone has been influenced in one way or another by either an exceptionally good instructor or an incompetent one. Drawing upon your own experience as a student, write a *paragraph* which begins with the sentence "Everyone should have an instructor like _____" or "No one should be forced to learn from an instructor like _____." Then support this statement by providing at least three examples illustrating why this instructor was either the best or the worst one you ever had. Maya Angelou's "Sister Flowers" (page 56) will show you how one writer conveys the special qualities of an influential teacher figure in her life.

2. Sherry finds serious fault with schools' tendency to grant diplomas to unprepared students. What criticisms do you have of education? Are you disturbed that unskilled teachers remain in the classroom? Do you detect an over-emphasis on athletics? Are you unhappy about the lack of effective sex-education programs? Select one of these problems or any other that concerns you. Then write an *essay* illustrating the extent of the problem. You may want to end the essay with suggestions for improving the situation.

⬭ 3. Sherry's son will probably never forget the day his mother told him he was going to flunk English if he didn't work harder. Think back to a specific memory, either positive or negative, you have from your school days. Then write an *essay* about this event. Perhaps you had a personality conflict with a teacher, were unjustly accused of cheating, won a prized academic award, or enjoyed a victory on the athletic field. Use plenty of vivid details so readers can understand how you felt about the experience. You may want to read Ben Carson's "Do It Better!" (page 45) or Dick Gregory's "Shame" (page 79) to see how another writer has depicted a formative school experience.

3

Family Life

Dad

Andrew H. Malcolm

When the author was a little boy, his father was an awesome being: enormous, impossibly wise, endlessly able. In the years that followed, his father assumed somewhat more ordinary dimensions, even acquired weaknesses. Yet Andrew Malcolm's regard for his father does not seem to have suffered. This selection was originally published in the "About Men" column in The New York Times Magazine. *In it, Malcolm, Chicago bureau chief for* The New York Times, *describes a warm father-son relationship that changed gradually, until the balance of roles was reversed.*

Words to Watch

yawning (1): deep and open
surveyed (1): viewed
uncanny (3): mysterious
fishy (5): expressionless
defused (6): reduced
heady (7): exciting
fedora (9): a type of hat
buttress (10): support
incumbent (11): officeholder
ostentatiously (12): in a showy manner

The first memory I have of him—of anything, really—is his   1
strength. It was in the late afternoon in a house under construction

near ours. The unfinished wood floor had large, terrifying holes whose yawning darkness I knew led to nowhere good. His powerful hands, then age 33, wrapped all the way around my tiny arms, then age 4, and easily swung me up to his shoulders to command all I surveyed.

The relationship between a son and his father changes over time. It may grow and flourish in mutual maturity. It may sour in resented dependence or independence. With many children living in single-parent homes today, it may not even exist.   2

But to a little boy right after World War II, a father seemed a god with strange strengths and uncanny powers enabling him to do and know things that no mortal could do or know. Amazing things, like putting a bicycle chain back on, just like that. Or building a hamster cage. Or guiding a jigsaw so it formed the letter F; I learned the alphabet that way in those pretelevision days, one letter or number every other evening plus a review of the collection. (The vowels we painted red because they were special somehow.)   3

He seemed to know what I thought before I did. "You look like you could use a cheeseburger and chocolate shake," he would say on hot Sunday afternoons. When, at the age of 5, I broke a neighbor's garage window with a wild curve ball and waited in fear for ten days to make the announcement, he seemed to know about it already and to have been waiting for something.   4

There were, of course, rules to learn. First came the handshake. None of those fishy little finger grips, but a good firm squeeze accompanied by an equally strong gaze into the other's eyes. "The first thing anyone knows about you is your handshake," he would say. And we'd practice it each night on his return from work, the serious toddler in the battered Cleveland Indians cap running up to the giant father to shake hands again and again until it was firm enough.   5

When my cat killed a bird, he defused the anger of a nine-year-old with a little chat about something called "instinked." The next year, when my dog got run over and the weight of sorrow was just too immense to stand, he was there, too, with his big arms and his own tears and some thoughts on the natural order of life and death, although what was natural about a speeding car that didn't stop always escaped me.   6

As time passed, there were other rules to learn. "Always do   7
your best." "Do it now." "NEVER LIE!" And, most importantly,
"You can do whatever you have to do." By my teens, he wasn't
telling me what to do anymore, which was scary and heady at the
same time. He provided perspective, not telling me what was
around the great corner of life but letting me know there was a lot
more than just today and the next, which I hadn't thought of.

When the most important girl in the world—I forget her name   8
now—turned down a movie date, he just happened to walk by the
kitchen phone. "This may be hard to believe right now," he said,
"but someday you won't even remember her name."

One day, I realize now, there was a change. I wasn't trying to   9
please him so much as I was trying to impress him. I never asked
him to come to my football games. He had a high-pressure career,
and it meant driving through most of Friday night. But for all the
big games, when I looked over at the sideline, there was that familiar fedora. And, by God, did the opposing team captain ever get a
firm handshake and a gaze he would remember.

Then, a school fact contradicted something he said.   10
Impossible that he could be wrong, but there it was in the book.
These accumulated over time, along with personal experiences, to
buttress my own developing sense of values. And I could tell we
had each taken our own, perfectly normal paths.

I began to see, too, his blind spots, his prejudices and his   11
weaknesses. I never threw these up at him. He hadn't to me, and,
anyway, he seemed to need protection. I stopped asking his advice;
the experiences he drew from no longer seemed relevant to the decisions I had to make. On the phone, he would go on about politics
at times, why he would vote the way he did or why some incumbent
was a jerk. And I would roll my eyes to the ceiling and smile a little, though I hid it in my voice.

He volunteered advice for a while. But then, in more recent   12
years, politics and issues gave way to talk of empty errands and, always, to ailments—his friends', my mother's and his own, which
were serious and included heart disease. He had a bedside oxygen
tank, and he would ostentatiously retire there during my visits, asking my help in easing his body onto the mattress. "You have very
strong arms," he once noted.

From his bed, he showed me the many sores and scars on his   13
misshapen body and all the bottles for medicine. He talked of the
pain and craved much sympathy. He got some. But the scene was
not attractive. He told me, as the doctor had, that his condition
would only deteriorate. "Sometimes," he confided, "I would just
like to lie down and go to sleep and not wake up."

After much thought and practice ("You can do whatever you   14
have to do"), one night last winter, I sat down by his bed and remembered for an instant those terrifying dark holes in another
house thirty-five years before. I told my father how much I loved
him. I described all the things people were doing for him. But, I
said, he kept eating poorly, hiding in his room and violating other
doctor's orders. No amount of love could make someone else care
about life, I said: it was a two-way street. He wasn't doing his best.
The decision was his.

He said he knew how hard my words had been to say and how   15
proud he was of me. "I had the best teacher," I said. "You can do
whatever you have to do." He smiled a little. And we shook hands,
firmly, for the last time.

Several days later, at about 4 a.m., my mother heard Dad   16
shuffling about their dark room. "I have some things I have to do,"
he said. He paid a bundle of bills. He composed for my mother a
long list of legal and financial what-to-do's "in case of emergency."
And he wrote me a note.

Then he walked back to his bed and laid himself down. He   17
went to sleep, naturally. And he did not wake up.

Understanding Content

1. What is the selection's main idea? If it is stated directly, locate
   the relevant sentence(s). If it is implied, state the main idea in
   your own words.

2. What are some of the things Malcolm, as a child, learned from
   his father?

3. Why does Malcolm gently scold his dying father? What effect
   does the reprimand have on Malcolm's father?

Understanding Technique

1. In the selection's first paragraph, Malcolm recalls his first memory of his father. What are some of the sensory details the author uses in this paragraph? How do these details reinforce the author's main idea?

2. Locate the three sentence fragments in paragraph 3. Why might Malcolm have decided to use fragments in this spot? What do they convey about the way Malcolm, as a child, regarded his father?

3. In paragraph 12, Malcolm recalls that his father told him, "You have very strong arms." Why do you think Malcolm includes this detail? What important truth about parents and children does this detail reveal?

Thinking About Ideas

1. Consider the way your relationship with your father, your mother, or another important adult has changed over the years. In what ways was your relationship with the person like Malcolm's with his father? How was it different?

2. Often, our opinions of other people change because we ourselves change. How do Malcolm's feelings about his father correspond to changes within himself? When have changes in your feelings about others corresponded to changes within yourself?

3. As a young adult, Malcolm decides not to confront his father about the older man's prejudices. Do you think Malcolm made the right decision? Why or why not? Do you think children should point out their parents' blind spots? Explain.

Writing About Ideas

1. Malcolm recalls some difficult lessons his father taught him as a child, such as accepting the death of a pet and learning about

violence in the world. Write a *paragraph* about a hard lesson you learned as a child or a teenager. Include vivid details from the experience to illustrate how difficult the lesson was for you.

2. Malcolm describes his growing understanding that his father was not a god, but rather a man with his own prejudices and weaknesses. Have you known anyone who turned out to have qualities other than what you expected? For example, some people may not seem particularly strong but demonstrate great strength during a difficult or challenging time; others whom we originally admire may turn out to have negative traits we dislike. Write an *essay* illustrating how someone surprised you by being different from what you expected. Be sure to establish at the beginning of the essay how you initially viewed the person. Then provide specific examples to show how your opinion of this person changed. At the end, reach some conclusion about what you learned from the experience.

3. Even during his adolescence, Malcolm and his father seem to get along. In many families, though, the relationship between parents and teenagers is troubled and stormy. Write an *essay* detailing three things either teens or their parents could do to get along better during this stressful period in their lives. Illustrate each of your suggestions with at least one real-life or hypothetical example, and be sure to explain what the effect would be if teens or parents followed your advice. Jade Snow Wong's "Fifth Chinese Daughter" (page 121) might give you some ideas about conflicts between parents and adolescents.

For My Indian Daughter

Lewis Sawaquat

In America today it is possible to live a normal life without being in close touch with one's personal roots. That was Lewis Sawaquat's experience—until he decided to learn more about his Native American heritage. When this essay was originally published on the "My Turn" page of Newsweek *magazine, it was under the author's former name, Lewis Johnson. Taking back his Indian name has been one step in Sawaquat's journey toward reclaiming his heritage. He explains in this reading how researching his roots led him to discover not only the unique culture of his people, but also his connection with all people.*

Words to Watch

guttural (2): spoken in harsh sounds
grub (3): a thick, wormlike larva
comeuppance (7): punishment
irony (7): inconsistency between what is expected and what actually happens
lore (8): collection of facts, beliefs, and traditions
iridescent (9): displaying shiny rainbowlike colors
culminated (12): reached its highest point
discomfiting (13): disturbing

My little girl is singing herself to sleep upstairs, her voice   1
mingling with the sounds of the birds outside in the old maple trees.

She is two and I am nearly fifty, and I am very taken with her. She came along late in my life, unexpected and unbidden, a startling gift.

Today at the beach my chubby-legged, brown-skinned daugh-   2
ter ran laughing into the water as fast as she could. My wife and I laughed watching her, until we heard behind us a low guttural curse and then an unpleasant voice raised in an imitation war whoop.

I turned to see a fat man in a bathing suit, white and soft as a   3
grub, as he covered his mouth and prepared to make the Indian war cry again. He was middle-aged, younger than I, and had three little children lined up next to him, grinning foolishly. My wife suggested we leave the beach, and I agreed.

I knew the man was not unusual in his feelings against   4
Indians. His beach behavior might have been socially unacceptable to more civilized whites, but his basic view of Indians is expressed daily in our small town, frequently on the editorial pages of the county newspaper, as white people speak out against Indian fishing rights and land rights, saying in essence, "Those Indians are taking our fish, our land." It doesn't matter to them that we were here first, that the U.S. Supreme Court has ruled in our favor. It matters to them that we have something they want, and they hate us for it. Backlash is the common explanation of the attacks on Indians, the bumper stickers that say, "Spear an Indian, Save a Fish," but I know better. The hatred of Indians goes back to the beginning when white people came to this country. For me it goes back to my childhood in Harbor Springs, Michigan.

Theft. Harbor Springs is now a summer resort for the very af-   5
fluent, but a hundred years ago it was the Indian village of my Ottawa ancestors. My grandmother, Anna Showanessy, and other Indians like her, had their land there taken by treaty, by fraud, by violence, by theft. They remembered how whites had burned down the village at Burt Lake in 1900 and pushed the Indians out. These were the stories in my family.

When I was a boy my mother told me to walk down the alleys   6
in Harbor Springs and not to wear my orange football sweater out of the house. This way I would not stand out, not be noticed, and not be a target.

I wore my orange sweater anyway and deliberately avoided the   7
alleys. I was the biggest person I knew and wasn't really afraid. But I

met my comeuppance when I enlisted in the U.S. Army. One night all the men in my barracks gathered together and, gang-fashion, pulled me into the shower and scrubbed me down with rough brushes used for floors, saying, "We won't have any dirty Indians in our outfit." It is a point of irony that I was cleaner than any of them. Later in Korea I learned how to kill, how to bully, how to hate Koreans. I came out of the war tougher than ever and, strangely, white.

I went to college, got married, lived in La Porte, Indiana, 8 worked as a surveyor and raised three boys. I headed Boy Scout groups, never thinking it odd when the Scouts did imitation Indian dances, imitation Indian lore.

One day when I was thirty-five or thereabouts I heard about 9 an Indian powwow. My father used to attend them and so with great curiosity and a strange joy at discovering a part of my heritage, I decided the thing to do to get ready for this big event was to have my friend make me a spear in his forge. The steel was fine and blue and iridescent. The feathers on the shaft were bright and proud.

In a dusty state fairground in southern Indiana, I found white 10 people dressed as Indians. I learned they were "hobbyists," that is, it was their hobby and leisure pastime to masquerade as Indians on weekends. I felt ridiculous with my spear, and I left.

It was years before I could tell anyone of the embarrassment 11 of this weekend and see any humor in it. But in a way it was that weekend, for all its silliness, that was my awakening. I realized I didn't know who I was. I didn't have an Indian name. I didn't speak the Indian language. I didn't know the Indian customs. Dimly I remembered the Ottawa word for dog, but it was a baby word, *kahgee,* not the full word, *muhkahgee,* which I was later to learn. Even more hazily I remembered a naming ceremony (my own). I remembered legs dancing around me, dust. Where had that been? Who had I been? "Sawaquat," my mother told me when I asked, "where the tree begins to grow."

That was 1968, and I was not the only Indian in the country 12 who was feeling the need to remember who he or she was. There were others. They had powwows, real ones, and eventually I found them. Together we researched our past, a search that for me culminated in the Longest Walk, a march on Washington in 1978. Maybe because I now know what it means to be Indian, it surprises me that others don't. Of course there aren't very many of us left. The chances of an average person knowing an average Indian in an average lifetime are pretty slim.

    Circle. Still, I was amused one day when my small, four-year-   13
old neighbor looked at me as I was hoeing in my garden and said, "You aren't a real Indian, are you?" Scotty is little, talkative, likable. Finally I said, "I'm a real Indian." He looked at me for a moment and then said, squinting into the sun, "Then where's your horse and feathers?" The child was simply a smaller, whiter version of my own ignorant self years before. We'd both seen too much TV, that's all. He was not to be blamed. And so, in a way, the moronic man on the beach today is blameless. We come full circle to realize other people are like ourselves, as discomfiting as that may be sometimes.

    As I sit in my old chair on my porch, in a light that is fading   14
so the leaves are barely distinguishable against the sky, I can picture my girl asleep upstairs. I would like to prepare her for what's to come, take her each step of the way saying, there's a place to avoid, here's what I know about this, but much of what's before her she must go through alone. She must pass through pain and joy and solitude and community to discover her own inner self that is unlike any other and come through that passage to the place where she sees all people are one, and in so seeing may live her life in a brighter future.

Understanding Content

1. What is the selection's main idea? If it is stated directly, locate the relevant sentence(s). If it is implied, state the main idea in your own words.

2. How does Sawaquat feel about the man on the beach who mocks his daughter? Does he think the man's attitude is unusual? Why is it significant that the man has three children with him?

3. Why does Sawaquat find the first powwow he attends both embarrassing and insulting? In what ways does the experience have a positive effect on him? Is the effect temporary or permanent? How can you tell?

Understanding Technique

1. Sawaquat opens and closes his essay by referring to his small daughter asleep upstairs. What effect do you think he intends this image to have on readers? How might this effect reinforce the essay's main idea?

2. Reread paragraph 9. What words does Sawaquat use to describe his spear? What do these particular words suggest about Sawaquat's attitude toward his heritage?

3. Sawaquat uses the first person ("I") in his essay and relates highly personal memories. What is the effect of these choices? What would have been lost had his approach been less subjective?

Thinking About Ideas

1. Like almost everyone, you have probably witnessed an incident in which someone revealed strong prejudice. Perhaps the person told a racist joke, made an ethnic slur, or related a sexist anecdote. How did the situation affect you? How did you react? Were you pleased with your reaction? Explain.

2. Despite his earlier attempts to blend in and become almost "white," Sawaquat eventually decides to learn about his heritage and, in the process, comes to take great pride in being a Native American. How might learning about one's heritage be a source of strength?

3. Sawaquat states, "We come full circle to realize other people are like ourselves, as discomfiting as that may be sometimes." Why might the idea that we're all essentially alike be troubling? Think of people you have met who initially seemed very different from you. As you got to know them, did they seem more like you? What might be the implications of your changing awareness?

Writing About Ideas

⊂⊃ 1. The author illustrates how crucial it can be to discover one's basic, or core, identity. Write a *paragraph* showing the powerful effect your ethnic heritage, family roots, or religious background has on your life. You could, for instance, write about one or two of the following: how you eat special foods, listen to certain music, dress in a particular way, celebrate specific rituals. Be sure to explain how this connection with your ethnic identity affects your life. To see how one author reveals his ethnic background, read Andrew Lam's "They Shut My Grandmother's Door" (page 116).

2. Sawaquat believes that his young neighbor was not to be blamed for having stereotypical views about Native Americans. Rather, Sawaquat explains, the youngster simply watches too much television. Focusing on two or three TV shows (or commercials), write an *essay* developing the point that television inaccurately portrays a particular group of people. You might, for example, focus on TV's flawed depiction of elderly people, homemakers, or Asians. Name the shows (or commercials), and provide specific examples to show how erroneous the portrayal is.

3. Sawaquat believes that prejudice occurs because we do not realize how alike all of us are. Focusing on a racial, sexual, class, or ethnic tension in your community or on your campus, write an *essay* detailing the steps that a specific group of people (for example, community leaders, residents of a neighborhood, college administrators, college students) could take to encourage people to see their common humanity. Consider beginning the essay with a vivid example that dramatizes the nature of the problem.

Living Up the Street

Gary Soto

To a poor Hispanic boy growing up on reruns of Leave It to
Beaver, *the life of Anglo families seemed serene, cool, and
uncomplicated. Nowhere on TV did he see children like
him, scrambling towards maturity as they ate beans and
tortillas and played amidst rusted car fenders and broken
glass. To poet and author Gary Soto, it seemed that if his
family would only imitate the habits of the ideal sitcom family, a magical transformation might take place. As you read
this excerpt from Soto's autobiography,* Living Up the
Street, *consider the impact of television on his self-image.*

Words to Watch

egg candlers (4):   workers who examine eggs by holding
                                them before a bright light
muu-muu (5):   a long, loose dress
contorted (8):   twisted
palsied (8):   shaking
host (10):   holy ritual bread
converged (12):   met
feigned (12):   pretended
rifts (16):   breaks in friendly relations

One July, while killing ants on the kitchen sink with a rolled   1
newspaper, I had a nine-year-old's vision of wealth that would save
us from ourselves. For weeks I had drunk Kool-Aid and watched

107

morning reruns of *Father Knows Best,* whose family was so uncomplicated in its routine that I very much wanted to imitate it. The first step was to get my brother and sister to wear shoes at dinner.

"Come on, Rick—come on, Deb," I whined. But Rick mimicked me and the same day that I asked him to wear shoes he came to the dinner table in only his swim trunks. My mother didn't notice, nor did my sister, as we sat to eat our beans and tortillas in the stifling heat of our kitchen. We all gleamed like cellophane, wiping the sweat from our brows with the backs of our hands as we talked about the day: Frankie our neighbor was beat up by Faustino; the swimming pool at the playground would be closed for a day because the pump was broken.

Such was our life. So that morning, while doing-in the train of ants which arrived each day, I decided to become wealthy, and right away! After downing a bowl of cereal, I took a rake from the garage and started up the block to look for work.

We lived on an ordinary block of mostly working class people: warehousemen, egg candlers, welders, mechanics, and a union plumber. And there were many retired people who kept their lawns green and the gutters uncluttered of the chewing gum wrappers we dropped as we rode by on our bikes. They bent down to gather our litter, muttering at our evilness.

At the corner house I rapped the screen door and a very large woman in a muu-muu answered. She sized me up and then asked what I could do.

"Rake leaves," I answered, smiling.

"It's summer, and there ain't no leaves," she countered. Her face was pinched with lines; fat jiggled under her chin. She pointed to the lawn, then the flower bed, and said: "You see any leaves there—or there?" I followed her pointing arm, stupidly. But she had a job for me and that was to get her a Coke at the liquor store. She gave me twenty cents, and after ditching my rake in a bush, off I ran. I returned with an unbagged Pepsi, for which she thanked me and gave me a nickel from her apron.

I skipped off her porch, fetched my rake, and crossed the street to the next block where Mrs. Moore, mother of Earl the retarded man, let me weed a flower bed. She handed me a trowel and for a good part of the morning my fingers dipped into the moist dirt, ripping up runners of Bermuda grass. Worms surfaced in my search for deep roots, and I cut them in halves, tossing them to Mrs. Moore's cat, who pawed them playfully as they dried in the sun. I made out Earl, whose face was pressed to the back window of the house, and although he was calling to me I couldn't understand what he was trying to say. Embarrassed, I worked without looking up, but I imagined his contorted mouth and the ring of keys attached to his belt—keys that jingled with each palsied step. He scared me and I worked quickly to finish the flower bed. When I did finish Mrs. Moore gave me a quarter and two peaches from her tree, which I washed there but ate in the alley behind my house.

I was sucking on the second one, a bit of juice staining the front of my T-shirt, when Little John, my best friend, came walking down the alley with a baseball bat over his shoulder, knocking over trash cans as he made his way toward me. 9

Little John and I went to St. John's Catholic School, where we sat among the "stupids." Miss Marino, our teacher, alternated the rows of good students with the bad, hoping that by sitting side-by-side with the bright students the stupids might become more intelligent, as though intelligence were contagious. But we didn't progress as she had hoped. She grew frustrated when one day, while dismissing class for recess, Little John couldn't get up because his arms were stuck in the slats of the chair's backrest. She scolded us with a shaking finger when we knocked over the globe, denting the already troubled Africa. She muttered curses when Leroy White, a real stupid but a great softball player with the gift to hit to all fields, openly chewed his host when he made his First Communion; his hands swung at his sides as he returned to the pew looking around with a big smile. 10

Little John asked what I was doing, and I told him that I was taking a break from work, as I sat comfortably among high weeds. He wanted to join me, but I reminded him that the last time he'd gone door-to-door asking for work his mother had whipped him. I was with him when his mother, a New Jersey Italian who could rise up in anger one moment and love the next, told me in a polite but matter-of-fact voice that I had to leave because she was going to beat her son. She gave me a homemade popsicle, ushered me to the door, and said that I could see Little John the next day. But it was 11 sooner than that. I went around to his bedroom window to suck my popsicle and watch Little John dodge his mother's blows, a few hitting their mark but many whirring air.

It was midday when Little John and I converged in the alley,   12
the sun blazing in the high nineties, and he suggested that we go to Roosevelt High School to swim. He needed five cents to make fifteen, the cost of admission, and I lent him a nickel. We ran home for my bike and when my sister found out that we were going swimming, she started to cry because she didn't have the fifteen cents but only an empty Coke bottle. I waved for her to come and three of us mounted the bike—Debra on the cross bar, Little John on the handle bars and holding the Coke bottle which we would cash for a nickel and make up the difference that would allow all of us to get in, and me pumping up the crooked streets, dodging cars and pot holes. We spent the day swimming under the afternoon sun, so that when we got home our mom asked us what was darker, the floor or us? She feigned a stern posture, her hands on her hips and her mouth puckered. We played along. Looking down, Debbie and I said in unison, "Us."

That evening at dinner we all sat down in our bathing suits to   13
eat our beans, laughing and chewing loudly. Our mom was in a good mood, so I took a risk and asked her if sometime we could have turtle soup. A few days before I had watched a television program in which a Polynesian tribe killed a large turtle, gutted it, and then stewed it over an open fire. The turtle, basted in a sugary sauce, looked delicious as I ate an afternoon bowl of cereal, but my sister, who was watching the program with a glass of Kool-Aid between her knees, said, "*Caca*[1]."

My mother looked at me in bewilderment. "Boy, are you a   14
crazy Mexican. Where did you get the idea that people eat turtles?"

"On television," I said, explaining the program. Then I took it   15
a step further. "Mom, do you think we could get dressed up for dinner one of these days? David King does."

"*Ay, Dios*[2]," my mother laughed. She started collecting the   16
dinner plates, but my brother wouldn't let go of his. He was still

_____

[1]Spanish for "excrement."

[2]Spanish for "Oh, Lord."

drawing a picture in the bean sauce. Giggling, he said it was me,
but I didn't want to listen because I wanted an answer from Mom.
This was the summer when I spent the mornings in front of the television that showed the comfortable lives of white kids. There were
no beatings, no rifts in the family. They wore bright clothes; toys
tumbled from their closets. They hopped into bed with kisses and
woke to glasses of fresh orange juice, and to a father sitting before
his morning coffee while the mother buttered his toast. They hurried through the day making friends and gobs of money, returning
home to a warmly lit living room, and then dinner. *Leave It to
Beaver* was the program I replayed in my mind:

"May I have the mashed potatoes?" asks Beaver with a smile.   17
"Sure, Beav," replies Wally as he taps the corners of his   18
mouth with a starched napkin.

The father looks on in his suit. The mother, decked out in ear-   19
rings and a pearl necklace, cuts into her steak and blushes. Their
conversation is politely clipped.

"Swell," says Beaver, his cheeks puffed with food.   20
Our own talk at dinner was loud with belly laughs and marked   21
by our pointing forks at one another. The subjects were commonplace.

"Gary, let's go to the ditch tomorrow," my brother suggests.   22
He explains that he has made a life preserver out of four empty de-
tergent bottles strung together with twine and that he will make me
one if I can find more bottles. "No way are we going to drown."

"Yeah, then we could have a dirt clod fight," I reply, so happy   23
to be alive.

Whereas the Beaver's family enjoyed dessert in dishes at the   24
table, our mom sent us outside, and more often than not I went into
the alley to peek over the neighbor's fences and spy out fruit, apri-
cot or peaches.

I had asked my mom and again she laughed that I was a crazy   25
chavalo[1] as she stood in front of the sink, her arms rising and
falling with suds, face glistening from the heat. She sent me outside
where my brother and sister were sitting in the shade that the fence
threw out like a blanket. They were talking about me when I

An informal Spanish word for "boy."

plopped down next to them. They looked at one another and then Debbie, my eight-year-old-sister, started in.

"What's this crap about getting dressed up?" 26

She had entered her profanity stage. A year later she would 27 give up such words and slip into her Catholic uniform, and into squealing on my brother and me when we "cussed this" and "cussed that."

I tried to convince them that if we improved the way we 28 looked, we might get along better in life. White people would like us more. They might invite us to places, like their homes or front yards. They might not hate us so much.

My sister called me a "craphead," and got up to leave with a 29 stalk of grass dangling from her mouth. "They'll never like us."

My brother's mood lightened as he talked about the ditch— 30 the white water, the broken pieces of glass, and the rusted car fenders that awaited our knees. There would be toads, and rocks to smash them.

David King, the only person we knew who resembled the 31 middle class, called from over the fence. David was Catholic, of Armenian and French descent, and his closet was filled with toys. A bear-shaped cookie jar, like the ones on television, sat on the kitchen counter. His mother was remarkably kind while she put up with the racket we made on the street. Evenings, she often watered the front yard and it must have upset her to see us—my brother and I and others—jump from trees laughing, the unkillable kids of the very poor, who got up unshaken, brushed off, and climbed into another one to try again.

David called again. Rick got up and slapped grass from his 32 pants. When I asked if I could come along he said no. David said no. They were two years older so their affairs were different from mine. They greeted one another with foul names and took off down the alley to look for trouble.

I went inside the house, turned on the television, and was able 33 to sit down with a glass of Kool-Aid when Mom shooed me outside.

"It's still light," she said. "Later you'll bug me to let you stay 34 out longer. So go on."

I downed my Kool-Aid and went outside to the front yard. No 35 one was around. The day had cooled and a breeze rustled the trees. Mr. Jackson, the plumber, was watering his lawn and when he saw me he turned away to wash off his front steps. There was more than an hour of light left, so I took advantage of it and decided to look for work. I felt suddenly alive as I skipped down the block in search of an overgrown flower bed and the dime that would end the day right.

Understanding Content

1. What is the selection's main idea? If it is stated directly, locate the relevant sentence(s). If it is implied, state the main idea in your own words.

2. What did Soto, as a child, admire about David King? About the white kids on television?

3. Soto yearns for a life that is different from the one he and his family live. Does he dislike his family and his life? What evidence can you find to support your view?

Understanding Technique

1. Soto narrates one day in his life as a nine-year-old. Reread the essay's first three paragraphs as well as the last one, noting that Soto relates his search for work in both the beginning and the end of the essay. Why do you suppose Soto opens and closes the essay in this manner?

2. Soto uses vivid details to depict his boyhood. Locate at least three spots where Soto's specifics are especially vivid. What do these details convey about Soto's boyhood?

3. Paragraphs 17–20 interrupt Soto's chronological account of his day. Why do you think Soto includes this material? What would have been lost if it hadn't been included?

Thinking About Ideas

1. As a child, Soto drew his impression of middle-class white American life from 1950s television shows like *Leave It to Beaver* and *Father Knows Best*. These shows presented a com-

fortable, cozy view of family life: Parents were wise and understanding, children were respectful, and problems were solved with minimal effort. What television programs today represent "typical" American families? How do these shows differ from those Soto watched?

2. The adults in Soto's boyhood represent a complex mix: Neighbors generously indulge Soto's drive to earn money; Miss Marino, the teacher, callously labels children "stupid"; Little John's mother "could rise up in anger one moment and love the next." How do you think children deal with these conflicting messages about what to expect from adults? How, as a child, did you make sense of similar contradictions?

3. Speaking to his brother and sister, Soto argued that "if we improved the way we looked, we might get along better in life. White people would like us more." Soto's sister isn't convinced that a deliberate attempt to look different would make them more "acceptable." Explain why you think her conclusion is or is not valid. To what extent do you—or people—in general judge others by how they look?

Writing About Ideas

1. Soto paints a vivid picture of his boyhood, using many concrete details to describe his family, neighborhood, and friends. Think of one particular scene from your childhood and write a *paragraph* about it, using a similar wealth of detail to make the scene come alive for readers. Andrew H. Malcolm's "Dad" (page 95) might suggest additional kinds of childhood scenes to describe.

2. Based in part on the television shows he watched, the nine-year-old Soto concluded that something was wrong with his family, not realizing that TV's depiction of family life was heavily idealized. Pick a single kind of TV program (for example, soap operas, news "magazine" shows, situation comedies) and write an *essay* showing that TV presents a distorted view of life. You might, for example, point out that soap operas convey an erro-

neous picture of male-female relationships or that situation comedies misrepresent what college life is like. Support your point with detailed references to two or three shows.

3. Many high school students want to work during the academic year because they believe, as Soto did as a child, that having a job offers significant advantages. However, a growing number of educators and psychologists contend that high school students shouldn't hold jobs during the school year. They argue that jobs distract young people from their studies, force them to adopt an employee role at too early an age, and encourage a preoccupation with money and what money can buy. Write an *essay* explaining why you think teenagers should or should not work during the school year. No matter which position you take, you should, at some point, address briefly the opposing viewpoint. To gather material for the paper, interview several people, including those who agree and those who disagree with your viewpoint.

They Shut
My Grandmother's Door

Andrew Lam

In traditional, family-oriented societies, death is viewed
without alarm. Babies are born, farm animals live and die,
and old people's lives end, all in the familiar surroundings
of the village. In Vietnam, particularly, decades of conflict
have forced the people to face death as a daily reality.
Vietnamese immigrant Andrew Lam, associate editor for
the Pacific News Service, is in a good position to comment
on the contrast between America's and Vietnam's ways of
dealing with death. He believes that a society's attitude towards death says much about its culture.

Words to Watch

quips (2): jokes
disjointed (4): disconnected
filial (6): due from a son or daughter
piety (6): devotion to and honor of family
pervaded (7): filled
rendered (9): made
embellished (10): exaggerated
satirized (10): made fun of
monsoon rain (13): seasonal heavy rains in Asia
wafting (13): drifting through the air

When someone died in the convalescent home where my   1
grandmother lives, the nurses rush to close all the patients' doors.
Though as a policy death is not to be seen at the home, she can always tell when it visits. The series of doors being slammed shut
remind her of the firecrackers during Tet[1].

The nurses' efforts to shield death are more comical to my   2
grandmother than reassuring. "Those old ladies die so often," she
quips in Vietnamese, "every day's like new year."

Still, it is lonely to die in such a place. I imagine some wasted   3
old body under a white sheet being carted silently through the
empty corridor on its way to the morgue. While in America a person may be born surrounded by loved ones, in old age one is often
left to take the last leg of life's journey alone.

Perhaps that is why my grandmother talks now mainly of her   4
hometown, Bac-Lieu; its river and green rich rice fields. Having
lost everything during the war, she can now offer me only her dis-
tant memories: Life was not disjointed back home; one lived in a
gentle rhythm with the land; people died in their homes surrounded
by neighbors and relatives. And no one shut your door.

So it goes. The once gentle, connected world of the past is but   5
the language of dreams. In this fast-paced society of disjointed lives,
we are swept along and have little time left for spiritual comfort.
Instead of relying on neighbors and relatives, on the river and land,
we deal with the language of materialism: overtime, stress, down
payment, credit cards, tax shelter. Instead of going to the temple to
pray for good health we pay life and health insurance religiously.

My grandmother's children and grandchildren share a certain   6
pang of guilt. After a stroke which paralyzed her, we could no
longer keep her at home. And although we visit her regularly, we
are not living up to the filial piety standard expected of us in the old
country. My father silently grieves and my mother suffers from
headaches. (Does she see herself in such a home in a decade or
two?)

Once, a long time ago, living in Vietnam we used to stare   7
death in the face. The war in many ways had heightened our sensi-

---

[1]The lunar new year as celebrated in Vietnam.

bilities toward living and dying. I can still hear the wails of widows
and grieving mothers. Though the fear of death and dying is a uni-
versal one, the Vietnamese did not hide from it. Instead, we dwelt in
its tragedy. Death pervaded our poems, novels, fairy tales and songs.

But if agony and pain are part of Vietnamese culture, pleasure   8
is at the center of America's culture. While Vietnamese holidays are
based on death anniversaries, birthdays are celebrated here.
American popular culture translates death with something like nau-
seating humor. People laugh and scream at blood and guts movies.
The wealthy freeze their dead relatives in liquid nitrogen.
Cemeteries are places of big business, complete with colorful
brochures. I hear there are even drive-by funerals where you don't
have to get out of your own car to pay your respects to the de-
ceased.

That America relies upon the pleasure principle and happy   9
endings in its entertainments does not, however, assist us in evading
suffering. The reality of the suffering of old age is apparent in the
convalescent home. There is an old man, once an accomplished
concert pianist, now rendered helpless by arthritis. Every morning
he sits staring at the piano. One feeble woman who outlived her
children keeps repeating, "My son will take me home." Then there
are those mindless, bedridden bodies kept alive through a series of
tubes and pulsating machines.

But despair is not newsworthy. Death itself must be embel-   10
lished or satirized or deep-frozen in order to catch the public's
attention.

Last week on her eighty-second birthday I went to see my   11
grandmother. She smiled her sweet sad smile.

"Where will you end up in your old age?" she asked me, her   12
mind as sharp as ever.

The memories of monsoon rain and tropical sun and relatives   13
and friends came to mind. Not here, not here, I wanted to tell her.
But the soft moaning of a patient next door and the smell of alcohol
wafting from the sterile corridor brought me back to reality.

"Anywhere is fine," I told her instead, trying to keep up with   14
her courageous spirit. "All I am asking for is that they don't shut
my door."

Understanding Content

1. What is the selection's main idea? If it is stated directly, locate the relevant sentence(s). If it is implied, state the main idea in your own words.

2. What, according to Lam, are the major differences between the Vietnamese and American attitudes toward death? How does Lam account for these differences?

3. What do you think Lam means when he implies that life in America is "disjointed" (paragraph 4)? According to Lam, how does this type of life compare to the life his grandmother remembers in Vietnam?

Understanding Technique

1. To help readers understand the similarities and differences between American and Vietnamese cultures, Lam uses a number of examples. Locate several of his most vivid examples. How do they help Lam support his main point?

2. What do you think Lam's purpose is for writing this essay? Given this purpose, for whom does he seem to have written the essay? How can you tell?

3. A symbol is a concrete object used to represent an intangible or abstract concept. What does the closed door symbolize in Lam's essay?

Thinking About Ideas

1. Have you ever visited a nursing home? If so, did you see anything there that upset you? Was anything a pleasant surprise? What things could be done to improve the quality of life in nursing homes?

2. Lam states that in Vietnam it is the children's responsibility to care for aging parents until their death. In America, many children place their parents in nursing homes to be cared for by

nurses and doctors. Do you think it should be the children's responsibility to care for aging parents? Why or why not? When a family is overwhelmed trying to tend an aging parent, what alternative approaches could be created that would not require putting the elderly person in a nursing home?

3. Lam notes the popularity of "blood and guts" movies in America. Have you seen any of these movies? Which ones? What made you want to see them? Do you agree with Lam that such movies distance people from death and dull their response to it? Explain.

Writing About Ideas

1. Lam contrasts two very different cultural perspectives on death. In a *paragraph,* contrast two people's opposing views toward another topic—perhaps education, exercise, or music. Provide enough specifics so your reader will understand how and why the two people hold such differing perspectives.

2. Think about some of the specific problems and concerns that the elderly face. Areas to consider include lack of transportation, failing health, loneliness, life on a fixed income, and the feeling of being a burden. In an *essay,* discuss one or two of these problems as fully as you can. Use specific examples to help your readers understand each problem. In your final paragraph(s), describe briefly what could be done to improve the overall situation.

○○ 3. Lam writes, "But if agony and pain are part of Vietnamese culture, pleasure is at the center of America's culture." Prepare an *essay* agreeing or disagreeing with Lam's point about American culture. Before formulating your position, think about Americans' attitudes toward work, family, leisure, sex, possessions, and so on. Then, drawing upon the most convincing examples, show that Americans do—or do not—value pleasure above everything else. Reading Donna Barron's "American Family Life: The Changing Picture" (page 128) will give you some perspective on the way Americans live today.

Fifth Chinese Daughter

Jade Snow Wong

Immigrants and their families often wrestle with the problem of maintaining their cultural identity while adapting to life in the new country. That was certainly the case with Jade Snow Wong's family, as Wong explains in this selection from her autobiography, Fifth Chinese Daughter. *Her parents brought with them from China an ancient, and inflexible, set of family traditions. They had a vision of their children reaping the economic benefits of life in the United States while remaining untouched by the Western-style emphasis on the individual. As Wong began to view her family's expectations from an American perspective, conflict inevitably followed.*

Words to Watch

oblige (2): accommodate
adamant (3): unyielding
edict (3): command
incurred (4): acquired
mounted (5): increased
nepotism (7): favoritism shown to relatives
incredulous (12): unbelieving
unfilial (12): not respectful to parents
ingrate (12): an ungrateful person
innuendos (14): belittling suggestions
perplexed (16): puzzled

By the time I was graduating from high school, my parents   1
had done their best to produce an intelligent, obedient daughter,
who would know more than the average Chinatown girl and should
do better than average at a conventional job, her earnings brought
home to them in repayment for their years of child support. Then,
they hoped, she would marry a nice Chinese boy and make him a
good wife, as well as an above-average mother for his children.
Chinese custom used to decree that families should "introduce"
chosen partners to each other's children. The groom's family should
pay handsomely to the bride's family for rearing a well-bred daughter. They should also pay all bills for a glorious wedding banquet
for several hundred guests. Then the bride's family could consider
their job done. Their daughter belonged to the groom's family and
must henceforth seek permission from all persons in his home before returning to her parents for a visit.

But having been set upon a new path, I did not oblige my par-   2
ents with the expected conventional ending. At fifteen, I had moved
away from home to work for room and board and a salary of twenty
dollars per month. Having found that I could subsist independently,
I thought it regrettable to terminate my education. Upon graduating
from high school at the age of sixteen, I asked my parents to assist
me in college expenses. I pleaded with my father, for his years of
encouraging me to be above mediocrity in both Chinese and
American studies had made me wish for some undefined but
brighter future.

My father was briefly adamant. He must conserve his re-   3
sources for my oldest brother's medical training. Though I desired
to continue on an above-average course, his material means were
insufficient to support that ambition. He added that if I had the talent, I could provide for my own college education. When he had
spoken, no discussion was expected. After his edict, no daughter
questioned.

But this matter involved my whole future—it was not simply   4
asking for permission to go to a night church meeting (forbidden
also). Though for years I had accepted the authority of the one I
honored most, his decision that night embittered me as nothing ever
had. My oldest brother had so many privileges, had incurred unusual expenses for luxuries which were taken for granted as his

birthright, yet these were part of a system I had accepted. Now I suddenly wondered at my father's interpretation of the Christian code: was it intended to discriminate against a girl after all, or was it simply convenient for my father's economics and cultural prejudice? Did a daughter have any right to expect more than a fate of obedience, according to the old Chinese standard? As long as I could remember, I had been told that a female followed three men during her lifetime: as a girl, her father; as a wife, her husband; as an old woman, her son.

My indignation mounted against that tradition and I decided   5
then that my past could not determine my future. I knew that more education would prepare me for a different expectation than my other female schoolmates, few of whom were to complete a college degree. I, too, had my father's unshakable faith in the justice of God, and I shared his unconcern with popular opinion.

So I decided to enter junior college, now San Francisco's City   6
College, because the fees were lowest. I lived at home and supported myself with an after-school job which required long hours of housework and cooking but paid me twenty dollars per month, of which I saved as much as possible. The thrills derived from reading and learning, in ways ranging from chemistry experiments to English compositions, from considering new ideas of sociology to the logic of Latin, convinced me that I had made a correct choice. I was kept in a state of perpetual mental excitement by new Western subjects and concepts and did not mind long hours of work and study. I also made new friends, which led to another painful incident with my parents, who had heretofore discouraged even girlhood friendships.

The college subject which had most jolted me was sociology. The instructor fired my mind with his interpretation of family rela-   7
tionships. As he explained to our class, it used to be an economic asset for American farming families to be large, since children were useful to perform agricultural chores. But this situation no longer applied and children should be regarded as individuals with their own rights. Unquestioning obedience should be replaced with parental understanding. So at sixteen, discontented as I was with my parents' apparent indifference to me, those words of my sociology professor gave voice to my sentiments. How old-fashioned was the dead-end attitude of my parents! How ignorant they were of

modern thought and progress! The family unit had been China's strength for centuries, but it had also been her weakness, for corruption, nepotism, and greed were all justified in the name of the family's welfare. My new ideas festered; I longed to release them.

One afternoon on a Saturday, which was normally occupied 8 with my housework job, I was unexpectedly released by my employer, who was departing for a country weekend. It was a rare joy to have free time and I wanted to enjoy myself for a change. There had been a Chinese-American boy who shared some classes with me. Sometimes we had found each other walking to the same 8:00 a.m. class. He was not a special boyfriend, but I had enjoyed talking to him and had confided in him some of my problems. Impulsively, I telephoned him. I knew I must be breaking rules, and I felt shy and scared. At the same time, I was excited at this newly found forwardness, with nothing more purposeful than to suggest another walk together.

He understood my awkwardness and shared my anticipation. 9 He asked me to "dress up" for my first movie date. My clothes were limited but I changed to look more graceful in silk stockings and found a bright ribbon for my long black hair. Daddy watched, catching my mood, observing the dashing preparations. He asked me where I was going without his permission and with whom.

I refused to answer him. I thought of my rights! I thought he 10 surely would not try to understand. Thereupon Daddy thundered his displeasure and forbade my departure.

I found a new courage as I heard my voice announce calmly 11 that I was no longer a child, and if I could work my way through college, I would choose my own friends. It was my right as a person.

My mother heard the commotion and joined my father to face 12 me; both appeared shocked and incredulous. Daddy at once demanded the source of this unfilial, non-Chinese theory. And when I quoted my college professor, reminding him that he had always felt teachers should be revered, my father denounced that professor as a foreigner who was disregarding the superiority of our Chinese culture, with its sound family strength. My father did not spare me; I was condemned as an ingrate for echoing dishonorable opinions which should only be temporary whims, yet nonetheless inexcusable.

The scene was not yet over. I completed my proclamation to   13
my father, who had never allowed me to learn how to dance, by
adding that I was attending a movie, unchaperoned, with a boy I
met at college.

My startled father was sure that my reputation would be sub-   14
ject to whispered innuendos. I must be bent on disgracing the
family name; I was ruining my future, for surely I would yield to
temptation. My mother underscored him by saying that I hadn't any
notion of the problems endured by parents of a young girl.

I would not give in. I reminded them that they and I were not   15
in China, that I wasn't going out with just anybody but someone I
trusted! Daddy gave a roar that no man could be trusted, but I devastated them in declaring that I wished the freedom to find my own
answers.

Both parents were thoroughly angered, scolded me for being   16
shameless, and predicted that I would some day tell them I was
wrong. But I dimly perceived that they were conceding defeat and
were perplexed at this breakdown of their training. I was too old to
beat and too bold to intimidate.

Understanding Content

1. What is the selection's main idea? If it is stated directly, locate
   the relevant sentence(s). If it is implied, state the main idea in
   your own words.

2. What does the selection reveal about the traditional Chinese
   view of men's and women's roles? How do Wong's views differ
   from the traditional ones?

3. How important was education to Wong? How can you tell?
   Which one of her academic experiences affected her most?
   Explain.

Understanding Technique

1. Wong is primarily concerned with describing her rebellion against her parents. How does the selection's first paragraph help Wong achieve her goal?

2. Although Wong struggles to free herself from her father's authority, she has positive feelings for him. How and where does she reveal these feelings?

3. Reread the last two sentences in paragraph 3 and the final sentence in paragraph 16, noting the way Wong uses parallel structure (paired items in matching form) in both places. How does this parallelism reinforce Wong's main idea?

Thinking About Ideas

1. Do you think Wong was correct in going out with her friend from school? Or should she have respected her parents' wishes? Explain your answer.

2. Wong writes that her parents "were perplexed at this breakdown of their training" (paragraph 16). What didn't they understand? Is their lack of understanding due to their cultural background, or are all parents apt to have this problem? Why or why not?

3. Wong wanted to go on to college "for some undefined but brighter future." Why are you going to college? How has college influenced you so far? How do you expect it to affect you in the future?

Writing About Ideas

1. Wong held a difficult after-school job to earn money to finance her college education. Write a *paragraph* describing what you did to get something you wanted badly. Perhaps you worked hard to develop an athletic skill, rent your own apartment, or become a stronger student. Provide vivid details that show your determination to achieve your goal.

⊂⊃ 2. When children grow up, they often accept parental ideas they once resented. What household rule, or parental idea, did you resent when you were younger but now feel was appropriate? In an *essay,* contrast your point of view then and now on one or more parental rules or guidelines. Near the beginning, state your general point, perhaps "Now that I am a parent, I impose rules on my children that I resented when I was their age" or "Some of my parents' ideas that I once thought made no sense seem reasonable to me today." Then discuss the particular parental ideas you used to resist. To illustrate that earlier response, describe specific incidents, confrontations, and conversations. End by explaining the reasons for your changed attitude. Andrew H. Malcolm's "Dad" (page 95) provides insight into the way our views of parents change over time.

3. As a college student, you—like Wong—undoubtedly recognize the value of a college education. Write an *essay* illustrating the point "There are several benefits to going to college." Explain in full each advantage that you cite, and illustrate it with one or more examples based on your own experiences or those of people you know—or of people who did not go to college. To generate ideas for this paper, think about your own motives for going to college, and speak to other students about the pluses they see in attending college.

American Family Life: The Changing Picture

Donna Barron

We Americans have always valued our independence. In recent decades, however, personal independence threatens another beloved American value—family life. With changes in our economic and social environment, family members have found reasons to live increasingly separate lives. Today, both Mom and Dad are busy with their careers, and the kids are absorbed in school activities, sports, and MTV. In this essay, freelance writer Donna Barron reflects on how and why we have changed, and what steps we can take to reclaim our sense of family.

Words to Watch

operate (6): function
mushroomed (7): grown rapidly
array (18): impressive collection

It's another evening in an American household. 1

The door swings open at 5:30 sharp. "Hi, honey! I'm home!" 2
In walks dear old Dad, hungry and tired after a long day at the office. He is greeted by Mom in her apron, three happy children, and the aroma of a delicious pot roast.

After a leisurely meal together, Mom does the dishes. That, 3
after all, is part of her job. The whole family then moves to the living

128

room. There they spend the evening playing Scrabble or watching
TV.

Then everyone is off to bed. And the next morning they wake 4
up to the sounds and smells of Mom preparing pancakes and
sausage for breakfast.

What? You say that doesn't sound like life in your house? 5
Well, you're not alone. In fact, you're probably in the majority.

A few years ago, the above household might have been typical. You can still visit such a home—on television. Just watch 6
reruns of old situation comedies. *Leave It to Beaver,* for example,
shows Mom doing housework in pearls and high heels. Dad keeps
his suit and tie on all weekend. But the families that operate like
Beaver Cleaver's are fewer and fewer. They're disappearing because three parts of our lives have changed. These are the way we
work, the way we eat, and the way we entertain ourselves.
Becoming aware of the effects of those changes may help us improve family life.

Let's look first at the changes in the way we work. Today the 7
words "Hi, honey! I'm home!" might not be spoken by dear old
Dad. Dear old Mom is just as likely to be saying them. A generation ago, most households could get by on one paycheck—Dad's.
Mom stayed home, at least until the children started school. But
today, over half the mothers with young children go to work. Even
a greater percentage of mothers of older children are in the work
force. And the number of single-parent homes has mushroomed in
the last thirty years.

These changes in work have affected children as well as par- 8
ents. When only Dad went out to work, children came home from
school to Mom. (In TV situation comedies, they came home to
Mom and home-baked cookies.) Today, we'll find them at an after-
school program or a neighbor's house. Or they may come home to
no one at all. In every community, children are caring for themselves until their parents return from work. Are these children
missing out on an important part of childhood? Or are they developing a healthy sense of self-reliance? These are questions that
Mrs. Cleaver never had to deal with.

In addition, Dad—and now Mom—are often gone from home 9
longer than ever. Not too long ago, most men worked close to

home. The office or factory was just downtown. Dad often walked
to work or hitched a ride with a friendly neighbor. But no more.

Today's working men and women are commuters. They travel   10
distances to work that would have made their parents gasp.
Commutes of forty-five minutes or an hour are common. Workers
travel on buses, subways, and crowded highways. Many leave their
suburban homes at dawn and don't return until dark. No running
home for lunch in the 1990s.

And speaking of lunch, there's been a second big change in   11
American family life. If both parents are away from home for long
hours, who's whipping up those delicious meals in the kitchen? The
answer, more and more, is nobody.

These days, few people have time to shop for and prepare   12
"home-style" meals. The Cleavers were used to dinners of pot roast
or chicken. Potatoes, salad, and vegetables went with the main
course, with pie or cake for dessert. But this kind of meal takes several hours to fix. People can't spend hours in the kitchen if they get
home at 5:30.

So what does the working family eat? They choose meals that   13
are easy to prepare or are already prepared. Fast food, take-out, and
heat-n-serve dishes make up much of the modern American diet.
Dad may arrive home with a bag of Big Macs and shakes. Mom
may phone out for Chinese food or ask the local pizza parlor to de-
liver. And more and more people rely on microwaves to thaw
frozen food in minutes.

One consequence of these quickly prepared meals is that fam-   14
ilies spend less time dining together. It's hard to make single
servings on aluminum trays special. And classic fast foods, like
hamburgers and fries, are meant to be eaten on the run, not slowly
enjoyed at the dinner table. The '90s family no longer shares the
evening meal. As a result, it no longer shares the day's news . . . or
the feeling of togetherness.

Finally, what about after dinner? Is the family evening at least   15
something the Cleavers could relate to?

Not a chance.   16

We don't even have to look outside the home to see the   17
changes. The modern American family entertains itself in ways the
Cleavers would never have dreamed of.

Thirty years ago, families gathered around a radio each   18
evening. Later, television took over. Most families had just one set,
which they watched together. Today, television and computers bring
a dizzying array of entertainments into the home. Cable television
provides everything from aerobics classes to Shakespeare. VCRs
expand the choices even more. If there's nothing good on network
TV or cable, the video store offers the best and worst of
Hollywood: recent movies, cartoons, "adult" films, exercise programs, travel, sports, how-to tapes. Computer games, which make
viewers part of the action, also provide excitement. Players can
compete in the Olympics, search out aliens, or wipe out entire civi-
lizations on their little screens.

With all these choices, it makes sense to own more than one   19
television set. The two-or-more-TV family used to be rare.
Nowadays, Dad might want to rent an action movie when Mom's
cable shopping service is on. Or Junior is playing a let's-blow-up-
Saturn video game while Sis wants to see the Cosby show. Why not
invest in several sets? Then each family member can enjoy himself
or herself in peace.

What's wrong with this picture of today's family?   20

Only this. Today's Cleavers spend their evenings in front of   21
their separate TV screens. Then they go to bed. The next morning,
they rush off to their separate jobs (work and school). They come
home at separate times. They eat separately. Finally, they return to
their separate TV screens for another evening's entertainment.
During all of these times, when do they talk to each other or even
see each other? When are they a family?

Certain realities of modern life cannot change. One is the   22
need, in most families, for both parents to bring home a paycheck.
Another is the distance many of us must travel to work or to school.
But must everything change? And must we lose the family structure
in the process?

No one is suggesting that we go back to the 1950s. The   23
Cleaver household was a fantasy even then, not reality. But we
might borrow one important lesson from the Cleavers. It is that
family life is just as important as work or play. If we agree, we'll
find ways of spending more time together. We'll find things to
share. And then there will be something *right* with the picture.

Understanding Content

1. What is the selection's main idea? If it is stated directly, locate the relevant sentence(s). If it is implied, state the main idea in your own words.

2. Barron discusses changes that have occurred in three critical areas of American life. What are the three areas? What has been the single most important effect of the changes in these areas?

3. According to Barron, what changes have occurred in parents' work lives? How do these changes affect children?

Understanding Technique

1. To clarify and emphasize her points—and to make her piece more colorful—Barron uses the Cleavers as a symbol. What do the Cleavers represent? How does Barron set up and use this symbolism?

2. Why do you think Barron organizes her points—first about work, then about eating, and finally about entertainment—in the order she does?

3. Barron uses a casual, often conversational tone in her essay. Identify specific places where this easy, informal tone is evident. Why do you think she adopts this tone? What is its effect?

Thinking About Ideas

1. How much time, on the average weekday, does your family spend together? Do you think it's enough time? Why or why not? If not, what do you think your family is losing by not having more time together?

2. Barron points out that today's workers "travel distances to work that would have made their parents gasp." What changes in the United States help to explain such long commutes? Why do you think people are willing to spend so much time going back and forth to work?

3. What changes in the workplace would make it easier for parents to spend more time with their children? Do you know businesses that have implemented any of these changes? Which changes have they adopted, and what has been their effect?

Writing About Ideas

⊂⊃ 1. Like Barron, many people feel that the evening meal provides an important opportunity for families to be together. Write a *paragraph* illustrating at least two benefits to a family of a leisurely dinner hour. Drawing upon your own experiences and observations, provide colorful, convincing examples of the benefits you discuss. Before planning your paper, you might want to read Gary Soto's "Living Up the Street" (page 107), an essay that contains a lively description of a family's dinnertime.

2. Barron writes that if we believe that family life is important, "we'll find ways of spending more time together." Focus on the three areas of life (work, eating, entertainment) that Barron discusses, and write an *essay* showing specifically what families could do to spend more time together. You may want to brainstorm with others to gather material for your paper.

3. Barron contrasts the typical lifestyle of a 1950s family with that of a family today. Write an *essay* contrasting two lifestyles of your own—perhaps your eating habits before and after you discovered health foods or your life before and after marriage. Once you choose which two times of your life to write about, decide on several contrasting points to discuss. For an essay on your life before and after marriage, for example, you might contrast how you now socialize, spend money, and perform housekeeping chores with the way you used to. If you like, use exaggeration and a humorous tone to highlight the amusing aspects of the differences you describe.

4

Television, Movies, and Entertainment

Rudeness at the Movies

Bill Wine

Do the loud conversations of your neighbors, the crinkling of candy wrappers, and the wailing of children make you wish you'd gone bowling instead of to the movies? Do you slump in your seat, despairing, when your fellow viewers announce plot twists moments before they happen? You'll find a comrade in suffering in film critic and columnist Bill Wine, who thinks people have come to feel all too at home in theaters. In the following essay, which first appeared in the New Jersey Courier-Post, *Wine wittily describes what the movie-going experience all too often is like these days.*

Words to Watch

spritzes (4): sprays
engulfed (9): swallowed up
galling (14): irritating
malodorous (15): bad-smelling
superfluous (16): unnecessary
prescient (20): knowing what will happen beforehand
waxing (21): becoming
provocation (23): urging
gregarious (25): sociable
Fascist-like (27): like dictators

Is this actually happening or am I dreaming?   1
I am at the movies, settling into my seat, eager with anticipation   2

137

at the prospect of seeing a long-awaited film of obvious quality. The theater is absolutely full for the late show on this weekend evening, as the reviews have been ecstatic for this cinema masterpiece.

Directly in front of me sits a man an inch or two taller than   3
the Jolly Green Giant. His wife, sitting on his left, sports the very latest in fashionable hairdos, a gathering of her locks into a shape that resembles a drawbridge when it's open.

On his right, a woman spritzes herself liberally with perfume   4
that her popcorn-munching husband got her for Valentine's Day, a scent that should be renamed "Essence of Elk."

The row in which I am sitting quickly fills up with members   5
of Cub Scout Troop 432, on an outing to the movies because rain has cancelled their overnight hike. One of the boys, demonstrating the competitive spirit for which Scouts are renowned worldwide, announces to the rest of the troop the rules in the Best Sound Made from an Empty Good-n-Plenty's Box contest, about to begin.

Directly behind me, a man and his wife are ushering three   6
other couples into their seats. I hear the woman say to the couple next to her: "You'll love it. You'll just love it. This is our fourth time and we enjoy it more and more each time. Don't we, Harry? Tell them about the pie-fight scene, Harry. Wait'll you see it. It comes just before you find out that the daughter killed her boyfriend. It's great."

The woman has more to say—much more—but she is   7
drowned out at the moment by the wailing of a six-month-old infant in the row behind her. The baby is crying because his mother, who has brought her twins to the theater to save on babysitting costs, can change only one diaper at a time.

Suddenly, the lights dim. The music starts. The credits roll.   8
And I panic.

I plead with everyone around me to let me enjoy the movie.   9
All I ask, I wail, is to be able to see the images and hear the dialogue and not find out in advance what is about to happen. Is that so much to expect for six bucks, I ask, now engulfed by a cloud of self-pity. I begin weeping unashamedly.

Then, as if on cue, the Jolly Green Giant slumps down in his   10
seat, his wife removes her wig, the Elk lady changes her seat, the

Scouts drop their candy boxes on the floor, the play-by-play commentator takes out her teeth, and the young mother takes her two bawling babies home.

Of course I am dreaming, I realize, as I gain a certain but 11 shaky consciousness. I notice that I am in a cold sweat. Not because the dream is scary, but from the shock of people being that cooperative.

I realize that I have awakened to protect my system from hav- 12 ing to handle a jolt like that. For never—NEVER—would that happen in real life. Not on this planet.

I used to wonder whether I was the only one who feared bad 13 audience behavior more than bad moviemaking. But I know now that I am not. Not by a long shot. The most frequent complaint I have heard in the last few months about the moviegoing experience has had nothing to do with the films themselves.

No. What folks have been complaining about is the audience. 14 Indeed, there seems to be an epidemic of galling inconsiderateness and outrageous rudeness.

It is not that difficult to forgive a person's excessive height, or 15 malodorous perfume, or perhaps even an inadvisable but understandable need to bring very young children to adult movies.

But the talking: that is not easy to forgive. It is inexcusable. 16 Talking—loud, constant, and invariably superfluous—seems to be standard operating procedure on the part of many movie patrons these days.

It is true, I admit, that after a movie critic has seen several 17 hundred movies in the ideal setting of an almost-empty screening room with no one but other politely silent movie critics around him, it does tend to spoil him for the packed-theater experience.

And something is lost viewing a movie in almost total isola- 18 tion—a fact that movie distributors acknowledge with their reluctance to screen certain audience-pleasing movies for small groups of critics. Especially with comedies, the infectiousness of laughter is an important ingredient of movie-watching pleasure.

But it is a decidedly uphill battle to enjoy a movie—no matter 19 how suspenseful or hilarious or moving—with non-stop gabbers sitting within earshot. And they come in sizes, ages, sexes, colors and motivations of every kind.

Some chat as if there is no movie playing. Some greet friends 20
as if at a picnic. Some alert those around them to what is going to
happen, either because they have seen the film before, or because
they are self-proclaimed experts on the predictability of plotting
and want to be seen as prescient geniuses.

Some describe in graphic terms exactly what is happening as 21
if they were doing the commentary for a sporting event on radio.
("Ooh, look, he's sitting down. Now he's looking at that green car.
A banana—she's eating a banana.") Some audition for film critic
Gene Shalit's job by waxing witty as they critique the movie right
before your very ears.

And all act as if it is their Constitutional or God-given right. 22
As if their admission price allows them to ruin the experience for
anyone and everyone else in the building. But why?

Good question. I wish I knew. Maybe rock concerts and ball 23
games—both environments which condone or even encourage
hootin' and hollerin'—have conditioned us to voice our approval
and disapproval and just about anything else we can spit out of our
mouths at the slightest provocation when we are part of an audience.

But my guess lies elsewhere. The villain, I'm afraid, is the 24
tube. We have seen the enemy and it is television.

We have gotten conditioned over the last few decades to 25
spending most of our screen-viewing time in front of a little box in
our living rooms and bedrooms. And when we watch that piece of
furniture, regardless of what is on it—be it commercial, Super
Bowl, soap opera, funeral procession, prime-time sitcom,
Shakespeare play—we chat. Boy, do we chat. Because TV viewing
tends to be an informal, gregarious, friendly, casually interruptible
experience, we talk whenever the spirit moves us. Which is often.

All of this is fine. But we have carried behavior that is perfectly acceptable in the living room right to our neighborhood 26
movie theater. And that *isn't* fine. In fact, it is turning lots of people
off to what used to be a truly pleasurable experience: sitting in a
jammed movie theater and watching a crowd-pleasing movie. And
that's a first-class shame.

Nobody wants Fascist-like ushers, yet that may be where 27
we're headed of necessity. Let's hope not. But something's got to
give.

Movies during this Age of Television may or may not be bet- 28
ter than ever. About audiences, however, there is no question.
They are worse.   29

Understanding Content

1. What is the selection's main idea? If it is stated directly, locate
   the relevant sentence(s). If it is implied, state the main idea in
   your own words.

2. What specific rude behavior does Wine object to most strongly
   in movie theaters? Why does he consider that behavior so objectionable?

3. According to Wine, what are some possible causes for people's
   rude behavior at movies? Of these, which does Wine consider
   the most likely cause?

Understanding Technique

1. Wine provides exaggerated descriptions of audience members—
   for example, he refers to the tall man sitting in front of him as
   "an inch or two taller than the Jolly Green Giant." Find other
   examples of this humorous exaggeration. Besides making readers smile, why might Wine have described the audience in this
   way?

2. Wine's style is casual and informal. Locate examples that illustrate this style, paying special attention to Wine's word choice
   and sentence structure. Do you think Wine's style is appropriate
   for his topic and audience? Why or why not?

3. Although Wine's essay is characterized by an easy informality,
   it nonetheless has four distinct sections: paragraphs 1–12,
   13–22, 23–26, 27–29. What is the purpose or focus of each section? What would have been lost if Wine had begun the essay
   with paragraph 13? Explain.

Thinking About Ideas

1. Do you agree with Wine's theory about why some people are rude at the movies? Why or why not? What might theater operators and other audience members do to control the problem?

2. Certain movies seem to bring out the worst in people. Which movies? Why?

3. Where else besides movie theaters do you find evidence of rude behavior in everyday life? What factors do you think contribute to this rudeness?

Writing About Ideas

⊂⊃ 1. Using humorous exaggeration as Wine does, write a *paragraph* describing your impressions of people's behavior at a specific event. For instance, you might describe how people act at a rock concert, in an elevator, in a singles' hangout, or in a library. Be sure to provide lots of lively details about people's appearance, speech, and actions. For examples of vivid details and dialogue, read Linda Ellerbee's "Television Changed My Family Forever" (page 149).

2. Rudeness seems to be on the rise nationwide. Focus on an objectionable behavior you have observed in a specific context—for example, in a supermarket line, at a sports event, on the highway, at a party. Then write an *essay* describing people's objectionable behavior in that context. Explain why you think people act this way and what should be done about it. To gather material for your paper, consider brainstorming ideas with other individuals who share your concern.

3. Which do you prefer—watching a movie on your VCR at home or seeing it in a movie theater? Drawing upon your own experiences, write an *essay* in which you explain why you prefer one viewing location over the other. Provide plentiful examples to support your reasons.

One Poke Over the Line

John Leo

Have you ever imagined taking a visitor from another planet to the movies with you? "This is fun," you explain to your little green friend, as you settle down for two hours of destruction, gore, and popcorn. Do you think the visitor might be surprised at what we consider entertainment? In this selection, originally one of John Leo's columns in U.S. News and World Report, *Leo asks why we like what we like and what our tastes imply about our society.*

Words to Watch

revel (1): delight
meander (1): wander
sadism (3): great cruelty
bludgeons (4): hits with a heavy club, or as if with a heavy club
implicitly (4): indirectly
impales (6): pierces through with something sharp
machete (6): a large knife with a heavy blade
decapitates (6): beheads
flip (6): disrespectful
cathartic (7): relieving tension
decorously (9): politely
nihilism (9): a rejection of usual moral beliefs
cynicism (9): a bitter, mocking attitude
parody (9): ridicule

As a critic of violent entertainment, I have a flaw: I've al-   1
ways enjoyed it. When my wife heads for Cinema One to revel in
some deeply empathetic movie about meaningful relationships,
usually starring Meryl Streep or Shirley MacLaine, I meander off to
Cinema Two for a film with more action, a higher body count and a
few mandatory car crashes and explosions.

This is an absolutely conventional male attitude. If a meaning-   2
ful relationship breaks out on screen, men usually go for popcorn.
Most of us want action stories based on quest, challenge and danger
(and therefore the likelihood of some violence). Like many males, I
am especially partial to cartoon-like shoot'em-ups, such as the
RoboCop and *Terminator* movies. If someone has to die, let it be a
villainous stick figure rather than a recognizable human.

Now, however, I am bailing out. The dial has been turned up   3
too far on gruesomeness and sadism, even in comic-book films. The
most innocent-looking male action movie must be checked in advance for stomach-churning brutality. I knew I would not be going
to see *Cape Fear* when a reviewer informed me that the DeNiro
character "bites into the cheek of a handcuffed woman and spits out
a Dinty Moore Chunky Stew-sized piece of flesh." Over-the-top
hair-raising violence that would have been unthinkable in mainstream movies a decade or so ago now seems routine.

What's worse, the attitude toward the justification of violence   4
has changed. At the beginning of *Terminator 2,* Arnold Schwarze-
negger arrives from the future, naked and programmed for violence.
He enters a bar and casually bludgeons a few pool players whose
only offense is refusing to give him their clothes and a motorcycle.
This is uncomfortably close to the common urban crime of attacking youngsters for their bikes or Starter jackets. Here that kind of
violence is implicitly but rather clearly endorsed. After all, Arnold
is bigger, stronger and has a nuclear war to stop. So beating up bystanders is OK.

Codes of the West.   In the old Hollywood, the code was dif-   5
ferent. On the whole, violence among heroes was limited and a last
resort. The deck was usually stacked to make nonviolence a nonop-
tion at the end. But at least sympathetic characters were rarely
shown enjoying violence or overdoing it. Now, as the social critic
Mark Crispin Miller has written in *The Atlantic,* screen violence "is

used primarily to invite the viewer to enjoy the *feel* of killing, beating, mutilating." The movie is set up for the viewer to identify with the hero and the fulfillment that violence brings him. Often, Miller says, the hero's murderous rage has no point "other than its open invitation to *become him* at that moment." This is not violence as last resort but as deeply satisfying lifestyle.

Michael Medved's book, *Hollywood vs. America,* is very sharp on another aspect of the new violence: It is often played for laughs. In the first *Predator* movie, the hero impales a man against a tree with his machete, then urges the victim to "stick around." In *Lethal Weapon 2,* Danny Glover jokes, "I nailed 'em both," after holding a nail gun to the heads of villains and puncturing their skulls. And in *Hudson Hawk,* Bruce Willis decapitates a bad guy and jokes, "I guess you won't be attending that hat convention in July." This is hardly hilarious humor, but it serves to suppress the moviegoer's normal emotional response to agony and mutilation. This flip attitude, very common in films now, is essentially sadistic.   6

In response to snowballing protests about screen violence, Hollywood has frequently tried to argue that fictional violence has a useful, cathartic effect: "I think it's a kind of purifying experience to see violence," says Paul Verhoeven, director of *Total Recall.* But a growing number of studies from the social sciences point away from this comforting thesis. The studies show that children exposed to violent entertainment tend to be more violent themselves and less sensitive to the pain of others. This makes screen violence a social problem and not, as Hollywood likes to argue, an individual problem for consumers. ("If you don't like the movie, don't go.")   7

Cardinal Roger Mahony, the Roman Catholic archbishop of Los Angeles, terrified the industry last winter by talking about a tough Hollywood film-rating code. But he dropped the idea and instead has issued a pastoral letter defending artistic freedom and asking Hollywood, ever so politely, to clean up its act. When violence is portrayed, he asks, "Do we feel the pain and dehumanization it causes to the person on the receiving end *and* to the person who engages in it? . . . Does the film cater to the aggressive and violent impulses that lie hidden in every human heart? Is there danger its viewers will be desensitized to the horror of violence by seeing it?" Good questions and no threat of censorship. Just an invitation to grow up.   8

Todd Gitlin, the Berkeley sociologist, put it less decorously,   9
talking at a recent conference about "the rage and nihilism" that
Hollywood is tossing on screen. He said: "The industry is in the
grip of inner forces which amount to a cynicism so deep as to defy
parody," reveling "in the means to inflict pain, to maim, disfigure,
shatter the human image." Message to Hollywood from cardinal
and sociologist: Try something else.

Understanding Content

1. What is the selection's main idea? If it is stated directly, locate
   the relevant sentence(s). If it is implied, state the main idea in
   your own words.

2. For Leo, some violence in movies is acceptable. What kinds of
   movie violence don't disturb him? In what ways do today's
   movies exceed that acceptable level?

3. What argument in defense of violent movies does Hollywood
   commonly advance? Do statistics support this argument?
   Explain.

Understanding Technique

1. Although Leo criticizes the violence in today's movies, he begins his essay with the admission that he has always enjoyed
   violent films. Why might he have begun his essay with this confession?

2. Like many writers advancing a controversial position, Leo acknowledges the opposing viewpoint. Where does he cite the
   opposing opinion? What does he gain by mentioning this position?

3. Locate at least three places where Leo's examples create vivid
   visual pictures. How does the sharpness of these images help
   Leo reinforce his main point?

Thinking About Ideas

1. Have you recently witnessed a violent scene in a movie or television program? How did the scene make you feel? Do you know anyone whose response to the scene was different from yours? If you do, how do you explain this difference in response?

2. Films are currently rated for age appropriateness. For example, a film rated G (General) is considered acceptable for all viewers, a film rated PG-13 (Parental Guidance-13) is judged not appropriate for people under the age of thirteen, and one rated R (Restricted) is deemed not appropriate for people under the age of seventeen. Is this film-rating system effective? Why or why not? How could the system be made more effective?

3. Do you think violence in movies should be regulated? Why or why not? If you believe it should, who should do the regulating (movie producers, critics, viewers, parent groups, the government)? What regulations would be appropriate?

Writing About Ideas

1. In a *paragraph,* describe as vividly as you can the violence you have seen in a specific movie, television program, or video game. Use specific details to convey what was depicted, and be sure to clarify how you felt about the violence. Did it upset you, or did you feel it was harmless?

2. Leo cites a study arguing that children who watch violent entertainment become more violent themselves. Write an *essay* suggesting how either parents or teachers could influence children not to watch violent movies (or television shows) or not to play violent video games. What reasons could the adults give? What alternatives could they suggest? To gather ideas for your essay, talk to parents, teachers, or counselors who are concerned about the issue. Include some of their most helpful comments in your essay.

⊂⊃ 3. Leo focuses on a problem that calls for serious attention. Write an *essay* about a problem that cries out for action in your community or on your campus. Start, as Leo does, by presenting dramatic details that illustrate the problem. Then recommend a course of action for dealing with the situation. Who should act? What specifically should be done? What are the benefits of what you propose? Before planning your paper, you may want to read Pete Hamill's "Crack and the Box" (page 156), an essay that focuses on another media-created problem that demands a remedy.

Television Changed My Family Forever

Linda Ellerbee

Everyone realizes that television has changed our lives greatly. But how? People who never lived in a world without TV may not fully understand its impact on our lives. Television producer and writer Linda Ellerbee has no such disadvantage. In this selection taken from her book Move On, *she tells what her childhood was like before and after her family had a television set. In the process, she brings readers back to a time when family activities were really active and the people communicating were not on a screen.*

Words to Watch

cadence (2): rhythmic flow
ambrosia (19): dish often made with coconut, oranges, cherries, sour cream, and pineapple
inconsequential (20): unimportant

Santa Claus brought us a television for Christmas. See, said   1
my parents, television doesn't eat people. Maybe not. But television changed people. Television changed my family forever. We stopped eating dinner at the dining-room table after my mother found out about TV trays. We kept the TV trays behind the kitchen door and served ourselves from pots on the stove. Setting and clearing the dining-room table used to be my job; now, setting and clearing meant unfolding and wiping out TV trays, then, when we'd fin-

149

ished, wiping and folding our TV trays. Dinner was served in time
for one program and finished in time for another. During dinner we
used to talk to one another. Now television talked to us. If you had
something you absolutely had to say, you waited until the commercial, which is, I suspect, where I learned to speak in thirty-second
bursts. As a future writer, it was good practice in editing my
thoughts. As a little girl, it was lonely as hell. Once in a while, I'd
pass our dining-room table and stop, thinking I heard our ghosts sitting around talking to one another, saying stuff.

    Before television, I would lie in bed at night listening to my   2
parents come upstairs, enter their bedroom and say things to one
another that I couldn't hear, but it didn't matter, their voices rocked
me to sleep. My first memory, the first one ever, was of my parents
and their friends talking me to sleep when we were living in Bryan
and my bedroom was right next to the kitchen. I was still in my crib
then. From the kitchen I could hear them, hear the rolling cadence
of their speech, the rising and falling of their voices and the sound
of chips.

    "Two pair showing."   3
    "Call?"   4
    "Check."   5
    "Call?"   6
    "Call." *Clink.*   7
    "I raise." *Clink Clink.*   8
    "See your raise and raise you back." *Clink clink clink.*   9
    "Call." *Clink Clink.*   10
    "I'm in." *Clink.*   11
    "I'm out."   12
    "Let's see 'em."   13

    It was a song to me, a lullaby. Now Daddy went to bed right   14
after the weather and Mama stayed up to see Jack Paar (later she
stayed up to see Steve Allen and Johnny Carson and even Joey
Bishop, but not David Letterman). I went to sleep alone, listening to
voices in my memory.

    Daddy stopped buying Perry Mason books. Perry was on tele-   15
vision and that was so much easier for him, Daddy said, because he
could never remember which Perry Mason books he'd read and was
always buying the wrong ones by mistake, then reading them all the
way to the end before he realized he'd already read them.

Television fixed that, he said, because although the stories weren't as good as the stories in the books, at least he knew he hadn't already read them. But it had been Daddy and Perry who'd taught me how fine it could be to read something you liked twice, especially if you didn't know the second time wasn't the first time. My mother used to laugh at Daddy. She would never buy or read the same book again and again. She had her own library card. She subscribed to magazines and belonged to the Book-of-the-Month Club. Also, she hated mystery stories. Her favorite books were about doctors who found God and women who found doctors. Her most favorite book ever was *Gone with the Wind,* which she'd read before I was born. Read it while she vacuumed the floor, she said. Read it while she'd ironed shirts. Read it while she'd fixed dinner and read it while she'd washed up. Mama sure loved that book. She dropped Book-of-the-Month after she discovered *As the World Turns.* Later, she stopped her magazine subscriptions. Except for *TV Guide.* I don't know what she did with her library card. I know what she didn't do with it.

Mom quit taking me to the movies about this time, not that she'd ever take me to the movies very often after Mr. Disney let Bambi's mother get killed, which she said showed a lack of imagination. She and Daddy stopped going to movies, period. Daddy claimed it was because movies weren't as much fun after Martin broke up with Lewis, but that wasn't it. Most movies he cared about seeing would one day show up on television, he said. Maybe even Martin & Lewis movies. All you had to do was wait. And watch. 16

After a while, we didn't play baseball anymore, my daddy and me. We didn't go to baseball games together, either, but we watched more baseball than ever. That's how Daddy perfected The Art of Dozing to Baseball. He would sit down in his big chair, turn on the game and fall asleep within five minutes. That is, he appeared to be asleep. His eyes were shut. He snored. But if you shook him and said, Daddy, you're asleep, he'd open his eyes and tell you what the score was, who was up and what the pitcher ought to throw next. The Art of Dozing to Baseball. I've worked at it myself, but have never been able to get beyond waking up in time to see the instant replay. Daddy never needed instant replay and, no, I don't know how he did it; he was a talented man and he had his secrets. 17

Our lives began to seem centered around, and somehow mea-   18
sured by, television. My family believed in television. If it was on
TV, it must be so. Calendars were tricky and church bells might
fool you, but if you heard Ed Sullivan's[1] voice you knew it was
Sunday night. When four men in uniforms sang that they were the
men from Texaco who worked from Maine to Mexico, you knew it
was Tuesday night. Depending on which verse they were singing,
you knew whether it was seven o'clock or eight o'clock on Tuesday
night. It was the only night of the week I got to stay up until eight
o'clock. My parents allowed this for purely patriotic reasons. If you
didn't watch Uncle Milty[2] on Tuesday nights, on Wednesday mornings you might have trouble persuading people you were a real
American and not some commie pinko[3] foreigner from Dallas. I
wasn't crazy about Milton Berle, but I pretended I was; an extra
hour is an extra hour, and if the best way to get your daddy's attention is to watch TV with him, then it was worth every joke Berle
could steal.

Television was taking my parents away from me, not all the   19
time, but enough, I believed. When it was on, they didn't see me, I
thought. Take holidays. Although I was an only child, there were always grandparents, aunts, uncles and cousins enough to fill the
biggest holiday. They were the best times. White linen and old silver and pretty china. Platters of turkey and ham, bowls of cornbread
dressing and sweet potatoes and ambrosia. Homemade rolls. Glass
cake stands holding pineapple, coconut, angel food and devil's food
cakes, all with good boiled icing. There was apple pie with cheese.
There were little silver dishes with dividers for watermelon pickles,
black olives and sliced cranberry jelly. There was all the iced tea
you'd ever want. Lord, it was grand. We kids always finished first
(we weren't one of those families where they make the kids eat last
and you never get a drumstick). After we ate, we'd be excused to go

------

[1]Host of *The Ed Sullivan Show,* broadcast on CBS Sunday evenings from
1948–1971.

[2]Milton Berle, popular TV comedian of the same era.

[3]Communist.

outside, where we'd play. When we decided the grown-ups had spent enough time sitting around the table after they'd already finished eating, which was real boring, we'd go back in and make as much noise as we could, until finally four or five grown-ups would come outside and play with us because it was just easier, that's all. We played hide-and-seek or baseball or football or dodge ball. Sometimes we just played *ball*. Sometimes we just played. Once in a while, there would be fireworks, which were always exciting ever since the Christmas Uncle Buck shot off a Roman candle and set the neighbor's yard on fire, but that was before we had a television.

Now, holiday dinners began to be timed to accommodate the kickoff, or once in a while the halftime, depending on how many games there were to watch; but on Thanksgiving or New Year's there were always games so important they absolutely could not be missed under any circumstances, certainly not for something as inconsequential as being "it" and counting to ten while you pretended not to see six children climb into the back seat of your car. 20

"Ssshhh, not now, Linda Jane. The Aggies have the ball." 21

"But you said . . . you promised. . . ." 22

"Linda Jane, didn't your daddy just tell you to hush up? We can't hear the television for you talking." 23

Understanding Content

1. What is the selection's main idea? If it is stated directly, locate the relevant sentence(s). If it is implied, state the main idea in your own words.

2. What was Ellerbee's family's life like before her parents bought a television?

3. Ellerbee writes, "Our lives began to seem centered around, and somehow measured by, television" (paragraph 18). What does she mean by the words "centered around" and "measured by"?

Understanding Technique

1. Ellerbee uses eleven short paragraphs to present "the rising and falling" of voices and "the sound of chips" as she fell asleep as a young child (paragraphs 3–13). Why do you think she gives so much space to the sounds of the poker game? What might she be trying to convey?

2. In paragraph 19, Ellerbee describes her childhood holiday meals in great detail. What does she accomplish with such a detailed description? What is the effect of the short, often incomplete sentences she uses in the description?

3. After the brief narration of the poker game, Ellerbee uses direct quotations only one other time in this selection—at the very end (paragraphs 21–23). What is the effect of the dialogue there?

Thinking About Ideas

1. How important is television in your family? Has its effect on you and your family been at all like its effects on Ellerbee's family? Explain.

2. Although the Ellerbees stopped going to baseball games, they didn't stop watching them. What are the differences between going to a sports event and watching it on TV? Which do you prefer, and why?

3. Ellerbee is unhappy about the negative effects of television on her family. However, many people argue that television is not all that bad. What do you consider some of the positive aspects of television?

Writing About Ideas

1. Paragraph 19 gives readers a detailed picture of typical Ellerbee holiday meals and activities. Write a *paragraph* describing a typical gathering in your family. Like Ellerbee, provide numerous colorful details to help readers experience the event you're writing about. You may describe any kind of get-together, in-

cluding holiday celebrations, family reunions, or birthday parties. Begin with a general statement that covers all the details of your paragraph, such as "Fourth-of-July picnics in my family meant a lot of food, fun, and fighting."

2. Critics often claim that television offers only the "lightweight" benefits of relaxation and entertainment. Brainstorm with others to identify some of the "weightier" beneficial effects of television. Review the brainstorming material, and select one positive effect you feel strongly about. Perhaps you feel strongly about television's ability to teach skills or to inform about social issues. Write an *essay* explaining how television provides this advantage. To support your point, discuss specific shows and the effects of these shows on you and on those you know.

3. Ellerbee shows that television brought about a significant change in her life. In an *essay,* show how the introduction of some other technological device changed your life (or someone else's). You could, for instance, write about the impact of a car, microwave, fax machine, remote control, or computer game. Your essay may be serious or humorous, but, in either case, be sure to provide vigorous details to illustrate the influence of the device on everyday life. You may find it helpful to read "Crack and the Box" (page 156), in which Pete Hamill discusses television's influence on drug addiction.

Crack and the Box

Pete Hamill

It is a rare reporter whose work has not been touched by the fact of drug addiction. Crime stories, stories about accidents, stories about gang life, poverty, child abuse, domestic violence, suicide—all are likely to be about drugs, to some degree or another. Drug-related stories had become commonplace to Pete Hamill, who became a general assignment reporter for the New York Post *in 1960. What he hadn't gained in all those years was any satisfying answer to the question "Why use drugs?" In this essay, originally printed in* Esquire *magazine, the veteran reporter writes of a possible answer that occurred to him while researching yet another drug story.*

Words to Watch

stiletto (1): a dagger with a thin blade
squalor (1): misery
stupefied (3): dazed
inert (5): inactive
pox (7): curse
placid (8): calm
reefer (8): slang term for marijuana
horse (8): slang term for heroin
diverted (9): entertained
obliterate (18): destroy
exaltation (18): elevating
manipulation (20): influence; control

One sad rainy morning last winter, I talked to a woman who 1
was addicted to crack cocaine. She was twenty-two, stiletto-thin,
with eyes as old as tombs. She was living in two rooms in a welfare
hotel with her children, who were two, three, and five years of age.
Her story was the usual tangle of human woe: early pregnancy, dropping out of school, vanished men, smack and then crack, tricks with
johns in parked cars to pay for dope. I asked her why she did drugs.
She shrugged in an empty way and couldn't really answer beyond
"makes me feel good." While we talked and she told her tale of
squalor, the children ignored us. They were watching television.

Walking back to my office in the rain, I brooded about the 2
woman, her zombielike children, and my own callous indifference.
I'd heard so many versions of the same story that I almost never
wrote them anymore; the sons of similar women, glimpsed a dozen
years ago, are now in Dannemora or Soledad or Joliet[1]; in a hundred
cities, their daughters are moving into the same loveless rooms. As I
walked, a series of homeless men approached me for change, most of
them junkies. Others sat in doorways, staring at nothing. They were
additional casualties of our time of plague, demoralized reminders
that although this country holds only 2 percent of the world's population, it consumes 65 percent of the world's supply of hard drugs.

Why, for God's sake? Why do so many millions of Americans 3
of all ages, races, and classes choose to spend all or part of their
lives stupefied? I've talked to hundreds of addicts over the years;
some were my friends. But none could give sensible answers. They
stutter about the pain of the world, about despair or boredom, the
urgent need for magic or pleasure in a society empty of both. But
then they just shrug. Americans have the money to buy drugs; the
supply is plentiful. But almost nobody in power asks, Why? Least
of all, George Bush[2] and his drug warriors.

William Bennett[3] talks vaguely about the heritage of sixties 4
permissiveness, the collapse of Traditional Values, and all that. But

---

[1]Names of prisons.

[2]President of the United States from 1988 to 1992.

[3]Secretary of Education and "drug czar" during President Bush's administration.

he and Bush offer the traditional American excuse: It Is Somebody
Else's Fault. This posture set the stage for the self-righteous inva-
sion of Panama, the bloodiest drug arrest in world history. Bush
even accused Manuel Noriega[1] of "poisoning our children." But he
never asked *why* so many Americans demand the poison.

And then, on that rainy morning in New York, I saw another   5
one of those ragged men staring out at the rain from a doorway. I
suddenly remembered the inert postures of the children in that welfare hotel, and I thought: *television.*

Ah, no, I muttered to myself: too simple. Something as com-   6
plicated as drug addiction can't be blamed on television. Come on
. . . but I remembered all those desperate places I'd visited as a reporter, where there were no books and a TV set was always playing
and the older kids had gone off somewhere to shoot smack, except
for the kid who was at the mortuary in a coffin. I also remembered
when I was a boy in the forties and early fifties, and drugs were a
minor sideshow, a kind of dark little rumor. And there was one
major difference between that time and this: television.

We had unemployment then; illiteracy, poor living conditions,   7
racism, governmental stupidity, a gap between rich and poor. We
didn't have the all-consuming presence of television in our lives.
Now two generations of Americans have grown up with television
from their earliest moments of consciousness. Those same
American generations are afflicted by the pox of drug addiction.

Only thirty-five years ago, drug addiction was not a major   8
problem in this country. There were drug addicts. We had some at
the end of the nineteenth century, hooked on the cocaine in patent
medicines. During the placid fifties, Commissioner Harry Anslinger
pumped up the budget of the old Bureau of Narcotics with fantasies
of reefer madness. Heroin was sold and used in most major
American cities, while the bebop generation of jazz musicians got
jammed up with horse.

But until the early sixties, narcotics were still marginal to   9
American life; they weren't the $120-billion market they make up
today. If anything, those years have an eerie innocence. In 1955 there

[1]Former President of Panama; arrested to stand trial for participation in
drug sales to the United States.

were 31,700,000 TV sets in use in the country (the number is now past 184 million). But the majority of the audience had grown up without the dazzling new medium. They embraced it, were diverted by it, perhaps even loved it, but they weren't *formed* by it. That year, the New York police made a mere 1,234 felony drug arrests; in 1988 it was 43,901. They confiscated ninety-seven *ounces* of cocaine for the entire year; last year it was hundreds of pounds. During each year of the fifties in New York, there were only about a hundred narcotics-related deaths. But by the end of the sixties, when the first generation of children *formed* by television had come to maturity (and thus to the marketplace), the number of such deaths had risen to 1,200. The same phenomenon was true in every major American city.

In the last Nielsen survey of American viewers, the average 10 family was watching television seven hours a *day*. This has never happened before in history. No people has even been entertained for seven hours a day. The Elizabethans didn't go to the theater seven hours a day. The pre-TV generation did not go to the movies seven hours a day. Common sense tells us that this all-pervasive diet of instant imagery, sustained now for forty years, must have changed us in profound ways.

Television, like drugs, dominates the lives of its addicts. And 11 though some lonely Americans leave their sets on without watching them, using them as electronic companions, television usually absorbs its viewers the way drugs absorb their users. Viewers can't work or play while watching television; they can't read; they can't be out on the streets, falling in love with the wrong people, learning how to quarrel and compromise with other human beings. In short, they are asocial. So are drug addicts.

One Michigan State University study in the early eighties of- 12 fered a group of four- and five-year-olds the choice of giving up television or giving up their fathers. Fully one third said they would give up Daddy. Given a similar choice (between cocaine or heroin and father, mother, brother, sister, wife, husband, children, job), almost every stoned junkie would do the same.

There are other disturbing similarities. Television itself is a 13 consciousness-altering instrument. With the touch of a button, it takes you out of the "real" world in which you reside and can place you at a basketball game, the back alleys of Miami, the streets of Bucharest, or the cartoony living rooms of Sitcom Land. Each move from channel to channel alters moods, usually with music or a laugh track. On any given evening, you can laugh, be frightened, feel tension, thump with excitement. You can even tune in *MacNeil/Lehrer*[1] and feel sober.

But none of these abrupt shifts in mood is *earned.* They are   14
attained as easily as popping a pill. Getting news from television, for example, is simply not the same experience as reading it in a newspaper. Reading is *active.* The reader must decode little symbols called words, then create images or ideas and make them connect; at its most basic level, reading is an act of the imagination. But the television viewer doesn't go through that process. The words are spoken to him by Dan Rather or Tom Brokaw or Peter Jennings[2]. There isn't much decoding to do when watching television, no time to think or ponder before the next set of images and spoken words appears to displace the present one. The reader, being active, works at his or her own pace; the viewer, being passive, proceeds at a pace determined by the show. Except at the highest levels, television never demands that its audience take part in an act of imagination. Reading always does.

In short, television works on the same imaginative and intel-   15
lectual level as psychoactive drugs. If prolonged television viewing makes the young passive (dozens of studies indicate that it does), then moving to drugs has a certain coherence. Drugs provide an unearned high (in contrast to the earned rush that comes from a feat accomplished, a human breakthrough earned by sweat or thought or love).

And because the television addict and the drug addict are   16
alienated from the hard and scary world, they also feel they make no difference in its complicated events. For the junkie, the world is reduced to him and the needle, pipe, or vial; the self is absolutely isolated, with no desire for choice. The television addict lives the same way. Many Americans who fail to vote in presidential elections must believe they have no more control over such a choice than they do over the casting of *L.A. Law.*

----

[1]A nightly news program broadcast on the Public Broadcasting System.

[2]Anchors of the three major networks' nightly news shows.

The drug plague also coincides with the unspoken assumption   17
of most television shows: Life should be *easy.* The most complicated events are summarized on TV news in a minute or less. Cops
confront murder, chase the criminals, and bring them to justice
(usually violently) within an hour. In commercials, you drink the
right beer and you get the girl. *Easy!* So why should real life be a
grind? Why should any American have to spend years mastering a
skill or a craft, or work eight hours a day at an unpleasant job, or
endure the compromises and crises of a marriage? Nobody *works*
on television (except cops, doctors, and lawyers). Love stories on
television are about falling in love or breaking up; the long, steady
growth of a marriage—its essential *dailiness*—is seldom explored,
except as comedy. Life on television is almost always simple: good
guys and bad, nice girls and whores, smart guys and dumb. And if
life in the real world isn't that simple, well, hey, man, have some
dope, man, be happy, feel good.

The doper always whines about how he *feels;* drugs are used to   18
enhance his feelings or obliterate them, and in this the doper is very
American. No other people on earth spend so much time talking
about their feelings; hundreds of thousands go to shrinks, they buy
self-help books by the millions, they pour out intimate confessions to
virtual strangers in bars or discos. Our political campaigns are about
emotional issues now, stated in the simplicities of adolescence. Even
alleged statesmen can start a sentence, "I feel that the Sandinistas[1]
should. . ." when they once might have said, "I *think.* . . ." I'm convinced that this exaltation of cheap emotions over logic and reason is
one by-product of hundreds of thousands of hours of television.

Most Americans under the age of fifty have now spent their   19
lives absorbing television; that is, they've had the structures of
drama pounded into them. Drama is always about conflict. So news
shows, politics, and advertising are now all shaped by those structures. Nobody will pay attention to anything as complicated as the
part played by Third World debt in the expanding production of cocaine; it's much easier to focus on Manuel Noriega, a character
right out of *Miami Vice,* and believe that even in real life there's a
Mister Big.

---

[1]Members of the former ruling party of Nicaragua.

What is to be done? Television is certainly not going away, but   20
its addictive qualities can be controlled. It's a lot easier to "just say
no" to television than to heroin or crack. As a beginning, parents
must take immediate control of the sets, teaching children to watch
specific television *programs,* not "television," to get out of the house
and play with other kids. Elementary and high schools must begin
teaching television as a subject, the way literature is taught, showing
children how shows are made, how to distinguish between the true
and the false, how to recognize cheap emotional manipulation. All
Americans should spend more time reading. And thinking.

For years, the defenders of television have argued that the net-   21
works are only giving the people what they want. That might be
true. But so is the Medellin cartel[1].

Understanding Content

1. What is the selection's main idea? If it is stated directly, locate
   the relevant sentence(s). If it is implied, state the main idea in
   your own words.

2. Hamill discusses a number of similarities between TV addiction
   and drug addiction. What are some of these similarities? How,
   according to Hamill, might TV addiction also be a cause of drug
   addiction?

3. What does Hamill believe parents and teachers should do to
   fight TV addiction among children?

Understanding Technique

1. Hamill's title is a pun, a play on words that suggests more than
   one association or meaning. Why might Hamill have given his
   essay this title? How does it prepare readers for the essay's main
   idea?

---

[1]The largest group of drug suppliers in Colombia.

2. Not until paragraph 5 does Hamill state his belief that TV may be a cause of drug addiction. How do the two immediately preceding paragraphs prepare readers for Hamill's assertion?

3. Beginning in paragraph 11, Hamill discusses a number of similarities between drug addiction and TV addiction. The comparisons, however, aren't balanced; Hamill devotes more space to TV than to drugs. Why might he have chosen to do this? Do you think the imbalance weakens the essay? Why or why not?

Thinking About Ideas

1. Do you agree with Hamill that heavy television viewing can lead to drug addiction? Where does evidence in support of Hamill's viewpoint seem strong? Where does it seem weak?

2. In paragraph 9, Hamill writes that even though many Americans watched and even "loved" television in the 1950s, "they weren't *formed* by it." In what ways are viewers nowadays "formed" by TV?

3. Hamill suggests (paragraph 21) that the television networks are, in a way, as guilty as the Medellin cartel; both appeal to what's worst in human nature. Do you think this is a fair comparison? Why or why not? Should the networks be held accountable for the programming they schedule? How?

Writing About Ideas

1. Most of us have experienced temporary "addictions" to enjoyable activities; we may, for instance, become obsessed with playing video games, participating in a sport, playing a musical instrument, using a computer, eating take-out food. In a *paragraph,* describe your life before and after you became addicted to a particular activity. Your tone may be serious or light-spirited.

2. In his next-to-last paragraph, Hamill gives general advice to parents and teachers about ways to protect children from becoming television addicts. Focusing on either parents or teachers, write

an *essay* in which you describe the specific steps that group can take to regulate children's TV viewing. To gather material for your paper, you may find it helpful to interview several people who are concerned about children's viewing habits.

CD 3. Hamill writes that the 1950s and 1960s were very different decades. In an *essay,* contrast two time periods that interest you—for instance, the 1980s and 1990s, childhood and old age, or your parents' or grandparents' generation and your own. Use vivid examples to make a point about the key differences between the two time periods. To see one author's comparison of two time periods, read "Television Changed My Family Forever" (page 149), Linda Ellerbee's account of her family life without TV and then with it.

Is Sex All That Matters?

Joyce Garity

Few of us would choose to return to the days when sex was a dirty word, when "decent" people kept their sexuality so tightly under wraps that a natural part of life was made invisible. But is today's sexual atmosphere a healthier one? When children are bombarded by a never-ending stream of sexual images from babyhood on up, can they escape the conclusion that sex should be the center of their lives? Joyce Garity, a social worker, reflects on the experience of one teenage girl and the forces that have influenced her developing sense of sexuality—and of self.

Words to Watch

leering (3): looking in a manner suggesting sexual desire
waif-thin (3): thin as an abandoned child
abandon (6): complete surrender; giving up any controls on behavior
pedestrian (6): ordinary
irony (7): inconsistency between what is expected and what actually happens
Shangri-la (7): an imaginary paradise
cynical (8): full of contempt
scantily (8): inadequately
euphemisms (8): indirect, vague terms
double talk (8): purposely unclear language
innuendo (8): suggestion

vestige (9): trace; remainder
simulated (9): pretended
copulation (9): intercourse
promiscuity (10): lacking standards in selection of
sexual partners

A few years ago, a young girl lived with me, my husband,   1
and our children for several months. The circumstances of Elaine's
coming to us don't matter here; suffice it to say that she was troubled and nearly alone in the world. She was also pregnant—hugely,
clumsily pregnant with her second child. Elaine was seventeen. Her
pregnancy, she said, was an accident; she also said she wasn't sure
who had fathered her child. There had been several sex partners and
no contraception. Yet, she repeated blandly, gazing at me with clear
blue eyes, the pregnancy was an accident, and one she would certainly never repeat.

Eventually I asked Elaine, after we had grown to know each   2
other well enough for such conversations, why neither she nor her
lovers had used birth control. She blushed— porcelain-skinned girl
with one child in foster care and another swelling the bib of her
fashionably faded overalls—stammered, and blushed some more.
Birth control, she finally got out, was "embarrassing." It wasn't "romantic." You couldn't be really passionate, she explained, and
worry about birth control at the same time.

I haven't seen Elaine for quite a long time. I think about her   3
often, though. I think of her as I page through teen fashion magazines in the salon where I have my hair cut. Although mainstream
and relatively wholesome, these magazines trumpet sexuality page
after leering page. On the inside front cover, an advertisement for
Guess jeans features junior fashion models in snug denim dresses,
their legs bared to just below the crotch. An advertisement for Liz
Claiborne fragrances shows a barely clad young couple sprawled on
a bed, him painting her toenails. An advertisement for Obsession
cologne displays a waif-thin girl draped stomach-down across a
couch, naked, her startled expression suggesting helplessness in the
face of an unseen yet approaching threat.

I think of Elaine because I know she would love these ads.   4
"They're so beautiful," she would croon, and of course they are.

The faces and bodies they show are lovely. The lighting is superb. The hair and makeup are faultless. In the Claiborne ad, the laughing girl whose toenails are being painted by her handsome lover is obviously having the time of her life. She stretches luxuriously on a bed heaped with clean white linen and fluffy pillows. Beyond the sheer blowing curtains of her room, we can glimpse a graceful wrought-iron balcony. Looking at the ad, Elaine could only want to be her. Any girl would want to be her. Heck, *I* want to be her.

But my momentary desire to move into the Claiborne picture, to trade lives with the exquisite young creature pictured there, is just that—momentary. I've lived long enough to know that what I see is a marketing invention. A moment after the photo session was over, the beautiful room was dismantled, and the models moved on to their next job. Later, the technicians took over the task of doctoring the photograph until it reached full-blown fantasy proportions.

Not so Elaine. After months of living together and countless hours of watching her yearn after magazine images, soap-opera heroines, and rock goddesses, I have a pretty good idea of why she looks at ads like Claiborne's. She sees the way life—her life—is *supposed* to be. She sees a world characterized by sexual spontaneity, playfulness, and abandon. She sees people who don't worry about such unsexy details as birth control. Nor, apparently, do they spend much time thinking about such pedestrian topics as commitment or whether they should act on their sexual impulses. Their clean sunlit rooms are never invaded by the fear of AIDS, of unwanted pregnancy, of shattered lives. For all her apparent lack of defense, the girl on the couch in the Obsession ad will surely never experience the brutality of rape.

Years of exposure to this media-invented, sex-saturated universe have done their work on Elaine. She is, I'm sure, completely unaware of the irony in her situation: She melts over images from a sexual Shangri-la, never realizing that her attempts to mirror those images left her pregnant, abandoned, living in the spare bedroom of a stranger's house, relying on charity for rides to the welfare office and supervised visits with her toddler daughter.

Of course, Elaine is not the first to be suckered by the cynical practice of using sex to sell underwear, rock groups, or sneakers. Using sex as a sales tool is hardly new. At the beginning of this century, British actress Lily Langtry shocked her contemporaries by posing, clothed somewhat scantily, with a bar of Pear's soap. The advertisers have always known that the masses are susceptible to the notion that a particular product will make them more sexually attractive. In the past, however, ads used euphemisms, claiming that certain products would make people "more lovable" or "more popular." What is a recent development is the abandonment of any such polite double talk. Advertising today leaves no question about what is being sold along with the roasted peanuts or artificial sweetener. "Tell us about your first time," coyly invites the innuendo-filled magazine advertisement for Campari liquor. A billboard for Levi's shows two jeans-clad young men on the beach, hoisting a girl in the air. The boys' perfect, tan bodies are matched by hers, although we see a lot more of hers: bare midriff, short shorts, cleavage. She caresses their hair; they stroke her legs. A jolly gang-bang fantasy in the making. And a TV commercial promoting the Irish pop group The Cranberries blares nonstop the suggestive title of their latest album: "Everybody else is doing it, so why can't we?"

Indeed, just about everybody is doing it. Studies show that by   9 the age of 20, 75 percent of Americans have lost their virginity. In many high schools—and an increasing number of junior highs— virginity is regarded as an embarrassing vestige of childhood, to be disposed of as quickly as possible. Young people are immersed from their earliest days in a culture that parades sexuality at every turn and makes heroes of the advocates of sexual excess. Girls, from toddlerhood on up, shop in stores packed with clothing once thought suitable only for streetwalkers—lace leggings, crop tops, and wedge-heeled boots. Parents drop their children off at Madonna or Michael Jackson concerts, featuring simulated on-stage masturbation, or at Bobby Brown's show, where a fan drawn out of the audience is treated to a pretended act of copulation. Young boys idolize sports stars like Wilt Chamberlain, who claims to have bedded 20,000 women. And when the "Spur Posse," eight California high school athletes, were charged with systematically raping girls as young as 10 as part of a "scoring" ritual, the beefy young jocks were rewarded with a publicity tour of talk shows, while one father boasted to reporters about his son's "manhood."

In a late, lame attempt to counterbalance this sexual overload,   10 most schools offer sex education as part of their curriculums. (In 1993, forty-seven states recommended or required such courses.)

But sex ed classes are heavy on the mechanics of fertilization and birth control—sperm, eggs, and condoms—and light on any discussion of sexuality as only one part of a well-balanced life. There is passing reference to abstinence as a method of contraception, but little discussion of abstinence as an emotionally or spiritually satisfying option. Promiscuity is discussed for its role in spreading sexually transmitted diseases. But the concept of rejecting casual sex in favor of reserving sex for an emotionally intimate, exclusive, trusting relationship—much less any mention of waiting until marriage—is foreign to most public school settings. "Love and stuff like that really wasn't discussed" is the way one Spur Posse member remembers his high school sex education class.

Surely teenagers need the factual information provided by sex 11 education courses. But where is "love and stuff like that" talked about? Where can they turn for a more balanced view of sexuality? Who is telling young people like Elaine, my former houseguest, that sex is not an adequate basis for a healthy, respectful relationship? Along with warnings to keep condoms on hand, is anyone teaching kids that they have a right to be valued for something other than their sexuality? Madison Avenue, Hollywood, and the TV, music, and fashion industries won't tell them that. Who will?

No one has told Elaine—at least, not in a way she comprehends. 12 I haven't seen her for a long time, but I hear of her occasionally. The baby boy she bore while living in my house is in a foster home, a few miles from his older half-sister, who is also in foster care. Elaine herself is working in a local convenience store—and she is pregnant again. This time, I understand, she is carrying twins.

Understanding Content

1. What is the selection's main idea? If it is stated directly, locate the relevant sentence(s). If it is implied, state the main idea in your own words.

2. According to Garity, what do advertisements "teach" young people about sex? What do musical and athletic stars "teach" about sex? What's wrong with these messages? What dangers do they pose?

3. What, according to Garity, is lacking in school sex education programs? What do you think she feels would happen if those things were included?

Understanding Technique

1. Because she feels strongly about her subject, Garity doesn't hesitate to use emotionally charged language, such as stating that magazines "trumpet sexuality page after leering page." What attitude toward her subject do these words convey? Identify at least five other places where Garity's word choice conveys this attitude.

2. In paragraph 8, Garity contrasts earlier advertising with the ads of today. How does this contrast help to reinforce her main point?

3. Making a smooth, meaningful, and interesting transition from one paragraph to another is one of a writer's challenges. How does Garity connect paragraph 4 to paragraph 5? Paragraph 5 to paragraph 6? Paragraph 6 to paragraph 7? Paragraph 8 to paragraph 9?

Thinking About Ideas

1. When you were younger, did you attend a sex-education class? What did it teach? What didn't it teach? What changes do you think are needed to improve the course? If you didn't attend such a class, do you think you missed something important? Explain.

2. Do you feel that your attitudes towards sex and intimacy have been influenced by television, the movies, ads, and commercials? Explain.

3. What can parents do to counteract the influence of those aspects of our culture that glamorize casual sex and sexual excess? What can other authority figures or organizations do to present a healthier, more balanced view of sexuality?

Writing About Ideas

1. Assume that your community is debating whether to offer a sex education program to the town's middle-school children. Along with several other residents, you have been asked to explain why you think such a program should or should not be offered. Write a *paragraph* stating your position and several reasons for your position. Illustrate each reason with concrete, persuasive examples from your own and other people's experiences.

2. Write an *essay* developing Garity's point that advertisements contribute to careless, irresponsible sex. Begin by finding two or three ads that you feel have subtle—or not so subtle—messages about sex. In your essay, describe the ads and interpret their sexual messages. Keep the ads nearby as you write so that you can describe them with the same sort of vivid detail as Garity does. For inspiration, you may want to read John Leo's "One Poke Over the Line" (page 143), an essay criticizing another aspect of American culture.

3. Choose an issue other than sex—for example, family life, fitness, nutrition—and come to a conclusion about how that subject is treated in advertisements and/or commercials. Then write an *essay* in which you state your conclusion and support it with vivid, detailed references to several ads and/or commercials.

5

Human Connections and Disconnections

Thank You

Alex Haley

"Thank you" are words we use often in the course of the day. We express our appreciation to waitresses, ticket sellers, and cashiers. Our automatic "Thanks!" is polite, but barely felt. In contrast, how often do we thank the people who have made genuine contributions to our lives? Alex Haley, the celebrated author of Roots, *became bothered by his own failure to thank some significant figures in his life. Unlike most of us, he did something about it, as the following essay from* Parade *magazine explains.*

Words to Watch

afterdeck (4): the part of a ship's deck located towards the stern (rear) of the ship
draughts (4): inhalations
reflex (5): automatic reaction
waning (6): coming to an end
indelibly (10): permanently
rendezvous (18): meet at a prearranged time and place
jostling (19): pushing and shoving
nigh (25): nearly
buoyant (27): cheerful
paramount (29): most important

It was 1943, during World War II, and I was a young U.S. coastguardsman, serial number 212-548, a number we never seem to forget. My ship, the USS *Murzim,* had been under way for several days. Most of her holds contained thousands of cartons of canned or dried foods. The other holds were loaded with five-hundred-pound bombs packed delicately in padded racks. Our destination was a big base on the island of Tulagi in the South Pacific.

I was one of the *Murzim*'s several cooks and, quite the same   2
as for folk ashore, this Thanksgiving morning had seen us busily preparing a traditional dinner featuring roast turkey.

Well, as any cook knows, it's a lot of hard work to cook and   3
serve a big meal, and clean up and put everything away. But finally, around sundown, with our whole galley crew just bushed, we finished at last and were free to go flop into our bunks in the fo'c'sle[1].

But I decided first to go out on the *Murzim*'s afterdeck for a   4
breath of open air. I made my way out there, breathing in great, deep draughts while walking slowly about, still wearing my white cook's hat and the long apron, my feet sensing the big ship's vibrations from the deep-set, turbine diesels and my ears hearing that slightly hissing sound the sea makes in resisting the skin of a ship.

I got to thinking about Thanksgiving. In reflex, my thoughts   5
registered the historic imagery of the Pilgrims, Indians, wild turkeys, pumpkins, corn on the cob and the rest.

Yet my mind seemed to be questing for something else—   6
some way that I could personally apply to the waning Thanksgiving. It must have taken me a half hour to sense that maybe some key to an answer could result from reversing the word "Thanksgiving"—at least that suggested a verbal direction, "Giving thanks."

Giving thanks—as in praying, thanking God, I thought. Yes,   7
of course. Certainly.

Yet my mind continued nagging me. Fine. But something   8
else.

After awhile, like a dawn's brightening, a further answer did   9
come—that there were people to thank, people who had done so much for me that I could never possibly repay them. The embar-

---

[1]Abbreviation of *forecastle,* the crew's quarters on a merchant ship.

rassing truth was I'd always just accepted what they'd done, taken all of it for granted. Not one time had I ever bothered to express to any of them so much as a simple, sincere "Thank you."

At least seven people had been particularly and indelibly 10 helpful to me. I realized, with a gulp, that about half of them had since died—so they were forever beyond any possible expression of gratitude from me. The more I thought about it, the more ashamed I became. Then I pictured the three who were still alive and, within minutes, I was down in the fo'c'sle.

Sitting at a mess table with writing paper and memories of 11 things each had done, I tried composing genuine statements of heartfelt appreciation and gratitude to my dad, Simon A. Haley, a professor at the old AMNC (Agricultural Mechanical Normal College) in Pine Bluff, Arkansas, now a branch of the University of Arkansas; to my grandma, Cynthia Palmer, back in our little hometown of Henning, Tennessee; and to the Rev. Lonual Nelson, my grammar school principal, retired and living in Ripley, six miles north of Henning.

I couldn't even be certain if they would recall some of their 12 acts of years past, acts that I vividly remembered and saw now as having given me vital training, or inspiration, or directions, if not all of these desirables rolled into one.

The texts of my letters began something like, "Here, this 13 Thanksgiving at sea, I find my thoughts upon how much you have done for me, but I have never stopped and said to you how much I feel the need to thank you—" And briefly I recalled for each of them specific acts performed in my behalf.

For instance, something uppermost about my father was how 14 he had impressed upon me from boyhood to love books and reading. In fact, this graduated into a family habit of after-dinner quizzes at the table about books read most recently and new words learned. My love of books never diminished and later led me toward writing books myself. So many times I have felt a sadness when exposed to modern children so immersed in the electronic media that they have little to no awareness of the wondrous world to be discovered in books.

I reminded the Reverend Nelson how each morning he would 15 open our little country town's grammar school with a prayer over

---

his assembled students. I told him that whatever positive things I had done since had been influenced at least in part by his morning school prayers.

In the letter to my grandmother, I reminded her of a dozen 16
ways she used to teach me how to tell the truth, to be thrifty, to share, and to be forgiving and considerate of others. (My reminders included how she'd make me pull switches from a peach tree for my needed lesson.) I thanked her for the years of eating her good cooking, the equal of which I had not found since. (By now, though, I've reflected that those peerless dishes are most gloriously flavored with a pinch of nostalgia.) Finally, I thanked her simply for having sprinkled my life with stardust.

Before I slept, my three letters went into our ship's office mail 17
sack. They got mailed when we reached Tulagi Island.

We unloaded cargo, reloaded with something else, then again 18
we put to sea in the routine familiar to us, and as the days became weeks, my little personal experience receded. Sometimes, when we were at sea, a mail ship would rendezvous and bring us mail from home, which, of course, we accorded topmost priority.

Every time the ship's loudspeaker rasped, "Attention! Mail 19
call!" two-hundred-odd shipmates came pounding up on deck and clustered about the raised hatch atop which two yeomen, standing by those precious bulging gray sacks, were alternately pulling out fistfuls of letters and barking successive names of sailors who were, in turn, hollering "Here! Here!" amid the jostling.

One "mail call" brought me responses from Grandma, Dad 20
and the Reverend Nelson—and my reading of their letters left me not only astounded, but more humbled than before.

Rather than saying they would forgive that I hadn't previously 21
thanked them, instead, for Pete's sake, they were thanking *me*—for having remembered, for having considered they had done anything so exceptional.

Always the college professor, my dad had carefully avoided 22
anything he considered too sentimental, so I knew how moved he was to write me that, after having helped educate many young people, he now felt that his best results included his own son.

The Reverend Nelson wrote that his decades as a "simple, 23
old-fashioned principal" had ended with grammar schools undergo-

ing such swift changes that he had retired in self-doubt. "I heard more of what I had done wrong than what I did right," he said, adding that my letter had brought him welcome reassurance that his career had been appreciated.

A glance at Grandma's familiar handwriting brought back in a 24 flash memories of standing alongside her white wicker rocking chair, watching her "settin' down" some letter to relatives. Frequently touching her pencil's tip to pursed lips, character by character, each between a short, soft grunt, Grandma would slowly accomplish one word, then the next, so that a finished page would consume hours. I wept over the page representing my Grandma's recent hours invested in expressing her loving gratefulness to me—whom she used to diaper!

Much later, retired from the Coast Guard and trying to make a 25 living as a writer, I never forgot how those three "thank you" letters gave me an insight into something nigh mystical in human beings, most of whom go about yearning in secret for more of their fellows to express appreciation for their efforts.

I discovered in time that, even in the business world, probably 26 no two words are more valued than "thank you," especially among people at stores, airlines, utilities and others that directly serve the public.

Late one night, I was one of a half-dozen passengers who 27 straggled weary and grumbling off a plane that had been forced to land at the huge Dallas/Fort Worth Airport. Suddenly, a buoyant, cheerful, red-jacketed airline man waved us away from the regular waiting room seats, saying, "You sure look bushed. I know a big empty office where you can stretch out while you wait." And we surely did. When the weather improved enough for us to leave, "Gene Erickson" was in my notebook and, back home, I wrote the president of that airline describing his sensitivity and his courtesy. And I received a thank you!

I travel a good deal on lecture tours and I urge students espe- 28 cially to tell their parents, grandparents, and other living elders simply "thank you" for all they have done to make possible the lives they now enjoy. Many students have told me they found themselves moved by the response. It is not really surprising, if one only reflects how it must feel to be thanked after you have given for years.

Now, approaching Thanksgiving of 1982, I have asked myself   29
what will I wish for all who are reading this, for our nation, indeed
for our whole world—since, quoting a good and wise friend of
mine, "In the end we are mightily and merely people, each with
similar needs." First, I wish for us, of course, the simple common
sense to achieve world peace, that being paramount for the very
survival of our kind.

And there is something else I wish—so strongly that I have   30
had this line printed across the bottom of all my stationery: *"Find
the good—and praise it."*

Understanding Content

1. What is the selection's main idea? If it is stated directly, locate
   the relevant sentence(s). If it is implied, state the main idea in
   your own words.

2. How does Haley define "Thanksgiving"? How does he apply
   this definition to his own life?

3. What reaction do you think Haley expected his letters to produce? What happened instead?

Understanding Technique

1. Why do you suppose Haley provides so many details about the
   ship and his duties (paragraphs 1–4)? What about Haley do
   these details help explain?

2. Haley places examples about Reverend Nelson (paragraphs 15
   and 23) between the examples about his father (paragraphs 14
   and 22) and his grandmother (paragraphs 16 and 24). Why do
   you think he decided to sequence the examples in this order?

3. Haley could have closed his essay at the end of paragraph 25.
   What function do you suppose he wanted paragraphs 26–30 to
   serve?

Thinking About Ideas

1. Do you, like Haley and his shipmates, also look forward to the daily mail delivery? What makes getting mail so enjoyable? How is receiving a letter different from receiving a telephone call? Which do you prefer? Why?

2. Haley believes we need to say "thank you" more often. Have you ever found "thank you" to be overused, insincere, or manipulative? In what circumstances? Are there any other common expressions which, although intended to be pleasant, can produce negative reactions? What are they?

3. Haley urges readers, "Find the good—and praise it." Some people can do this easily; others cannot. Why do you think people have difficulty acknowledging the positive?

Writing About Ideas

1. Haley captures the joy we often experience when we follow our better instincts. In a *paragraph,* describe a time that you had to decide how to act and you chose to follow your finer impulses. What specifically did you do? Why did you make the decision you did? You might want to start the paragraph with a sentence like "I felt deep satisfaction the day I decided to _____." Before writing your paper, you might want to read Bob Greene's "Handled with Care" (page 200), an essay which presents an example of the better side of human nature.

2. As you look back on your life, to what one person are you especially grateful? Write an *essay* showing exactly how this person has made a difference in your life. To develop your paper, you may recount one especially dramatic example or several more subtle examples. In either case, provide plentiful details to illustrate this person's influence on you.

3. Most people, Haley writes, "go about yearning in secret for more of their fellows to express appreciation." Select one area of life (for example, on the job, in the classroom, in the family); then write an *essay* explaining what people in that context could

do to show their appreciation of other individuals' efforts. You may want to do some group brainstorming to identify steps people could take to be more appreciative. Begin the paper with an incident illustrating that people tend not to show gratitude or thanks.

Let's Get Specific

Beth Johnson

Some writing moves along energetically, gliding you through a rich, intriguing verbal landscape. Other writing just lies there, merely existing. Try as you might, you cannot summon up much interest in it. According to author and writing teacher Beth Johnson, the difference between the two types of writing is simple: one is full of concrete images, while the other is "blandly general."

Words to Watch

prospective (2): expected
intuitively (16): naturally
swayed (16): influenced
parody (16): an imitation meant to be amusing and/or
        mocking
shrilly (22): in a high-pitched, piercing tone
compelling (33): demanding and keeping one's attention
sustain (34): support

Imagine that you've offered to fix up your sister with a blind 1
date. "You'll like him," you tell her. "He's really nice." Would that
assurance be enough to satisfy her? Would she contentedly wait for
Saturday night, happily anticipating meeting this "nice" young
man? Not likely! She would probably bombard you with questions:
"But what's he like? Is he tall or short? Funny? Serious? Smart?
Kind? Shy? Does he work? How do you know him?"

Such questions reveal the instinctive hunger we all feel for   2
specific detail. Being told that her prospective date is "nice" does
very little to help your sister picture him. She needs concrete details
to help her vividly imagine this stranger.

The same principle applies to writing. Whether you are   3
preparing a research paper, a letter to a friend, or an article for the
local newspaper, your writing will be strengthened by the use of detailed, concrete language. Specific language energizes and informs
readers. General language, by contrast, makes their eyes glaze over.

The following examples should prove the point.   4

Dear Sir or Madam: 5

Please consider my application for a job with your   6
company. I am a college graduate with experience in
business. Part-time jobs that I have held during the
school year and my work over summer vacations make
me well-qualified for employment. My former employers have always considered me a good, reliable worker.
Thank you for considering my application.

Sincerely,   7
Bob Cole   8

Dear Sir or Madam: 9

I would like to be considered for an entry-level position   10
in your purchasing department. I graduated in June
from Bayside College with a 3.5 GPA and a bachelor's
degree in business administration. While at Bayside, I
held a part-time job in the college's business office,
where I eventually had responsibility for coordinating
food purchasing for the school cafeteria. By encouraging competitive bidding among food suppliers, I was
able to save the school approximately $2,500 in the
'92–'93 school year. During the last three summers
(1990–93), I worked at Bayside Textiles, where I was
promoted from a job in the mailroom to the position of
assistant purchasing agent, a position that taught me a
good deal about controlling costs. Given my back-

ground, I'm confident I could make a real contribution to your company. I will telephone you next Tuesday morning to ask if we might arrange an interview.

Sincerely,   11
Julia Moore   12

Which of the preceding letters do you think makes a more 13 convincing case for these job seekers? If you're like most people, you would choose the second. Although both letters are polite and grammatically acceptable, the first one suffers badly in comparison with the second for one important reason. It is *general* and *abstract,* while the second is *specific* and *concrete.*

Let's look at the letters again. The differing styles of the two 14 are evident in the first sentence. Bob is looking for "a job with your company." He doesn't specify what kind of job—it's for the employer to figure out if Bob wants to work as a groundskeeper, on an assembly line, or as a salesperson. By contrast, Julia is immediately specific about the kind of job she is seeking—"an entry-level position in your purchasing department." Bob tells only that he is "a college graduate." But Julia tells where she went to college, the kind of grades she received, and exactly what she studied.

The contrast continues as the two writers talk about their work 15 experience. Again, Bob talks in vague, general terms. He gives no concrete evidence to show how the general descriptions "well-qualified" and "good, reliable worker" apply to him. But Julia backs up her claims. She tells specifically what positions she's held (buyer for cafeteria, assistant purchasing clerk for textile company), gives solid evidence that she performed her jobs well (saved the school $2,500, was promoted from mail room), and explains what skills she has acquired (knows about controlling costs). Julia continues to be clear and concrete as she closes the letter. By saying, "I will telephone you next Tuesday morning," she leaves the reader with a helpful, specific piece of information. Chances are, her prospective employer will be glad to take her call. The chances are equally good that Bob will never hear from the company. His letter was so blandly general that the employer will hardly remember receiving it.

Julia's letter demonstrates the power of specific detail—a 16 power that we all appreciate intuitively. Indeed, although we may not always be aware of it, our opinions and decisions are frequently swayed by concrete language. On a restaurant menu, are you more tempted by a "green salad" or "a colorful salad bowl filled with romaine and spinach leaves, red garden-fresh tomatoes, and crisp green pepper rings"? Would being told that a movie is "good" persuade you to see it as much as hearing that it is "a hilarious parody of a rock documentary featuring a fictional heavy-metal band"? Does knowing that a classmate has "personal problems" help you understand her as well as hearing that "her parents are divorcing, her brother was just arrested for selling drugs, and she is scheduled for surgery to correct a back problem"?

When we read, all of us want—even crave—this kind of   17
specificity. Concrete language grabs our attention and allows us to witness the writer's world almost firsthand. Abstract language, on the other hand, forces us to try to fill in the blanks left by the writer's lack of specific imagery. Usually we tire of the effort. Our attention wanders. We begin to wonder what's for lunch and whether it's going to rain, as our eyes scan the page, searching for some concrete detail to focus upon.

Once you understand the power of concrete details, you will   18
gain considerable power as a writer. You will describe events so vividly that readers will feel they experienced them directly. You will sprinkle your essays with nuggets of detail that, like the salt on a pretzel, add interest and texture. Consider the following examples, and decide for yourself which came from a writer who has mastered the art of the specific detail.

Living at Home   19

Unlike many college students, I have chosen to   20
live at home with my parents. Naturally, the arrangement has both good and bad points. The most difficult part is that, even though I am an adult, my parents sometimes still think of me as a child. Our worst disagreements occur when they expect me to report to them as though I were still twelve years old. Another drawback to living with my parents is that I don't feel free to have friends over to "my place." It's not that my parents don't welcome my friends in their home, but I

can't tell my friends to drop in anytime as I would if I
lived alone. But in other ways, living at home works
out well. The most obvious plus is that I am saving a lot
of money. I pay room and board, but that doesn't compare to what renting an apartment would cost. There
are less measurable advantages as well. Although we do
sometimes fall into our old parent-child roles, my parents and I are getting to know each other in new ways.
Generally, we relate as adults, and I think we're all
gaining a lot of respect for one another.

The Pros and Cons of Living at Home   21

Most college students live in a dormitory or apart-   22
ment. They spend their hours surrounded by their own
stereos, blaring Pearl Jam or Arrested Development;
their own furnishings, be they leaking beanbag chairs
or Salvation Army sofas; and their own choice of foods,
from tofu-bean sprout casseroles to a basic diet of
Cheetos. My life is different. I occupy the same room
that has been mine since babyhood. My school pictures,
from gap-toothed first-grader to cocky senior, adorn
the walls. The music drifting through my door from
the living room ranges from Lawrence Welk to . . .
Lawrence Welk. The food runs heavily to Mid-American
Traditional: meatloaf, mashed potatoes, frozen peas.
Yes, I live with my parents. And the arrangement is not
always ideal. Although I am twenty-four years old, my
parents sometimes slip into a time warp and mentally
cut my age in half. "Where are you going, Lisa? Who
will you be with?" my mother will occasionally ask. I'll
answer patiently, "I'm going to have pizza with some
people from my psych class." "But where?" she continues. "I'm not sure," I'll say, my voice rising just a hair.
If the questioning continues, it will often lead to a
blowup. "You don't need to know where I'm going,
OK?" I'll say shrilly. "You don't have to yell at me,"
she'll answer in a hurt voice. Living at home also
makes it harder to entertain. I find myself envying

classmates who can tell their friends, "Drop in anytime." If a friend of mine "drops in" unexpectedly, it throws everyone into a tizzy. Mom runs for the dustcloth while Dad ducks into the bedroom, embarrassed to be seen in his comfortable, ratty bathrobe. On the other hand, I don't regret my decision to live at home for a few years. Naturally, I am saving money. The room and board I pay my parents wouldn't rent the tiniest, most roach-infested apartment in the city. And despite our occasional lapses, my parents and I generally enjoy each other's company. They are getting to know me as an adult, and I am learning to see them as people, not just as my parents. I realized how true this was when I saw them getting dressed up to go out recently. Dad was putting on a tie, and Mom one of her best dresses. I opened my mouth to ask where they were going when it occurred to me that maybe they didn't care to be checked up on any more than I did. Swallowing my curiosity, I simply waved goodbye and said, "Have a good time!"

Both passages could have been written by the same person. 23
Both make the same basic points. But the second passage is far more interesting because it backs up its writer's points with concrete details. While the first passage merely *tells* that the writer's parents sometimes treat her like a child, the second passage follows this point up with an anecdote that *shows* exactly what she means. Likewise with the point about inviting friends over: the first passage only states that there is a problem, but the second one describes in concrete terms what happens if a friend does drop in unexpectedly. The first writer simply says that her room and board costs wouldn't pay for an apartment, but the second is specific about just how inadequate the money would be. And while the first passage uses abstract language to say the writer and her parents are "getting to know each other in new ways," the second shows what that means by describing a specific incident.

Every kind of writing can be improved by the addition of con- 24
crete detail. Let's look at one final example: the love letter.

Dear April, 25

I can't wait any longer to tell you how I feel. I am crazy 26
about you. You are the most wonderful woman I've ever
met. Every time I'm near you I'm overcome with feelings of love. I would do anything in the world for you
and am hoping you feel the same way about me.

Love, 27
Paul 28

Paul has written a sincere note, but it lacks a certain some- 29
thing. That something is specific detail. Although the letter
expresses a lot of positive feelings, it could have been written by
practically any love-struck man about any woman. For this letter to
be really special to April, it should be unmistakably about her and
Paul. And that requires concrete details. Here is what Paul might
write instead.

Dear April, 30

Do you remember last Saturday, as we ate lunch in the 31
park, when I spilled my soda in the grass? You quickly
picked up a twig and made a tiny dam to keep the liquid from flooding a busy anthill. You probably didn't
think I noticed, but I did. It was at that moment that I
realized how totally I am in love with you and your passion for life. Before that I only thought you were the
most beautiful woman in the world, with your eyes like
sparkling pools of emerald water and your chestnut
hair glinting in the sun. But now I recognize what it
means when I hear your husky laugh and I feel a tight
aching in my chest. It means I could stand on top of the
Empire State Building and shout to the world, "I love
April Snyder." Should I do it? I'll be waiting for your
reply.

Paul 32

There's no guarantee that April is going to return Paul's feel- 33
ings, but she certainly has a better idea now just what it is about her

that Paul finds so lovable, as well as what kind of a guy Paul is. Concrete details have made this letter far more compelling.

Vague, general language is the written equivalent of baby   34
food. It is adequate; it can sustain life. But it isn't very interesting. For writing to have satisfying crunch, sizzle, and color, it must be generously supplied with specifics. Whether the piece is a job application, a student essay, or a love letter, it is concrete details that make it interesting, persuasive, and memorable.

Understanding Content

1. What is the selection's main idea? If it is stated directly, locate the relevant sentence(s). If it is implied, state the main idea in your own words.

2. Why would an employer react more favorably to Julia Moore's letter than to Bob Cole's? What personal and professional qualities does Julia project in her letter?

3. According to Johnson, how does abstract language affect readers? Why should writers use concrete details instead?

Understanding Technique

1. Johnson takes her own advice and uses numerous concrete details. Locate some particularly strong examples. How do these details support Johnson's point?

2. Johnson includes three pairs of examples: the job-application letters, the living-at-home passages, and the love letters. Why do you think she uses all three pairs? What does each pair contribute to the essay?

3. Essays often begin with an introduction that prepares readers for the author's main idea. How does Johnson begin her essay? Why do you suppose she opens in this manner?

Thinking About Ideas

1. What kinds of writing will you prepare over the next few weeks or months? How might you make that writing more concrete and detailed?

2. Johnson states, "Although we may not always be aware of it, our opinions and decisions are frequently swayed by concrete language." She illustrates her point by showing how persuasive the menu description of a salad can be. When else might you be influenced by concrete language—for example, when voting, shopping, or deciding what to do on the weekend?

3. "Let's Get Specific" is addressed to students, but what are some ways people might use the power of concrete details outside the classroom?

Writing About Ideas

1. Write a one-*paragraph* letter of application for a part-time or a full-time job. Describe the kind of job you seek, the positions you have held, and the skills you have acquired. Remember to include specific details about your on-the-job experiences and accomplishments. (For a good example of this kind of writing, review Julia's Moore's letter in the reading.)

2. Below are two boring, general paragraphs that are in great need of concrete details. Write an *essay* using one of these paragraphs as an outline. Support the general points with specific anecdotes from your own life. Be sure to include vivid specifics that allow readers to "see," "hear," and "feel" what your experiences were like. (For a good example of such writing, take another look at paragraph 22 of the reading.)

> Holidays are a time for gatherings with family and friends, for gifts, and for high hopes. It's no wonder, then, that many of my best [or worst] memories are associated with holidays. One holiday that brings to mind vivid memories is _____. Another holiday that provided many memories is _____. My most dramatic memories are associated with _____.

I am often very busy with work, school, and family. But
when I do have time to relax, there are several activities I
especially enjoy. I often like to _____. I also enjoy
_____. My favorite activity is _____.

3. Johnson uses vigorous details to make a point she feels strongly
about—that specific language lends power to writing. Prepare
an *essay* persuading readers of the virtues of something you believe in strongly. Perhaps you want to argue that college
students should exercise regularly. Bearing in mind that specific
details are more persuasive than generalities, include one or two
convincing examples for every point that you make. For instance, if you claim that one benefit of exercise is that it makes
college students healthier, you might tell how one friend's back
trouble improved once she started lifting weights and how another friend's headaches cleared after he began jogging.
Whatever evidence you provide, be sure to make it convincing
and concrete. For an example of an essay in which detailed examples support the main point, read Alex Haley's "Thank You"
(page 175).

The Fine Art of Complaining

Caroline Rego

How simple our lives would be if all people kept their promises, if all products performed as advertised, if service always came with a smile. And how unlikely it is, unfortunately, that our existence will ever be so easy. However, according to consumer affairs reporter Caroline Rego, we can minimize the aggravation that accompanies such problems. The key, says Rego, is to become an expert complainer. Here she provides a step-by-step guide.

Words to Watch

hapless (3): unfortunate
venture (3): dare to go
patsy (3): someone who is easily taken advantage of
milquetoasts (4): timid people
apoplectic rage (4): extreme anger
Neanderthal (4): a very rude person
indiscriminately (5): unselectively
disembodied (7): without a body
credible (23): believable

Y*ou waited forty-five minutes for your dinner, and when it* 1
came it was cold—and not what you ordered in the first place. You washed your supposedly machine-washable, pre-shrunk T-shirt (the one the catalogue claimed was "indestructible"), and now it's the

size of a napkin. Your new car broke down a month after you bought it, and the dealer says the warranty doesn't apply.

Life's annoyances descend on all of us—some pattering down   2
like gentle raindrops, others striking with the bruising force of hailstones. We dodge the ones we can, but inevitably, plenty of them make contact. And when they do, we react fairly predictably. Many of us—most of us, probably—grumble to ourselves and take it. We scowl at our unappetizing food but choke it down. We stash the shrunken T-shirt in a drawer, vowing never again to order from a catalogue. We glare fiercely at our checkbooks as we pay for repairs that should have been free.

A few of us go to the other extreme. Taking our cue from the   3
crazed newscaster in the 1976 movie *Network,* we go through life mad as hell and unwilling to take it any more. In offices, we shout at hapless receptionists when we're kept waiting for appointments. In restaurants, we make scenes that have fellow patrons craning their necks to get a look at us. In stores, we argue with salespeople for not waiting on us. We may notice after a while that our friends seem reluctant to venture into public with us, but hey—we're just standing up for our rights. Being a patsy doesn't get you anywhere in life.

It's true—milquetoasts live unsatisfying lives. However, peo-   4
ple who go through the day in an eye-popping, vein-throbbing state of apoplectic rage don't win any prizes either. What persons at both ends of the scale need—what could empower the silent sufferer and civilize the Neanderthal—is a course in the gentle art of *effective* complaining.

Effective complaining is not apologetic and half-hearted. It's   5
not making one awkward attempt at protest—"Uh, excuse me, I don't think I ordered the squid and onions"—and then slinking away in defeat. But neither is it roaring away indiscriminately, attempting to get satisfaction through the sheer volume of our complaint.

Effective complainers are people who act businesslike and im-   6
portant. Acting important doesn't mean puffing up your chest and saying, "Do you know who I am?"—an approach that would tempt anyone to take you down a peg or two. It doesn't mean shouting

and threatening—techniques that will only antagonize the person whose help you need. It does mean making it clear that you know your request is reasonable and that you are confident it will be taken care of. People are generally treated the way they expect to be treated. If you act like someone making a fair request, chances are that request will be granted. Don't beg, don't explain. Just state your name, the problem, and what you expect to have done. Remain polite. But be firm. "My car has been in your garage for three days, and a mechanic hasn't even looked at it yet," you might say. "I want to know when it is going to be worked on." Period. Now it is up to them to give you a satisfactory response. Don't say, "Sorry to bother you about this, but . . ." or "I, uh, was sort of expecting . . ." You're only asking people to remedy a problem, after all; that is not grounds for apology.

If your problem requires an immediate response, try to make   7
your complaint in person; a real, live, in-the-flesh individual has to be dealt with in some way. Complaining over the telephone, by contrast, is much less effective. When you speak to a disembodied voice, when the person at the other end of the line doesn't have to face you, you're more likely to get a runaround.

Most importantly, complain to the right person. One of the   8
greatest frustrations in complaining is talking to a clerk or receptionist who cannot solve your problem and whose only purpose seems to be to drive you crazy. Getting mad doesn't help; the person you're mad at probably had nothing to do with your actual problem. And you'll have to repeat everything you've said to the clerk once you're passed along to the appropriate person. So make sure from the start that you're talking to someone who can help—a manager or supervisor.

If your problem doesn't require an immediate response, com-   9
plaining by letter is probably the most effective way to get what you want. A letter of complaint should be brief, businesslike, and to the point. If you have a new vacuum cleaner that doesn't work, don't spend a paragraph describing how your Uncle Joe tried to fix the problem and couldn't. As when complaining in person, be sure you address someone in a position of real authority. Here's an example of an effective letter of complaint.

August 29, 1994   10

Ms. Anne Lublin, Manager   11
Mitchell Appliances
80 Front Street
Newton, MA 02159

Dear Ms. Lublin: 12

Paragraph #1: Explain the problem. Include facts to back up   13
your story.

On August 6, I purchased a new Perma-Kool freezer   14
from your store (a copy of my sales receipt is enclosed).
The freezer ran normally when it was installed, but
since then it has repeatedly turned off, causing the food
inside to spoil. During the three weeks I have owned
the freezer, I have had to call your repair department
three times in an attempt to get it running properly.
My calls to your repair department have not been responded to promptly. After I called the first time, on
August 10, I waited two days for the repair person to
show up. It took three days to get a repair person here
after my second call, on August 15. The freezer stopped
yet again on August 20. I called to discuss this recent
problem, but no one has responded to my call.

Paragraph #2: Tell how you trust the company and are confi-   15
dent that your reader will fix the problem. (This is to "soften up"
the reader a bit.)

I am surprised to receive such unprofessional service   16
and poor quality from Mitchell Appliances since I have
been one of your satisfied customers for fifteen years.
In the past, I have purchased a television, air condi-
tioner, and washing machine from your company. I
know that you value good relations with your customers, and I'm sure you want to see me pleased with
my most recent purchase.

Paragraph #3: Explain exactly what you want to be done—re-   17
pair, replacement, refund, etc.

Although your repair department initially thought that the freezer needed only some minor adjustments, the fact that no one has been able to permanently fix the problem convinces me that the freezer has some serious defect. I am understandably unwilling to spend any more time having repairs made. Therefore, I expect you to exchange the freezer for an identical model by the end of next week (September 7). Please call me to arrange for the removal of the defective freezer and the delivery of the new one.   18

Sincerely,   19
Janice Becker   20

P.S.: Readers always notice a P.S. State again when you expect the problem to be taken care of, and what you will do if it isn't.   21

P.S. I am confident that we can resolve this problem by September 7. If the defective freezer is not replaced by then, however, I will report this incident to the Better Business Bureau.   22

Notice that the P.S. says what you'll do if your problem isn't solved. In other words, you make a threat—a polite threat. Your threat must be reasonable and believable. A threat to burn down the store if your purchase price isn't refunded is neither reasonable nor believable—or if it were believed, you could end up in jail. A threat to report the store to a consumer-protection agency, such as the Better Business Bureau, however, is credible.   23

Don't be too quick to make one of the most common—and commonly empty—threats: "I'll sue!" A full-blown lawsuit is more trouble, and more expensive, than most problems are worth. On the other hand, most areas have a small-claims court where suits involving modest amounts of money are heard. These courts don't use complex legal language or procedures, and you don't need a lawyer to use them. A store or company will often settle with you— if your claim is fair—rather than go to small-claims court.   24

Whether you complain over the phone, in person, or by letter, be persistent. One complaint may not get results. In that case, keep on complaining, and make sure you keep complaining to the same   25 person. Chances are he or she will get worn out and take care of the situation, if only to be rid of you.

Someday, perhaps, the world will be free of the petty annoy-   26
ances that plague us all from time to time. Until then, however, toasters will break down, stores will refuse to honor rainchecks, and bills will include items that were never purchased. You can depend upon it—there will be grounds for complaint. You might as well learn to be good at it.

Understanding Content

1. What is the selection's main idea? It if is stated directly, locate the relevant sentence(s). If it is implied, state the main idea in your own words.

2. According to Rego, why doesn't loud, angry complaining work? What kind of complaining works better? Why?

3. What four elements should a letter of complaint include? Why are these elements needed?

Understanding Technique

1. The essay is about effective complaining, yet Rego doesn't give advice on how to complain until paragraph 6. What does she gain by waiting until this point to present her advice?

2. Paragraphs 2 and 3 are written in the first person plural—that is, from the point of view of "us" and "we." Why do you suppose Rego uses this approach? What is its effect?

3. Why do you think Rego includes the italicized material in paragraphs 13, 15, 17, and 21? What would have been lost if she had used only the italicized material or only the model letter?

Thinking About Ideas

1. Have you ever experienced any of the types of annoyances Rego writes about? Did you complain? If so, what form did your complaint take, and what were the results?

2. Rego states that writing a letter is "the most effective way to get what you want" (paragraph 9). Why might a letter work so well?

3. Rego mentions two possible threats: reporting a company to a consumer-protection agency and taking a company to a small-claims court. What other threats might work?

Writing About Ideas

1. Rego writes, "Life's annoyances descend on all of us." What annoyances do you face? A nosy younger brother? A temperamental car? An inconsiderate boss? Focusing on one everyday nuisance in your life, write a *paragraph* that develops this sentence: "The most annoying irritation in my life right now is _____." Use lively examples to illustrate the annoyance and how you try to deal with it.

2. Rego shows how to complain effectively. Write an *essay* showing step by step how to do something else well. (You could title your essay "The Fine Art of _____.") Use a subject you know a good deal about—maybe growing a vegetable garden, keeping in good physical shape, training a dog, throwing a surprise birthday party, or sticking to a budget. Use dramatic, detailed examples to illustrate each piece of advice you give. To help readers understand what they should do, begin—as Rego does—by telling them what they shouldn't do. Your essay may be serious or light-spirited. Before planning your paper, you may want to read Beth Johnson's "Let's Get Specific" (page 183), which gives persuasively illustrated guidelines for making writing vigorous.

3. Using the format suggested by Rego, write a *letter* of complaint about a product or service that disappointed you. Before writing, take a few minutes to brainstorm information to include in the letter: What exactly is the problem? Why should the company make amends? What specifically do you want the company to do? What will you do if your complaint is ignored? As you write, try not to let your anger get the best of you; be firm but polite. Make sure you have the name and company address of the person to whom you plan to send the letter.

Handled with Care

Bob Greene

Columnist Bob Greene quotes author John Barth in asking, "Which snowflake triggers the avalanche?" Which, indeed? Which petty inconvenience, which minor dispute could make a person lose a grip on reality and commit a shocking act? In telling the story of the naked woman on Michigan Avenue, Greene doesn't speculate on what private miseries might have burdened her. Rather, he dwells on the sympathetic reaction of strangers who witnessed her "cry for help." Greene writes his syndicated column for the Chicago Tribune *and has authored a number of books, including* American Beat, *from which the following selection is taken.*

Words to Watch

titillation (7): excitement
premises (8): assumptions or rules
fabric (8): structure
fault (9): a break in a rock
resigned (9): accepting without a struggle
trifling (9): unimportant
assessment (9): tax

The day the lady took her clothes off on Michigan Avenue, 1 people were leaving downtown as usual. The workday had come to an end; men and women were heading for bus and train stations, in a hurry to get home.

200

She walked south on Michigan; she was wearing a white robe,   2
as if she had been to the beach. She was blond and in her thirties.

As she passed the Radisson Hotel, Roosevelt Williams, a   3
doorman, was opening the door of a cab for one of the hotel's
guests. The woman did not really pause while she walked; she
merely shrugged the robe off, and it fell to the sidewalk.

She was wearing what appeared to be the bottom of a blue   4
bikini bathing suit, although one woman who was directly next to
her said it was just underwear. She wore nothing else.

Williams at first did not believe what he was seeing. If you   5
hang around long enough, you will see everything: robberies, mug-
gings, street fights, murders. But a naked woman on North
Michigan Avenue? Williams had not seen that before and neither,
apparently, had the other people on the street.

It was strange; her white robe lay on the sidewalk, and by all   6
accounts she was smiling. But no one spoke to her. A report in the
newspaper the next day quoted someone: "The cars were stopping,
the people on the buses were staring, people were shouting, and
people were taking pictures." But that is not what other people who
were there that afternoon said.

The atmosphere was not carnival-like, they said. Rather, they   7
said, it was as if something very sad was taking place. It took only a
moment for people to realize that this was not some stunt designed
to promote a product or a movie. Without anything telling them,
they understood that the woman was troubled, and that what she
was doing had nothing to do with sexual titillation; it was more of a
cry for help.

The cry for help came in a way that such cries often come.   8
The woman was violating one of the basic premises of the social
fabric. She was doing something that is not done. She was not
shooting anyone, or breaking a window, or shouting in anger.
Rather, in a way that everyone understood, she was signaling that
things were not right.

The line is so thin between matters being manageable and   9
being out of hand. One day a person may be barely all right; the
next the same person may have crossed over. Here is something
from the author John Barth:

She paused amid the kitchen to drink a glass of water; at that instant, losing a grip of fifty years, the next-room-ceiling plaster crashed. Or he merely sat in an empty study, in March-day glare, listening to the universe rustle in his head, when suddenly a five-foot shelf let go. For ages the fault creeps secret through the rock; in a second, ledge and railings, tourists and turbines all thunder over Niagara. Which snowflake triggers the avalanche? A house explodes; a star. In your spouse, so apparently resigned, murder twitches like a fetus. At some trifling new assessment, all the colonies rebel.

The woman continued to walk past Tribune Tower. People   10
who saw her said that the look on her face was almost peaceful. She did not seem to think she was doing anything unusual; she was described as appearing "blissful." Whatever the reaction on the street was, she seemed calm, as if she believed herself to be in control.

She walked over the Michigan Avenue bridge. Again, people   11
who were there report that no one harassed her; no one jeered at her or attempted to touch her. At some point on the bridge, she removed her bikini bottom. Now she was completely undressed, and still she walked.

"It was as if people knew not to bother her," said one woman   12
who was there. "To tell it, it sounds like something very lewd and sensational was going on. But it wasn't like that at all. It was as if people knew that something very . . . fragile . . . was taking place. I was impressed with the maturity with which people were handling it. No one spoke to her, but you could tell that they wished someone would help her."

Back in front of the Radisson, a police officer had picked up   13
the woman's robe. He was on his portable radio, advising his colleagues that the woman was walking over the bridge.

When the police caught up with the woman, she was just   14
standing there, naked in downtown Chicago, still smiling. The first thing the police did was hand her some covering and ask her to put it on; the show was over.

People who were there said that there was no reaction from   15
the people who were watching. They said that the juvenile behavior you might expect in such a situation just didn't happen. After all,

when a man walks out on a ledge in a suicide attempt, there are always people down below who call for him to jump. But this day, by all accounts, nothing like that took place. No one called for her to stay undressed; no one cursed the police officers for stopping her.

"It was as if everyone was relieved," said a woman who saw   16
it. "They were embarrassed by it; it made them feel bad. They were glad that someone had stopped her. And she was still smiling. She seemed to be off somewhere."

The police charged her with no crime; they took her to Read   17
Mental Health Center, where she was reported to have signed herself in voluntarily. Within minutes things were back to as they always are on Michigan Avenue; there was no reminder of the naked lady who had reminded people how fragile is the everyday world in which we live.

Understanding Content

1. What is the selection's main idea? If it is stated directly, locate the relevant sentence(s). If it is implied, state the main idea in your own words.

2. Greene gives two very different accounts of how people reacted to the woman. Describe each account. Which version does Greene assume is more accurate? Why?

3. What does Greene mean when he writes, at the end, that the naked woman "reminded people how fragile is the everyday world in which we live"? How does this insight relate to the Barth quotation in paragraph 9?

Understanding Technique

1. Why do you think Greene decided to open his essay as he does? What mood does Greene create with the words "The day the lady took her clothes off on Michigan Avenue, people were leaving downtown as usual"? How does this mood contrast with what follows?

2. What specific details does Greene include about the woman's behavior? Her facial expression? Her clothing? What effect might he have hoped to create by providing these details?

3. Why do you think Greene titled his essay "Handled with Care"? How does the title reinforce Greene's main idea?

Thinking About Ideas

1. Are you surprised by the subdued reaction of the witnesses to this incident? Why or why not? Should the observers have acted differently in any way? How? What would you have done had you been there?

2. Greene writes that the woman's action, which violated a social taboo, was a "cry for help." Have you ever observed someone who sought help or attention by acting in socially unacceptable ways? What did the person do? What prompted the person's unusual behavior? Did the person get the needed help? Why or why not?

3. In what way might this incident be "a fable for our times"? What truths about our society does this incident suggest?

Writing About Ideas

1. Although most people never do something as socially unacceptable as the woman on Michigan Avenue, all of us have, at one time or another, done something unexpected and out of the ordinary. In a *paragraph,* write about a time you did something unusual. Perhaps you were prompted by anger, or impatience, or joy, or sheer playfulness. Be sure to provide lively details to convey the unusual nature of your behavior.

2. The woman in Greene's essay is apparently emotionally disturbed. Perhaps she is a victim of the stresses of modern life. Focus on a particular group of people—for example, college students, college athletes, working parents, fast-food employees. Then write an *essay* illustrating two or three of the serious

stresses afflicting this group. You'll also want to show the effects of these stresses. To gather information for your paper, speak to several people belonging to the group under discussion. Draw upon their experiences (as well as your own, if appropriate) to develop your points.

CD 3. Greene's article raises the question of how much responsibility we should have for the care or protection of others. Should we give assistance to a homeless person asleep on a sidewalk? Should we help accident victims or come to the aid of someone being attacked by a mugger or rapist? Drawing upon incidents you have witnessed or have heard about, write an *essay* explaining when we should—and, if appropriate, when we should not—get involved if we see someone in trouble. Be sure to provide specific reasons to explain why you feel as you do. Paul Keegan's "A Dangerous Party" (page 213) may provide some helpful perspective on the issue of moral accountability.

The Price of Hate

Rachel L. Jones

Reporters observe events in order to report on them. They are therefore usually on the sidelines. But when Rachel L. Jones, as a reporter with The Miami Herald, *covered a Ku Klux Klan rally, she became one of the rally's victims. In this essay, which first appeared in the* St. Petersburg Times, *she explains how that event changed her—and how it didn't change her.*

Words to Watch

mechanism (2): system of behavior
burly (5): heavy and muscular
fray (5): uproar
feigned (9): pretended
clinical (13): without feeling
proffered (16): offered
vitriol (31): bitterly abusive expression
visceral (32): instinctive
epithets (36): insults, terms of abuse
rabble (38): mob
ingenious (38): clever
diffuse (41): soften
demented (43): insane

I was sitting at my computer terminal when I overheard   1
someone in the office mention his concern because he thought a
black couple was moving into a house on his street.

He was standing only four feet away from me, yet lacked a 2
mechanism that would prevent him from making racist statements in
front of a black person. I stopped typing and stared at his back. He
froze momentarily, and the woman he was talking to glanced at me.

I didn't confront him. I had to transmit copy to St. Petersburg 3
and then leave to cover a graduation. Besides, my stomach was
churning. Just seven days earlier, at a Ku Klux Klan rally in
Clearwater, I had stood only four feet away from a Tarpon Springs
man who told me he was tired of "the n—s getting everything."

I'd be lying if I said that the possibility of covering a Ku Klux 4
Klan rally didn't cause me a few moments' concern about my physical well-being. But when another reporter came over to tell me
about the May 28th Klan rally in front of Clearwater City Hall, I
reasoned, "It's just another assignment. I am a reporter, and I know
my life isn't all budget meetings."

I must admit to a curiosity about the Klan, and it seemed a 5
good opportunity to take a look at that sideshow of human nature.
Now, I *could* have asked to be excused from that particular assignment. As a police reporter, my Saturdays are sometimes very busy.
Had I approached my editor to delicately decline, we could have
both made ourselves believe it was only natural to send a burly
young man into the fray. Anything could have happened that day—
traffic accidents, drownings, first-degree murders at the jail.

I couldn't be two places at once, could I? 6

But two days before the event, I turned to my editor and 7
asked, "I AM covering the rally on Saturday, aren't I?"

She didn't miss a beat. Yes, of course. Just a short story, un- 8
less the streets were running with blood or something.

I jokingly told her about the only slightly feigned horror of 9
my older sister, who shrieked into the phone, "They're letting a
black reporter cover the KLAN?"

At the Klan rally, the man from Tarpon Springs saw my press 10
badge and figured I was a part of something he called the "Black
Associated Press," which he swore was denying white journalism
graduates jobs. Mr. Tarpon told me that n—s weren't qualified to
get the jobs they were getting through affirmative action, and that
America is for white people.

I paused momentarily and asked what he thought should be 11
done about black people. He didn't know or care.

"Send 'em all to hell," he said, while I took notes.   12

It's funny—it was all so clinical. My voice held an even tone,   13
and while he talked I searched his contoured face for some glimmer
of recognition on his part that *I* was a human being, and the words
that he spat just might hurt me.

Just as I later waited for Mr. Welcome Wagon to turn around   14
and apologize for his blunder, I waited for the Tarpon Springs man
to show some spark of humanity, but he finished his conversation
and walked away.

My stomach was still churning hours later as I relived that   15
rally. The whole experience was like being scalded, like having
something sharp raked over my flesh until it was raw.

After it was over I went home and drank a shot from the bot-   16
tle of brandy I'd bought last Christmas. In Harlequin romances,
handsome princes always proffered hard liquor to soothe the jan-
gled nerves of a distraught heroine.

But I was alone, and I was no heroine. That night, every noise   17
from the apartment upstairs made me jump, and the pattern of trees
against the curtains frightened me as I tossed and turned. I called
three of my siblings, but other than offering sympathy, they felt
helpless to ease my trauma.

I had been so naive about the whole assignment. The thing is,   18
I never thought it would change me. I figured it would be difficult,
but I didn't want it to *change* me.

What you must understand about the Klan is that its members   19
and supporters have been stripped of their humanity. I gained that
insight and feel stronger for it. It was easy enough on one level to
say, "These people are stupid, so I shouldn't be bothered by what
they say."

But that was cold comfort as I walked across the City Hall   20
parking lot, feeling a numbness creep through my arms and legs. I
thought I must have been walking like the Scarecrow in *The Wizard
of Oz,* but figured if I could just make it to the church across the
street, I'd be fine.

At the church, I asked to use the phone and was sent down a   21
hall and to the left. My fingers felt like sausages as I tried to use the
rotary dial, muttering curses as I fouled up several times. Finally
managing to reach an editor, I was coherent enough to give her information for a brief summary of the rally.

But when the next editor picked up the phone, I dissolved in   22
tears after three words. He was puzzled, and I think unaware of
what was wrong at first. I whimpered that I was sorry and didn't
know what was wrong either. I gasped and caught a few breaths before describing in a wavering voice what had happened.

He tried calming me down to discuss the facts. How many   23
people attended? Had there been any clashes? What did police have
to say? I planned to write a full story.

The editor said maybe we should just ignore the event. He   24
asked if any of the Klan members had been abusive to me. I mumbled, "Uh hum," and the tears flowed fresh. He told me to get as
much police information as I could and to call him back later.

I placed the phone on the hook and buried my face in my   25
hands, letting the sobs come freely. The man who had let me use
the church phone brought me a box of tissues and a Coke.

After I splashed my face with cold water and controlled the   26
sobs, I headed back to the rally, just as the Klansmen were loading
up to leave. Shouts of "white supremacy" rang through the air as
they rolled out, and my photographer walked over to give me the
Klansmen's names. I turned away, telling her that I probably
wouldn't use them anyway.

"I didn't think it would affect me," I whispered.   27

"Don't cry. They aren't worth it, Rachel," she said.   28

But even then, it had started to change me. . . .   29

When you have stared into the twisted face of hate, you must   30
change. I remember watching the documentary *Eyes on the Prize,*
in particular the segment on the desegregation of Little Rock High
School in 1957, and being disturbed by the outpouring of rage
against those nine students.

The whites who snarled into the camera back then had no ex-   31
planation for their vitriol and violence other than that the students
were black, and they didn't care who knew it. They weren't going
to let those n—s into the school, no matter what.

I've struggled all my life against a visceral reaction to that   32
kind of racism. I have been mistreated because of my color, but
nothing ever came near to what those students went through on a
daily basis.

That and countless other examples let me know what I'd been   33
spared, and I decided to choose the path of understanding, realizing

that some people are always going to fear or even hate me because of my color alone.

It's a burden blacks must carry no matter how high a level of   34
achievement they reach, and I sought to incorporate that into my own striving. Watching films of what hate turned those people into made me choose to reject it, to deal with people individually and not tarnish all whites with the same obscene images. *I would not hate.*

But as one Klan supporter muttered, "N— b—," at me as I   35
weaved my way through the crowd, that resolve crumbled. It stung as much as if he *had* slapped me or thrown something.

The leader shouted taunts and epithets at a black woman who   36
was infuriated by the proceedings, and who had even lunged at several people in the small group of supporters.

As the black woman walked away, the leader shouted, "Why   37
don't you go back to Nee-gor Africa where you came from!" I laughed because he sounded foolish, but he saw me and sent a fresh stream of obscenity my way.

A Jewish woman who came to protest was heaped with sting-   38
ing abuse, and the rabble was ingenious in its varied use of sexual and racial obscenities directed toward her.

Other reporters and photographers eyed me warily throughout   39
the rally, watching for my reactions to the abuse. When the leader started passing out leaflets and avoided my outstretched hand, a photographer asked for two and brought me one.

I said thank you. He said quietly, "You're very, very wel-   40
come," and was embarrassed when I caught his eye.

When it was all over, several police officials called me brave.   41
But I felt cold, sick and empty. I felt like such a naive fool. I felt bitter. So this is what it feels like, I thought. Why *shouldn't* I just hate them right back, why couldn't I diffuse this punch in the gut?

What is noble about not flinching in the face of hate? Slavery,   42
lynchings, rape, inequality, was that not enough? If they want to send me to hell, shouldn't I want to take them along for the ride?

But I still couldn't hate. I was glad I had cried, though. It de-   43
fied their demented logic. It meant I was human.

Understanding Content

1. What is the selection's main idea? If it is stated directly, locate

the relevant sentence(s). If it is implied, state the main idea in your own words.

2. In paragraph 33, Jones writes that she "decided to choose the path of understanding." What does she mean by "the path of understanding"?

3. Jones comments that she had been "naive about the whole assignment" to cover the KKK rally and that she hadn't wanted it to change her. About what was she naive? How did the rally change her? How *didn't* it change her?

Understanding Technique

1. Although Jones focuses on the KKK rally, she begins her essay with three paragraphs that describe an incident at her office. What purpose do these introductory paragraphs serve? How do they reinforce Jones's key points?

2. Unlike most short narratives, Jones's account of the KKK rally does not follow a strict chronological order. She begins her description of the rally with the anecdote about the Tarpon Springs man (paragraphs 10–14), then moves to her reaction at home (paragraphs 15–18). Next she returns to the rally and her experience at the church (paragraphs 20–25), followed by a description of what happened afterwards (paragraphs 26–41). Why do you think Jones decided to narrate events in this order?

3. Her essay is mainly about the cruel behavior of racist whites, yet Jones also describes examples of kindnesses. Identify these examples. Why do you think she included them?

Thinking About Ideas

1. Jones's sister asked, "They're letting a black reporter cover the KLAN?" (9). Do you think assigning a black reporter to the rally was a good idea? Why or why not?

2. Jones burst into tears soon after one of her editors picked up the phone. The editor responded, "Maybe we should just ignore the event." Why might the editor have made that suggestion? Do

you think it would have been a good idea to ignore the event? Explain.

3. Have you ever been the target of racist behavior, or have you ever witnessed such behavior? What happened, and how did the event make you feel?

Writing About Ideas

1. Like Jones, focus on the effect of a significant event, and write a *paragraph* showing how the incident affected you or someone you know well. The event could be a positive one (such as the birth of a child, a wedding, even seeing a powerful film) or a negative one (perhaps a crime, an accident, or an encounter with rudeness). If you write about someone else's experience, interview your subject to gather details about the event and how it made that person feel.

2. Jones mentions several acts of kindness that managed to brighten, at least somewhat, the rally's overall grimness. Write an *essay* arguing that small acts of kindness can have considerable effects. Support that point by describing several instances of small actions that provided help and encouragement. To get ideas for your paper, ask friends and relatives for examples from their own experiences. Take notes, and try to include some of your subjects' more revealing quotations when you write your essay. For additional inspiration, you might want to read Alex Haley's "Thank You" (page 175), an essay that illustrates the positive effects of expressing gratitude.

3. Like most people, at one time or another, you have probably been subjected to unpleasant, even hostile behavior—perhaps someone criticized your appearance or abilities or taunted you about your gender or race. Write an *essay* about a specific insult that you experienced. Start by narrating what happened, being sure to provide vigorous details to convey the drama of the incident and your reaction to it. Were you satisfied with your reaction? If not, explain what would have been a more effective way to deal with the offensive behavior.

A Dangerous Party

Paul Keegan

On some college campuses, alcohol and sex are almost as common as textbooks. The result can be what is now known as "date rape" or "acquaintance rape." A representative example involves a group of drunk male students who took advantage of a drunk female student at the University of New Hampshire. Paul Keegan, an alumnus of that school, returned to explore the incident and what followed. In this article, which first appeared in longer form in New England Monthly Magazine, *he reconstructs the event and reports on the differing views of what it was that took place.*

Words to Watch

elicited (6): brought out
complied (10): did what was requested
confront (16): oppose
forestall (29): prevent
base (36): morally low

What happened on the traumatic night of February 19 I   1
pieced together from police records, the testimony of witnesses, and
conversations with most of the participants.

On that night, a freshman named Karen decided she was not   2
in the mood to party with the other girls on the fourth floor of Stoke
Hall. She was still upset about her grandfather, who had died in the

213

fall. Also, a boy she liked was not treating her well. Karen told the others she'd rather just stay in her room and study. Her friend Sara, however, would have none of it. "Come on," she told Karen. "You never have any fun. What you need is to go out with your friends and have a good time."

This was typical Sara. She was popular, cute, fun-loving, and   3
smart—she'd had a 3.9 grade point average the previous semester. She planned to be a biology major, and her friends marveled at how easily subjects like botany and chemistry came to her. But Sara was also a real partyer. It was not unusual for her to get everybody else on the floor psyched up to go out. And that night, excitement on the fourth floor was running high. There was a Ladies' Tea[1] at Pi Kappa Alpha, a fraternity behind Stoke. The mood was infectious. Finally, Karen smiled and gave in.

Sara was in her room with her best friend, Michele, drinking   4
rum and Cokes and listening to Steve Winwood. By the time they left for the party forty minutes later, Sara had consumed two rum and Cokes, and had finished up with a straight shot. Finally, a little after ten, Karen and two other girls, Noelle and Tracy, were ready, and all five headed out into the cold night. The temperature was hovering around zero as they walked to the three-story frat house they called Pike.

The basement wasn't yet crowded. Sara and Karen squeezed   5
up to the small curved bar. Each grabbed a plastic cup of beer and challenged the other to a chugging contest. Karen won. They laughed and went back for another. As the night wore on, Sara became preoccupied with a Pike brother named Hal who was pouring beer. Michele noticed that Sara was drinking fast so she'd have an excuse to return and talk with him. But Hal acted cold, which hurt Sara's feelings.

Within an hour, Michele saw Sara dancing wildly. Later, she   6
saw her leaning against a post, looking very spaced out. When Michele asked her something, Sara didn't seem to hear her. Linda, a freshman who also lived at Stoke, was looking for a friend when she noticed Sara leaning against the wall. "Where's Rachel?" Linda shouted. When Sara didn't respond, Linda repeated the question,

---

[1] A fraternity drinking party meant to attract women.

this time louder. Sara merely stared straight ahead. Finally, Linda shook her and screamed, *"Where is she?"* This elicited only a mumble, so Linda gave up.

At about twelve-thirty, Michele, Noelle, and Tracy decided to leave, but Sara said she wanted to stay longer. Karen and Sara agreed there was no reason to leave, since they were both having a good time. They assumed they'd go back together later. At length, Karen staggered upstairs, threw up, and passed out. When she awakened she was lying on the floor near the bathroom. By then, the party was over and Sara was gone.

That night, Jon, Chris, and Gordon were returning to Stoke after their night at the Wildcat[1]. The three sophomores were probably legally intoxicated but not out of control. Chris decided to go up to the fifth floor, while Jon and Gordon went to the fourth, where all three lived. They headed to one of the girls' wings, and on the way, dropped their pants around their ankles and raced down the hall, a favorite prank. They stopped to visit Laura, a dark-haired freshman who used to date Jon, and her roommate, Linda, who had tried to talk to Sara at the party. No one was in, so they left a note: "We came to see you in our boxer shorts—Jon and Chris."

On the way back to their wing, the two boys saw a girl in the hallway. She was looking for Scott, she said. Noticing her shirttail sticking out of the zipper of her pants, Gordon tugged on it playfully and said, "What's this?" Both boys laughed.

Before going into his room, Jon asked the girl if he could have a good-night hug, which, he says, she gave him. He then asked for a good-night kiss, and she complied. When the couple backed toward the door, Gordon decided to leave the two of them alone. Without exchanging a word with her, Jon had sex with the girl in his room. After about twenty minutes, he walked down the hall to Gordon's room, where Gordon was already in bed. "I just did it with a girl; she's really horny," Jon told him. Still in his underwear, Gordon decided to check out what was happening. He says he entered Jon's room out of curiosity, without any sexual intentions. But once inside, he changed his mind.

[2]A campus bar.

Meanwhile, Jon raced up to the fifth floor to tell his room-   11
mate, Chris, what was going on. The two went downstairs to their
room. When they reached the door, the boys were surprised to see
Linda and Laura, the girls they had left the note for about an hour
earlier.

Wordlessly, Chris slipped into the room while Jon, in jeans   12
and T-shirt, stayed outside with the girls, casually discussing the
night's partying. The girls saw nothing unusual about Chris going
into his own room at one-thirty in the morning, and Jon was being
his normal smooth-talking self. But when they drifted near the door,
according to the girls' account, Jon said, "Don't go in. Gordy's in
there doing really bad things with a drunk girl." (Jon denies using
the words *bad things* and *drunk*.)

Oh, *really*? the girls said. "We were kidding around with Jon,"   13
recalls Laura. "It wasn't like, 'Oh my God, that's awful.' Usually, if
you're in someone's room, it's because you want to be." Even
though Chris was in the room, too, it's not terribly unusual to go to
bed while two people are having sex in the bunk below you. What
the girls didn't know was that it was Chris having sex with the girl
while Gordon (whose activities with her had not included actual
penetration) waited inside for them to leave so he could sneak back
to his own room.

Soon Laura and Linda said good-night to Jon. As they passed   14
John Prescott's room, they saw that the sophomore resident assistant was at his desk studying. Laura was a good friend of his, so
they stopped in. After some small talk, the girls half-jokingly asked
him how he would let such wild stuff go on in his wing and told
him about Gordon and the drunk girl.

"It's not my job to monitor people's sex lives," Prescott told   15
them. "But I'll look into it anyway, out of the goodness of my
heart."

Prescott, a hotel administration and economics major from   16
Hudson, New Hampshire, went to the room and knocked. When no
one answered, he opened the door and saw two figures silhouetted
on a bed. (He would later learn it was Jon, having a second round
with the girl.) Prescott also saw Chris, sitting on a couch next to the
bed, watching. (Chris maintains he was simply getting dressed.)
According to Prescott, Chris looked up laughing and whispered,

"Get out," waving him away. After telling Chris several times to come out into the hall and being told to go away, Prescott barked, "Get out here *now*." Chris at last obeyed. "I was tense and nervous," Prescott remembers. "You don't confront your friends like that all the time."

Prescott asked if the girl had passed out, and Chris said no. "I 17 want that girl out of the room," Prescott said.

"Oh, come on," Chris replied. 18

"Is she really drunk?" Prescott asked. 19

Chris nodded and laughed, Prescott says, although Chris de- 20 nies this.

"Do you know that what you're doing could be considered 21 rape?" Prescott said.

"No, it's not," Chris answered. 22

"You guys are going to learn one of these days that someone 23 is going to wake up the next day and think that what happened was wrong, even if she wanted to be in there," Prescott said. "I want that girl out of the room." Chris finally agreed, but said he had to talk to her first.

Despite his role as the enforcer and voice of reason, Prescott 24 nonetheless thought the events on his floor were entertaining—so much so that he went to see two of his friends and told them what had happened. "Wow! No way! Unbelievable!" Prescott remembers them saying. "We were all laughing. It was funny, in a sick kind of way."

As Prescott and his friends went out into the hallway, Jon 25 emerged from the room and walked toward them. When he reached the group, two of the boys said, he gave Prescott's friends high fives. Then he continued past them, slapping the air at knee level, giving low fives to other members of the imaginary team.

Prescott says Jon proceeded to tell the three of them in great 26 detail what he had done with the girl and how he had gone to get Gordon and Chris. All three remember that during this conversation Jon told them he had a "train" going in his room. (Jon denies both the high fives and the train reference.) As the boys were talking, Linda and Laura returned, "not because we were worried about what had happened," Laura remembers. "We were still just hanging out." Then Joe, another freshman on the floor, joined the group. A discussion ensued between the five boys and two girls about whether the boys' behavior was wrong. "Someone said, 'Hey, a drunk girl is fair game,'" Laura recalls, "which made Linda and me a little defensive, obviously." One of the boys suggested that maybe Joe could "get lucky, too." Joe walked toward the door—just to see what was happening, he says.

Inside, Chris was now alone with the girl. She got dressed, 27 and for the first time there was verbal communication: Chris told her a lot of people were in the hallway talking about them and watching the door. He carefully explained how she could avoid them. Just as Joe reached the room, the door opened and the crowd saw a girl walk out, her shirt untucked. Without looking up, she disappeared into the stairwell.

To their astonishment, everyone recognized Sara, the girl who 28 lived on the same floor. They had all simply assumed it was someone they didn't know, maybe a high-school girl. Suddenly the atmosphere in the hallway changed. Linda and Laura were outraged. "You *assholes!*" one of them screamed. "How could you do such a thing?" No one was more shocked than Jon: "You mean you *know* her?" It was at that moment that Jon and Chris heard her name for the first time.

By now there were six witnesses, two of them girls who 29 didn't seem to understand the boys' point of view. This was trouble. Chris and Jon decided to talk to Sara to forestall misunderstanding.

When Giselle, Sara's roommate, heard voices calling, "Sara, 30 Sara, Sara," she thought she was dreaming. But when she looked up from her bed, she saw two boys bent over her roommate's bed, shaking Sara's shoulder. "What the hell are you doing in here?" she demanded.

"We have to talk to Sara," they said. "It's very important." 31

Giselle got up. Sara was lying on her side with a nightshirt on. 32 "You okay?" Giselle asked, shaking her gently. Sara nodded. "Do you want to get up?" she asked. Sara shook her head: no. "I don't think she should get up," Giselle said.

But they pleaded with her, so Giselle shrugged and went back 33 to bed. A moment later, she saw Sara standing in the middle of the room, wrapping herself in a blanket. One of the boys held her left arm with his right arm. This must have been, Giselle thought later, to prevent her from falling back into bed.

When the three were out in the hallway, Chris and Jon say, 34
they all agreed on what had happened so there could be no misunderstanding later. Chris then suggested that Jon leave so he could
talk to Sara more easily. Alone, they began kissing. They walked a
few steps and opened the stairwell door. Then, at some time between three and four in the morning, beneath a window through
which a slice of Pi Kappa Alpha was visible, near a heating vent
painted the same blue as the walls around them, Chris and Sara got
down on the landing and had sex again.

What is most puzzling about the way the kids in Stoke reacted 35
to the incident is that for at least three days, until Sara first spoke
with a counselor, no one called it rape. Even Prescott, who had used
the term when he talked to Chris outside the room, insists that his
main concern was the perception that it was rape, not whether it actually was. "These guys were my friends. My concern was not for
the woman in that room. My concern was for the men. But look
where it got me. Now when I see Gordon and say hi, he just gives
me a blank look."

Prescott is thin and earnest-looking, with short blond hair and 36
an angular face. Clearly, the incident has taken its toll on him, yet
he talks about it willingly. Over the weekend, he told a friend what
had happened, setting off the chain reaction of gossip that eventually led to Sara herself; only then did she go to the police. But
Prescott's motives, he freely admits, were entirely base. "You know
why I told him?" Prescott says today. "I wanted to astonish him."

But why didn't Prescott consider the possibility that the girl in 37
the room was raped? "I just assumed she was willing, since I didn't
know any differently," he says. "I saw her walk out of the room.
Look, that's how sex happens here. Most scoops happen after parties, and guys go to parties to scoop."

But three guys? "It doesn't surprise me that much," he says. 38
"You hear stories about that kind of thing all the time. I don't expect it to happen, but I'm not ignorant that it goes on. I'm not naive.
My fault was in not going to see her right away, when she walked
back to her room. Then there would be no question. I keep asking
myself why I didn't. I don't know. I was like a pendulum swinging
back and forth, and finally I just had to try to look at this objec-
tively and make a judgment." He stares into space. "You know, I
still can't make one."

Editors' Note: Keegan writes that five days after the night of the incident, Jon, Chris, and Gordon were arrested and charged with sexual assault.

At university Judicial Board proceedings, the three young men were judged not guilty of sexual assault. Jon and Chris, however, were found to have violated "a university rule entitled 'Respect for Others'" and were suspended for the summer and fall terms. Gordon was cleared of all charges.

A series of noisy campus demonstrations followed. At one demonstration, two hundred students showed up, and protesters demanded that the Judicial Board hearing be nullified, the boys expelled, and a public apology made to Sara. The president of the University of New Hampshire, "shaken," scheduled a special convocation in the fall for a "moral reexamination" of campus behavior. At the convocation, the president announced steps the university would take to prevent future cases of sexual assault, including publicizing sexual assault cases, improving lighting, and providing greater oversight of Stoke Hall and the fraternity houses.

At their court trial, Jon and Chris pleaded guilty to misdemeanor sexual assault, and each served two months in prison; the court also forced them to write a letter of apology to Sara. The charge against Gordon was dropped.

Sara transferred to another school.

Understanding Content

1. What is the selection's main idea? If it is stated directly, locate the relevant sentence(s). If it is implied, state the main idea in your own words.

2. What condition was Sara in during and after the party?

3. According to witnesses, after Jon emerged from his room, "he gave Prescott's friends high fives." And Prescott and his friends report that Jon said "he had a 'train' going in his room" (paragraphs 25–26). What do the high fives and the train comment imply about Jon's attitude toward sexual activity?

Understanding Technique

1. Keegan is upset by the incident he describes, but, as a journalist, he strives to be objective. What are some of the techniques he uses to make his report of the incident as fair as possible?

2. Why do you suppose Keegan frequently quotes the words of people involved in the incident? What do these direct quotations add to the selection?

3. Find places where Keegan puts words in italics. What several functions do the italics serve?

Thinking About Ideas

1. One definition of acquaintance rape is "forced sexual intercourse by a 'friend' or an acquaintance." Do you feel that Jon, Gordon, and Chris raped Sara? Why or why not? To what extent was Sara also at fault?

2. Keegan writes, "What is most puzzling about the way the kids in Stoke reacted to the incident is that for at least three days, until Sara first spoke with a counselor, no one called it rape." Why might a victim of date rape hesitate to accuse her attacker?

3. Do college students you know or know of do a great deal of drinking? If so, why do you think they drink so much? Is their drinking harmful? How?

Writing About Ideas

1. As Keegan's article demonstrates, the challenges of college aren't all related to the classroom. The college years are often a time of significant personal growth. Write a *paragraph* arguing that the benefits of college are not just academic. Illustrate your viewpoint with detailed examples from your own or your friends' experiences.

⊂⊃ 2. Keegan describes a situation that reveals ugly tensions between males and females. Fortunately, not all encounters between the sexes are so distressing. Write an *essay* making the point that men and women (or boys and girls) can and often do relate in positive, rewarding ways. Support your point with vivid examples drawn from your own experiences and observations. For inspiration, you might read Alex Haley's "Thank You" (page 175) and Bob Greene's "Handled with Care" (page 200), both of which focus on caring interactions between people.

3. In an *essay,* present your definition of date rape, explaining both what it is and what it is not. To gather material for your paper, interview friends of both sexes about their opinions and experiences. Draw upon this information when constructing your definition. Be sure to provide vivid examples to illustrate your point of view.

6

The Light
Side
of Life

Wait Divisions

Tom Bodett

In the following essay, humorist Tom Bodett addresses one of life's perennial annoyances. Although he hasn't discovered any cure for waiting, he has at least come up with an entertaining system of classifying "waits." When you next find yourself staring with unfocused eyes in the grip of a wait, you can amuse yourself by deciding which category your wait fits. This selection is taken from Bodett's book Small Comforts.

Words to Watch

staggering (2): causing great discouragement
disengages (3): frees itself
render (5): make
demise (6): death
expound on (8): explain in detail
interludes (9): times in between
potent (10): intense
aforementioned (11): mentioned before

I read somewhere that we spend a full third of our lives wait- 1
ing. I've also read where we spend a third of our lives sleeping, a third working, and a third at our leisure. Now either somebody's lying, or we're spending all our leisure time waiting to go to work or sleep. That can't be true or league softball and Winnebagos never would have caught on.

So where are we doing all of this waiting and what does it 2
mean to an impatient society like ours? Could this unseen waiting be
the source of all our problems? A shrinking economy? The staggering deficit? Declining mental health and moral apathy? Probably
not, but let's take a look at some of the more classic "waits" anyway.

The very purest form of waiting is what we'll call the *Watched-* 3
Pot Wait. This type of wait is without a doubt the most annoying of
all. Take filling up the kitchen sink. There is absolutely nothing you
can do while this is going on but keep both eyes glued to the sink
until it's full. If you try to cram in some extracurricular activity,
you're asking for it. So you stand there, your hands on the faucets,
and wait. A temporary suspension of duties. During these waits it's
common for your eyes to lapse out of focus. The brain disengages
from the body and wanders around the imagination in search of dis-
traction. It finds none and springs back into action only when the
water runs over the edge of the counter and onto your socks.

The phrase "a watched pot never boils" comes of this experi- 4
ence. Pots don't care whether they are watched or not; the problem
is that nobody has ever seen a pot actually come to a boil. While
they are waiting, their brains turn off.

Other forms of the Watched-Pot Wait would include waiting 5
for your drier to quit at the laundromat, waiting for your toast to
pop out of the toaster, or waiting for a decent idea to come to mind
at a typewriter. What they all have in common is that they render
the waiter helpless and mindless.

A cousin to the Watched-Pot Wait is the *Forced Wait*. Not for 6
the weak of will, this one requires a bit of discipline. The classic
Forced Wait is starting your car in the winter and letting it slowly
idle up to temperature before engaging the clutch. This is every bit
as uninteresting as watching a pot, but with one big difference. You
have a choice. There is nothing keeping you from racing to work
behind a stone-cold engine save the thought of the early demise of
several thousand dollars' worth of equipment you haven't paid for
yet. Thoughts like that will help you get through a Forced Wait.

Properly preparing packaged soup mixes also requires a 7
Forced Wait. Directions are very specific on these mixes. "Bring
three cups of water to boil, add mix, simmer three minutes, remove
from heat, let stand five minutes." I have my doubts that anyone has

actually done this. I'm fairly spineless when it comes to instant soups and usually just boil the bejeezus out of them until the noodles sink. Some things just aren't worth a Forced Wait.

All in all Forced Waiting requires a lot of a thing called *pa-* 8 *tience,* which is a virtue. Once we get into virtues I'm out of my element, and can't expound on the virtues of virtue, or even lie about them. So let's move on to some of the more far-reaching varieties of waiting.

The *Payday Wait* is certainly a leader in the long-term antici- 9 pation field. The problem with waits that last more than a few minutes is that you have to actually do other things in the meantime. Like go to work. By far the most aggravating feature of the Payday Wait is that even though you must keep functioning in the interludes, there is less and less you are able to do as the big day draws near. For some of us the last few days are best spent alone in a dark room for fear we'll accidentally do something that costs money. With the Payday Wait comes a certain amount of hope that we'll make it, and faith that everything will be all right once we do.

With the introduction of faith and hope, I've ushered in the 10 most potent wait class of all, the *Lucky-Break Wait,* or the *Wait for One's Ship to Come In.* This type of wait is unusual in that it is for the most part voluntary. Unlike the Forced Wait, which is also voluntary, waiting for your lucky break does not necessarily mean that it will happen.

Turning one's life into a waiting game of these proportions re- 11 quires gobs of the aforementioned faith and hope, and is strictly for the optimists among us. For these people life is the thing that happens to them while they're waiting for something to happen to them. On the surface it seems as ridiculous as following the directions on soup mixes, but the Lucky-Break Wait performs an outstanding service to those who take it upon themselves to do it. As long as one doesn't come to rely on it, wishing for a few good things to happen never hurt anybody.

In the end it is obvious that we certainly do spend a good deal 12 of our time waiting. The person who said we do it a third of the time may have been going easy on us. It makes a guy wonder how anything at all gets done around here. But things do get done, people grow old, and time boils on whether you watch it or not.

The next time you're standing at the sink waiting for it to fill 13 while cooking soup mix that you'll have to eat until payday or until a large bag of cash falls out of the sky, don't despair. You're probably just as busy as the next guy.

Understanding Content

1. What is the selection's main idea? If it is stated directly, locate the relevant sentence(s). If it is implied, state the main idea in your own words.

2. Bodett identifies four types of waiting. What are they? Which one does he call the "purest form of waiting," and why?

3. In paragraph 8, Bodett states that he will now move on to "more far-reaching" varieties of waiting. In what ways are the last two types of waiting "more far-reaching" than the others?

Understanding Technique

1. Bodett begins his essay with conflicting quotations from sources he's read. Why do you suppose he cites these contradictory sources? What insight do they provide into Bodett's attitude toward waiting?

2. Bodett identifies four types of waiting and then expands on the first two by using examples. What are some of these examples? Why might he have chosen these particular examples?

3. Other than its considerable length, what is significant about the first sentence in the essay's concluding paragraph? Why might Bodett have decided to begin his conclusion with this sentence? What is its effect?

Thinking About Ideas

1. Think about places or situations where you have to wait. How does this waiting make you feel? What strategies help you cope with the waiting?

2. Bodett quotes a source that claims we spend a third of our lives sleeping, a third working, and a third at our leisure. Does this division apply to you? How many hours a day (or a week) do you typically spend sleeping? studying? in class? working? exercising? watching television? socializing? How might you change these divisions to make your life more productive—or more enjoyable?

3. Besides waiting, what other pet peeves can you think of that deserve to be written about? Which of these pet peeves do you find particularly annoying? What makes them frustrating?

Writing About Ideas

1. Bodett admits that forced waiting requires patience—a virtue that he doesn't claim to possess. But some things are very much worth waiting for. Write a *paragraph* about something that you had to wait for but that was well worth the effort. You could, for example, write about a long-awaited special occasion (a birthday or vacation) or about a dream come true (a date with someone special or the birth of a child). Include vivid details that show dramatically what was so special about the event when it finally happened. Before planning your paper, you might want to read "Coping with Santa Claus" (page 236) to see how Delia Ephron builds suspense as she describes waiting for a special event.

2. Write an *essay* about a particularly frustrating experience you had that involved waiting for a long time. Perhaps you waited to get service (at a restaurant or bank), an item (a paycheck or a library book), or even information (a test grade or the results of a medical test). Tell why you were forced to wait, what you did while you waited, and how the wait made you feel. At the end of your essay, explain briefly how the situation should have been handled so you wouldn't have had such a long wait.

3 Focus on another activity that people spend a great deal of time doing, usually with little or no positive result—for example, worrying, watching television, or arguing. Write an *essay* showing how unproductive most people are during this activity. Begin with a brief anecdote about someone who wastes considerable

time in this way. Then present at least three reasons why this approach isn't productive, being sure to support your reasons with convincing examples. Close the essay by suggesting better ways for dealing with the situation.

Will You Go Out with Me?

Laura Ullman

The times they are a-changing, and nowhere is that change more evident than in the relations between the sexes. As unbalanced, unfair, and unsatisfying as some of the old patterns between men and women were, at least everybody understood the rules. If you were a woman, you waited to be asked out. If you were a man, you did the asking and picked up the check. Like many of her contemporaries, freelance writer and former University of California student Laura Ullman thinks dating shouldn't have to be that way. However, as the following essay from the "My Turn" page of Newsweek *magazine makes clear, believing something and acting on it are two different things.*

Words to Watch

anticipate (1): look forward to
initiative (2): first step
muster up (2): call forth
attire (3): clothing

Every day I anxiously wait for you to get to class. I can't   1
wait for us to smile at each other and say good morning. Some
days, when you arrive only seconds before the lecture begins, I'm
incredibly impatient. Instead of reading the *Daily Cal,* I anticipate
your footsteps from behind and listen for your voice. Today is one
of your late days. But I don't mind, because after a month of des-

231

perately desiring to ask you out, today I'm going to. Encourage me, because letting you know I like you seems as risky to me as skydiving into the sea.

I know that dating has changed dramatically in the past few   2
years, and for many women, asking men out is not at all daring. But I was raised in a traditional European household where simply the thought of my asking you out spells naughty. Growing up, I learned that men call, ask, and pay for the date. During my three years at Berkeley, I have learned otherwise. Many Berkeley women have brightened their social lives by taking the initiative with men. My girlfriends insist that it's essential for women to participate more in the dating process. "I can't sit around and wait anymore," my former roommate once blurted out. "Hard as it is, I have to ask guys out—if I want to date at all!" Wonderful. More women are inviting men out, and men say they are delighted, often relieved, that dating no longer solely depends on their willingness and courage to take the first step. Then why am I digging my nails into my hand trying to muster up courage?

I keep telling myself to relax, since dating is less stereotypical   3
and more casual today. A college date means anything from studying together to sex. Most of my peers prefer casual dating anyway because it's cheaper and more comfortable. Students have fewer anxiety attacks when they ask somebody to play tennis than when they plan a formal dinner date. They enjoy last-minute "let's make dinner together" dates because they not only avoid hassling with attire and transportation but also don't have time to agonize.

Casual dating also encourages people to form healthy friend-   4
ships prior to starting relationships. My roommate and her boyfriend were friends for four months before their chemistries clicked. They went to movies and meals and often got together with mutual friends. They alternated paying the dinner check. "He was like a girlfriend," my roommate once laughed—blushing. Men and women relax and get to know each other more easily through such friendships. Another friend of mine believes that casual dating is improving people's social lives. When she wants to let a guy know she is interested, she'll say, "Hey, let's go get a yogurt."

Who pays for it? My past dates have taught me some things: 5
you don't know if I'll get the wrong idea if you treat me for dinner,

and I don't know if I'll deny you pleasure or offend you by insisting on paying for myself. John whipped out his wallet on our first date before I could suggest we go Dutch. During our after-dinner stroll he told me he was interested in dating me on a steady basis. After I explained I was more interested in a friendship, he told me he would have understood had I paid for my dinner. "I've practically stopped treating women on dates," he said defensively. "It's safer and more comfortable when we each pay for ourselves." John had assumed that because I graciously accepted his treat, I was in love. He was mad at himself for treating me, and I regretted allowing him to.

Larry, on the other hand, blushed when I offered to pay for my meal on our first date. I unzipped my purse and flung out my wallet, and he looked at me as if I had addressed him in a foreign language. Hesitant, I asked politely, "How much do I owe you?" Larry muttered, "Uh, uh, you really don't owe my anything, but if you insist . . ." Insist, I thought, I only offered. To Larry, my gesture was a suggestion of rejection. 6

Men and women alike are confused about who should ask whom out and who should pay. While I treasure my femininity, adore gentlemen, and delight in a traditional formal date, I also believe in equality. I am grateful for casual dating because it has improved my social life immensely by making me an active participant in the process. Now I can not only receive roses but can also give them. Casual dating is a worthwhile adventure because it works. No magic formula guarantees "he" will say yes. I just have to relax, be Laura, and ask him out in an unthreatening manner. If my friends are right, he'll be flattered. 7

Sliding into his desk, he taps my shoulder and says, "Hi, Laura, what's up?" 8

"Good morning," I answer with nervous chills. "Hey, how would you like to have lunch after class on Friday?" 9

"You mean after the midterm?" he says encouragingly. "I'd love to go to lunch with you." 10

"We have a date," I smile. 11

Understanding Content

1. What is the selection's main idea? If it is stated directly, locate the relevant sentence(s). If it is implied, state the main idea in your own words.

2. According to Ullman, how does casual dating benefit both men and women?

3. Ullman indicates that uncertainty about who pays for a date may result in miscommunication. When did men she was dating misinterpret her feelings? What happened?

Understanding Technique

1. How does Ullman use her date with a classmate as an organizational device to structure her essay?

2. A writer may refer to someone else using either the third-person point of view ("he" or "she") or the second-person point of view ("you"). Which point of view does Ullman use when she initially refers to the young man she wants to date? Does she use the same point of view at the end of the essay? Why or why not?

3. Effective examples usually require more space than the general points they illustrate. Consider the first six sentences of paragraph 4. Which sentence presents a general point, and which sentences illustrate that point? In paragraphs 5 and 6, where is the general point, and which sentences illustrate it?

Thinking About Ideas

1. Have you or people you know tried the "more casual" dating Ullman writes about? What advantages and disadvantages have you experienced or heard about?

2. Why do you think there is such uncertainty these days over who pays for a date? How might such uncertainty be overcome?

3. What forces in society do you think have caused the changes in the way people date? What other changes do you see in the way men and women relate? What do you think has led to these changes?

Writing About Ideas

1. What was your best date like? Your worst one? Write a *paragraph* titled either "The Best Date of My Life" or "My Date from Hell." Begin by explaining how the date came about; then describe the event itself. Select only those details that show how good or how bad the experience was. To see how a skilled prose stylist recounts a memorable experience, read Annie Dillard's "The Chase" (page 247).

2. Ullman notes that it takes "willingness and courage to take the first step" in dating. What other activities take courage? Seeking help for a problem? Taking an unpopular position on an issue? Speaking in front of a group? Write an *essay* supporting the point that people sometimes have to "muster up courage" to do something that's important to them personally. Drawing upon your own and other people's experience, illustrate this point with three dramatic examples. Alternately, you may support your point with one especially powerful illustration. In either case, use vivid details so readers can appreciate the courage required to act.

3. Changes in dating stem partly from greater freedom in sexual roles. What other changes have resulted from the easing of gender roles? Consider changes in marriage, in the classroom, on the athletic field, in dormitory life, on the job, and so on. Focusing on one such area, write an *essay* supporting this point: "Increased freedom in men's and women's roles has led to significant changes in _____." To gather ideas for your paper, talk to several people of varying ages about the changes they have experienced. When you write, be sure either to imply or to state directly how you feel about the changes described.

Coping with Santa Claus
Delia Ephron

The innocent faith of children—in the Easter bunny, in the tooth fairy, and in the endless wisdom of adults—is a delight to parents. But as youngsters grow older, we expect them to put away those childish beliefs and face reality. What can be done, then, when a child clings to a belief in a beloved but fictional character? Is it up to parents to set the record straight? In this piece from Delia Ephron's book of essays Funny Sauce, the author tells how she and her husband handled—or mishandled—such a situation.

Words to Watch

hedgy (2): avoiding a direct answer
pretentious (2): puffed up and pompous
opted for (8): chose
modicum (10): small amount
reproachfully (32): in a disapproving way

Julie had turned 8 in October and as Christmas approached,   1
Santa Claus was more and more on her mind. During the week before Christmas, every night she announced to her father, "I know
who really brings the presents. You do!" Then, waiting a moment,
she added, "Right?"

Jerry didn't answer. Neither he nor I, her stepmother, was sure   2
she really wanted the truth. We suspected she did, but couldn't
bring ourselves to admit it to her. And we both felt uncomfortable

saying something hedgy. Something pretentious. Something like, "But Santa does exist dear, he exists in spirit—in the spirit of giving in all of us." That sounded like some other parents in some other house with some other child.

I actually resented Julie for putting us on the spot. Wasn't the truth about Santa something one learned from a classmate? The same classmate who knows a screwed-up version of the facts of life. Or else from a know-it-all older sister—as I did. Mine sneaked into my room on Christmas Eve, woke me and said, "Go into the hall and look. You'll see who really puts out the presents." 3

There was another problem. Jerry and I were reluctant to give up Santa Claus ourselves. We got to tell Julie and her younger brother, Adam, to put out the cookies in case Santa was hungry. We made a fuss about the fire being out in the fireplace so he wouldn't get burned. We issued a few threats about his list of good children and bad. It was all part of the tension and thrill of Christmas Eve— the night the fantasy comes true. And that fantasy of a fat jolly man who flies through the sky in a sleigh drawn by reindeer and arrives via chimney with presents—that single belief says everything about the innocence of children. How unbearable to lose it. For them and for us. So Jerry and I said nothing. And the next night Julie announced it again. 4

Christmas Eve Julie appeared with a sheet of yellow, lined paper. At the top she had written, "If you are real, sign here." It was, she said, a letter to Santa. She insisted that on this letter each of us—her father, Adam and I—write the words "Santa Claus," so if Santa were to sign it, she could compare our handwriting with his. Then she would know she had not been tricked. 5

Jerry signed. I signed. Adam, who was 5 and couldn't write, gave up after the letter "S." Julie folded the paper into quarters, wrote "Santa Claus"on the outside and stuck it on a ledge inside the chimney along with two Christmas cookies. 6

After much fuss, Julie and Adam were tucked into bed. Jerry and I put out the presents. We were not sure what to do about the letter. 7

After a short discussion, and mostly because we couldn't resist, we opted for deceit. Jerry took the note and, in the squiggliest printing imaginable, wrote "Merry Christmas, Santa Claus." He put the note back in the fireplace and ate the cookies. 8

The next morning, very early, about six, we heard Julie and   9
Adam tear down the hall. Jerry and I, in bed, listened for the first
ecstatic reactions to the presents. Suddenly, we heard a shriek.
"He's real! He's real! He's really real!!!!" The door to our room
flew open. "He's REAL!!!" she shouted. Julie showed us the paper
with the squiggly writing.

Somehow, this was not what we had bargained for. I had ex-   10
pected some modicum of disbelief—at least a "Dad, is this for
real?"

Julie clasped the note to her chest. Then she dashed back to   11
the presents.

That afternoon, our friend Deena came over to exchange gifts.   12
"Santa Claus is real," said Julie.

"Oh," said Deena.   13

"I know for sure, for really, really sure. Look!" And Julie pro-   14
duced the proof.

Just then the phone rang. Knowing it was a relative calling   15
with Christmas greetings, Julie rushed to answer it. "Santa Claus is
real," I heard her say to my sister Nora, the same sister who had
broken the bad news about Santa Claus to me thirty years ago. Julie
handed me the phone.

"What is this about?" asked Nora.   16

I told her the story, trying to make it as funny as possible,   17
hoping she wouldn't notice how badly Jerry and I had handled what
I was beginning to think of as "the Santa issue." It didn't work.

"We may have made a mistake here," said Nora, diplomati-   18
cally including herself in the mess.

"You're telling me!" I said. "Do you think there's any chance   19
Julie will forget all this?" That was what I really wanted, of
course—for the whole thing to go away.

"I doubt it," said Nora.   20

We had a wonderful day—good food, good presents, lots of   21
visitors. Then it was bedtime.

"Dad?" said Julie, as he tucked her in.   22

"What?"   23

"If Santa's real, then Rudolph must be real, too."   24

"What!"   25

"If Santa's real—"   26

"I heard," said Jerry. He sat down on her bed and took a deep   27
breath. "You know, Julie," and then he stopped. I could see he was
trying to think of a way, any way, to explain our behavior so it
wouldn't sound quite as deceptive, wrong and stupid as it was. But
he was stumped.

"Yeah," said Julie.   28

"I wrote the note," said Jerry.   29

She burst into tears.   30

Jerry apologized. He apologized over and over while Julie   31
sobbed into her pillow. He said he was wrong, that he shouldn't
have tricked her, that he should have answered her questions about
Santa Claus the week before.

Julie sat up in bed. "I thought he was real," she said reproach-   32
fully. Then suddenly she leaned over the bed, pulled out a comic
from underneath and sat up again. "Can I read for five minutes?"
she said.

"Sure," said Jerry.   33

And that was it. One minute of grief at Santa's death, and life   34
went on.

Jerry and I left Julie's room terribly relieved. I immediately   35
got a craving for leftover turkey and headed for the kitchen. I was
putting the bird back in the refrigerator when I heard Adam crying.
I went down the hall. The door to his room was open and I heard
Julie, very disgusted, say: "Oh, Adam, you don't have to cry! Only
babies believe in Santa Claus."

Understanding Content

1. What is the selection's main idea? If it is stated directly, locate
   the relevant sentence(s). If it is implied, state the main idea in
   your own words.

2. How ready was Julie to give up the Santa Claus fantasy? How
   can you tell?

3. Ephron writes in paragraph 4 that the belief in Santa Claus
   "says everything about the innocence of children." What does
   she mean by the phrase "the innocence of children"? Why is
   that innocence so appealing to Ephron?

Understanding Technique

1. Even though "Coping with Santa Claus" is a brief essay, Ephron reveals quite a bit about the central characters in her narrative. For instance, what can you conclude about Julie's temperament? About Jerry's? Which narrative details support your conclusions?

2. Ephron describes some events briefly, others in considerable detail. For instance, compare paragraph 21 with paragraphs 22–33. What's different about the way Ephron narrates Christmas events in these two paragraphs? Why do you think Ephron decided to describe these two parts of Christmas Day so differently?

3. Ephron could have ended her essay with paragraph 34. What would have been lost had she done so?

Thinking About Ideas

1. Julie burst into tears when Jerry told her he had written the note from Santa. Why do you think he told her the truth then, instead of earlier? Do you think she would have cried had he told her the truth about Santa when she first asked? Why or why not?

2. How did you learn the truth about Santa Claus (or another fantasy figure like the tooth fairy)? How did you feel? If you have children, which fantasy figures do they believe in? How did they (or how will they) learn the truth?

3. Should children be told fantasies—even though they must eventually accept reality? Is the pleasure of the fantasy worth a temporary lie? Explain.

Writing About Ideas

1. Write a *paragraph* explaining why and how children should be told the truth about a particular fantasy figure. Support your point with examples from your own experiences or from those of people you know.

⚭ 2. Ephron suggests that learning the truth about Santa changes forever a child's perspective. Write an *essay* about an experience
that dramatically altered your view of someone or something.
Perhaps you discovered that you had a hidden talent, that someone was not as you imagined, that a job you wanted wasn't ideal
after all, or that a possession you had dreamed of owning turned
out to be a nuisance once it was yours. Use vivid details to describe how the experience affected you. Your essay may be
serious or humorous. To see how one author describes an experience that gave him a new perspective, read Isaac Asimov's
"What Is Intelligence, Anyway?" (page 242).

3. Julie's parents told her something untrue in order to preserve her
childlike enjoyment of Christmas. What other reasons might
there be for lying? To hide a painful truth? To prevent feelings
from being hurt? To protect privacy? Write an *essay* supporting
the idea that there may—at times—be valid reasons for with-
holding the truth. To gather material for your paper, discuss
with friends those situations in which lying is acceptable, even
desirable. Then develop your essay by citing several reasons,
and illustrate each reason with convincing examples.
Alternatively, you may cite one particularly compelling reason
and support that reason with two or three highly persuasive examples.

What Is Intelligence, Anyway?

Isaac Asimov

Haven't we all known people in school who had the reputation of being "brains"—but couldn't change a light bulb? And others who could barely make passing grades, yet seemed to understand instinctively how an engine worked? In this essay, noted science and science fiction writer Isaac Asimov places himself in the first category and questions the conventional definition of intelligence.

Words to Watch

KP (1): work with the "kitchen police," soldiers who assist the army cooks
complacent (2): self-satisfied
bents (2): talents
vitals (3): internal organs
pronouncements (3): statements by an authority
oracles (3): messages from the gods
academician (4): scholar
absolute (4): unchanging
foist (4): force
arbiter (4): judge
indulgently (6): done to go along with someone's wishes
raucously (6): loudly

What is intelligence, anyway? When I was in the Army, I re-   1
ceived a kind of aptitude test that all soldiers took and, against a

normal of 100, scored 160. No one at the base had ever seen a figure like that, and for two hours they made a big fuss over me. (It didn't mean anything. The next day I was still a buck private with KP as my highest duty.)

All my life I've been registering scores like that, so that I have   2 the complacent feeling that I'm highly intelligent, and I expect other people to think so, too. Actually, though, don't such scores simply mean that I am very good at answering the type of academic questions that are considered worthy of answers by the people who make up the intelligence tests—people with intellectual bents similar to mine?

For instance, I had an auto repairman once, who, on these in-   3 telligence tests, could not possibly have scored more than 80, by my estimate. I always took it for granted that I was far more intelligent than he was. Yet, when anything went wrong with my car, I hastened to him with it, watched him anxiously as he explored its vitals, and listened to his pronouncements as though they were divine oracles—and he always fixed my car.

Well then, suppose my auto repairman devised questions for   4 an intelligence test. Or suppose a carpenter did, or a farmer, or, indeed, almost anyone but an academician. By every one of those tests, I'd prove myself a moron. And I'd *be* a moron, too. In a world where I could not use my academic training and my verbal talents but had to do something intricate or hard, working with my hands, I would do poorly. My intelligence, then, is not absolute but is a function of the society I live in and of the fact that a small subsection of that society has managed to foist itself on the rest as an arbiter of such matters.

Consider my auto repairman, again. He had a habit of telling   5 me jokes whenever he saw me. One time he raised his head from under the automobile hood to say, "Doc, a deaf-and-dumb guy went into a hardware store to ask for some nails. He put two fingers together on the counter and made hammering motions with the other hand. The clerk brought him a hammer. He shook his head and pointed to the two fingers he was hammering. The clerk brought him nails. He picked out the sizes he wanted, and left. Well, doc, the next guy who came in was a blind man. He wanted scissors. How do you suppose he asked for them?"

Indulgently, I lifted my right hand and made scissoring mo-   6
tions with my first two fingers. Whereupon my auto repairman
laughed raucously and said, "Why, you dumb jerk, he used his
voice and asked for them." Then he said, smugly, "I've been trying
that on all my customers today." "Did you catch many?" I asked.
"Quite a few," he said, "but I knew for sure I'd catch *you*." "Why is
that?" I asked. "Because you're so goddamned educated, doc, I
knew you couldn't be very smart."

And I have an uneasy feeling he had something there.   7

Understanding Content

1. What is the selection's main idea? If it is stated directly, locate
the relevant sentence(s). If it is implied, state the main idea in
your own words.

2. What is a "normal" score on an IQ test? What was Asimov's
score, and how did he feel about it? How did others react to it?

3. What is wrong with Asimov's answer to the auto mechanic's
riddle? How does this incident reinforce Asimov's main idea?

Understanding Technique

1. Why might Asimov have decided to place parentheses around
the last two sentences in his first paragraph? What effect is pro-
duced by enclosing these sentences in parentheses? How does
this effect reinforce Asimov's main idea?

2. How does Asimov move readers from the essay's first example
(his Army test scores) to the second (his auto mechanic's intelligence) to the third (the auto mechanic's riddle)? Identify words
and phrases he uses to link these three parts of his essay. What
is the effect of these words and phrases?

3. Why do you suppose Asimov ends his essay with a one-sen-
tence conclusion? How does this concluding sentence
underscore Asimov's central point?

Thinking About Ideas

1. What are some ways we judge people's intelligence? Are these ways always accurate? Why or why not?

2. Have you ever taken an intelligence test? How did you feel knowing your intelligence was being assessed? Do you agree with Asimov that such tests are unfair? If so, what could be done to make them fairer?

3. The mechanic says to Asimov, "Because you're so goddamned educated, doc, I *knew* you couldn't be very smart." What is the difference between being educated and being smart? Which would you rather be? Why?

Writing About Ideas

⟳ 1. Do you know anyone like Asimov's mechanic—someone who has a kind of intelligence that is not easily measured by standardized tests? In a *paragraph,* describe this person. Include several convincing examples that illustrate the individual's intelligence. Your opening sentence could be similar to these: "My neighbor Joe Ventura is a genius at making people feel comfortable" or "My mother's skill with computers amazes me." For inspiration, read "Coping with Santa Claus" (page 236) to see how Delia Ephron vividly reveals the intelligence of an eight-year-old child.

2. As Asimov's Army experience shows, a high IQ score doesn't guarantee success; other factors play an equal, even more important role. In an *essay,* describe several traits you consider essential for success in a particular area of life. You could, for example, write about the qualities needed to succeed as a college student, parent, campus leader, boss, spouse, or friend. Drawing upon personal observations and other people's experience, illustrate the importance of each trait. Use a separate paragraph to discuss each trait.

3. Asimov answers the question "What is intelligence?" by presenting lively examples of what it is and what it isn't. Write an

essay defining another quality (for example, "devotion," "hypocrisy," "deceit," or "good taste"). Like Asimov, relate several vivid examples that illustrate what the quality is and what it is not. You may find newspaper accounts and television reports as well as your own experiences good sources of material for your essay.

The Chase

Annie Dillard

A snowy morning, a gang of kids, cars crawling along the slippery streets—a perfect opportunity. The children made the most of it, secure in the assumption that their existence and that of the motorists ran on parallel tracks that did not, could not, intersect. Then the unthinkable happened: an adult broke through the barrier separating the two worlds, and suddenly the children were running for their lives. In "The Chase," taken from Annie Dillard's autobiography, An American Childhood, *the poet and essayist captures a morning from her childhood, a morning memorable for its terror, but even more for the exhilaration of feeling wholly alive.*

Words to Watch

crenellated (5): indented
spherical (6): round
translucent (6): allowing light to come through
nigh (7): near
impelled (14): pushed
improvising (14): making decisions at the moment
labyrinths (15): mazes
obscure (16): remote
prow (16): a part that projects forward
perfunctorily (18): in a routine manner
cap (20): provide a finishing touch to
brooded (20): thought deeply

dismembered (20): torn apart
piecemeal (20): a little at a time
exalting (20): delighting

Some boys taught me to play football. This was fine sport.   1
You thought up a new strategy for every play and whispered it to
the others. You went out for a pass, fooling everyone. Best, you got
to throw yourself mightily at someone's running legs. Either you
brought him down or you hit the ground flat out on your chin, with
your arms empty before you. It was all or nothing. If you hesitated
in fear, you would miss and get hurt: you would take a hard fall
while the kid got away, or you would get kicked in the face while
the kid got away. But if you flung yourself wholeheartedly at the
back of his knees—if you gathered and joined body and soul and
pointed them diving fearlessly—then you likely wouldn't get hurt,
and you'd stop the ball. Your fate, and your team's score, depended
on your concentration and courage. Nothing girls did could compare with it.

Boys welcomed me at baseball, too, for I had, through enthu-   2
siastic practice, what was weirdly known as a boy's arm. In winter,
in the snow, there was neither baseball nor football, so the boys and
I threw snowballs at passing cars. I got in trouble throwing snowballs, and have seldom been happier since.

On one weekday morning after Christmas, six inches of new   3
snow had just fallen. We were standing up to our boot tops in snow
on a front yard on trafficked Reynolds Street, waiting for cars. The
cars traveled Reynolds Street slowly and evenly; they were targets
all but wrapped in red ribbons, cream puffs. We couldn't miss.

I was seven; the boys were eight, nine, and ten. The oldest   4
two Fahey boys were there—Mikey and Peter—polite blond boys
who lived near me on Lloyd Street, and who already had four
brothers and sisters. My parents approved Mikey and Peter Fahey.
Chickie McBride was there, a tough kid, and Billy Paul and Mackie
Kean too, from across Reynolds, where the boys grew up dark and
furious, grew up skinny, knowing, and skilled. We had all drifted
from our houses that morning looking for action, and had found it
here on Reynolds Street.

It was cloudy but cold. The cars' tires laid behind them on the   5
snowy street a complex trail of beige chunks like crenellated castle
walls. I had stepped on some earlier; they squeaked. We could have
wished for more traffic. When a car came, we all popped it one. In
the intervals between cars we reverted to the natural solitude of
children.

I started making an iceball—a perfect iceball, from perfectly   6
white snow, perfectly spherical, and squeezed perfectly translucent
so no snow remained all the way through. (The Fahey boys and I
considered it unfair actually to throw an iceball at somebody, but it
had been known to happen.)

I had just embarked on the iceball project when we heard tire   7
chains come clanking from afar. A black Buick was moving toward
us down the street. We all spread out, banged together some regular
snowballs, took aim, and, when the Buick drew nigh, fired.

A soft snowball hit the driver's windshield right before the   8
driver's face. It made a smashed star with a hump in the middle.

Often, of course, we hit our target, but this time, the only time   9
in all of life, the car pulled over and stopped. Its wide black door
opened; a man got out of it, running. He didn't even close the car
door.

He ran after us, and we ran away from him, up the snowy   10
Reynolds sidewalk. At the corner, I looked back; incredibly, he was
still after us. He was in city clothes: a suit and tie, street shoes. Any
normal adult would have quit, having sprung us into flight and
made his point. This man was gaining on us. He was a thin man, all
action. All of a sudden, we were running for our lives.

Wordless, we split up. We were on our turf; we could lose   11
ourselves in the neighborhood backyards, everyone for himself. I
paused and considered. Everyone had vanished except Mikey
Fahey, who was just rounding the corner of a yellow brick house.
Poor Mikey, I trailed him. The driver of the Buick sensibly picked
the two of us to follow. The man apparently had all day.

He chased Mikey and me around the yellow house and up a   12
backyard path we knew by heart: under a low tree, up a bank,
through a hedge, down some snowy steps, and across the grocery
store's delivery driveway. We smashed through a gap in another
hedge, entered a scruffy backyard and ran around its back porch and

tight between houses to Edgerton Avenue; we ran across Edgerton to an alley and up our own sliding woodpile to the Halls' front yard; he kept coming. We ran up Lloyd Street and wound through mazy backyards toward the steep hilltop at Willard and Lang.

He chased us silently, block after block. He chased us silently 13 over picket fences, through thorny hedges, between houses, around garbage cans, and across streets. Every time I glanced back, choking for breath, I expected he would have quit. He must have been as breathless as we were. His jacket strained over his body. It was an immense discovery, pounding into my hot head with every sliding, joyous step, that this ordinary adult evidently knew what I thought only children who trained at football knew: that you have to fling yourself at what you're doing, you have to point yourself, forget yourself, aim, dive.

Mikey and I had nowhere to go, in our own neighborhood or 14 out of it, but away from this man who was chasing us. He impelled us forward; we compelled him to follow our route. The air was cold; every breath tore my throat. We kept running, block after block; we kept improvising, backyard after backyard, running a frantic course and choosing it simultaneously, failing always to find small places or hard places to slow him down, and discovering always, exhilarated, dismayed, that only bare speed could save us—for he would never give up, this man—and we were losing speed.

He chased us through the backyard labyrinths of ten blocks 15 before he caught us by our jackets. He caught us and we all stopped.

We three stood staggering, half blinded, coughing, in an ob- 16 scure hilltop backyard: a man in his twenties, a boy, a girl. He had released our jackets, our pursuer, our captor, our hero: he knew we weren't going anywhere. We all played by the rules. Mikey and I unzipped our jackets. I pulled off my sopping mittens. Our tracks multiplied in the backyard's new snow. We had been breaking new snow all morning. We didn't look at each other. I was cherishing my excitement. The man's lower pants legs were wet; his cuffs were full of snow, and there was a prow of snow beneath them on his shoes and socks. Some trees bordered the little flat backyard, some messy winter trees. There was no one around: a clearing in a grove, and we the only players.

It was a long time before he could speak. I had some diffi- 17
culty at first, recalling why we were there. My lips felt swollen; I
couldn't see out of the sides of my eyes; I kept coughing.

"You stupid kids," he began perfunctorily. 18

We listened perfunctorily indeed, if we listened at all, for the 19
chewing out was redundant, a mere formality, and beside the point.
The point was that he had chased us passionately without giving up,
and so he had caught us. Now he came down to earth. I wanted the
glory to last forever.

But how could the glory have lasted forever? We could have 20
run through every backyard in North America until we got to
Panama. But when he trapped us at the lip of the Panama Canal,
what precisely could he have done to prolong the drama of the
chase and cap its glory? I brooded about this for the next few years.
He could only have fried Mikey Fahey and me in boiling oil, say, or
dismembered us piecemeal, or staked us to anthills. None of which
I really wanted, and none of which any adult was likely to do, even
in the spirit of fun. He could only chew us out there in the
Panamanian jungle, after months or years of exalting pursuit. He
could only begin, "You stupid kids," and continue in his ordinary
Pittsburgh accent with his normal righteous anger and the usual
common sense.

If in that snowy backyard the driver of the black Buick had 21
cut off our heads, Mikey's and mine, I would have died happy, for
nothing has required so much of me since as being chased all over
Pittsburgh in the middle of winter—running terrified, exhausted—
by this sainted, skinny, furious redheaded man who wished to have
a word with us. I don't know how he found his way back to his car.

Understanding Content

1. What is the selection's main idea? If it is stated directly, locate
   the relevant sentence(s). If it is implied, state the main idea in
   your own words.

2. Right before the black Buick comes along, Dillard is making an
   iceball, but she doesn't throw it at the car. Why not? What does
   Dillard's decision reveal about her?

3. How does Dillard feel about the man who chased her? About the outcome of the chase? Which passages convey how she feels?

Understanding Technique

1. Dillard relies heavily on play-by-play action and vivid descriptive details to create drama and suspense. Point out examples of these techniques, and comment on their effectiveness.

2. Why do you suppose Dillard begins her essay with a paragraph about learning to play football?

3. Dillard views the chase from the perspective of both an adult looking back on an important childhood event and a seven-year-old child experiencing the event. Find examples of both perspectives in the essay. What does Dillard gain by using both points of view?

Thinking About Ideas

1. Why did the man driving the Buick chase Dillard and her friends? If your car were hit by a snowball, would you stop the car? Why or why not? Would you be as determined as the man in your pursuit of the culprits? Explain.

2. Dillard found great pleasure participating in activities that many would consider inappropriate for girls. In the same way, boys are often discouraged form getting involved in activities traditionally associated with girls. Do you think these gender boundaries limit children's behavior and development? Why or why not?

3. In her final paragraph, Dillard writes, "If in that snowy backyard the driver of the black Buick had cut off our heads, . . . I would have died happy." Why might she have felt this way? What in your own life has given you—or could give you—a similar feeling of exhilaration? Explain.

Writing About Ideas

1. Dillard has never forgotten the experience of being chased by the Buick-driving stranger. Write a *paragraph* about a memorable encounter you had with a stranger. Perhaps someone was unusually rude and arrogant or surprisingly kind and compassionate. Begin with a brief description of the setting, and then tell what happened, providing vivid details that show why the incident was memorable. Be sure your attitude toward the incident is either stated directly or implied by your details.

2. Dillard remembers the chase as a successful test of her endurance and courage. In an *essay,* describe an occasion when you also felt good about the way you responded to some kind of test or challenge. Before writing, brainstorm details about why the challenge demanded much of you, where it occurred, who else was involved, how it turned out, and what you learned as a result. Like Dillard, use play-by-play action and colorful details to create drama and suspense.

3. As a young girl, Dillard felt joyously alive participating in what might be considered typically masculine activities. In an *essay,* tell about a time you acted in a way that crossed traditional gender lines. If you're a female, perhaps you fixed a flat tire. If you're a male, perhaps you babysat a young child. Provide vivid details to describe what the experience was like and how you (and others) felt about your defying gender boundaries. Before you write, you may want to read Laura Ullman's "Will You Go Out with Me?" (page 231), which presents an example of challenging a stereotyped role.

Acknowledgments

Adler, Mortimer. "How to Mark a Book." From *Saturday Review*, July 6, 1940. Reprinted by permission.

Angelou, Maya. "Sister Flowers." From *I Know Why the Caged Bird Sings*, copyright © 1969 by Maya Angelou. Reprinted by permission of Random House, Inc.

Asimov, Isaac. "What Is Intelligence, Anyway?" Reprinted by permission of the Estate of Isaac Asimov c/o Ralph M. Vicinanza, Ltd.

Barkin, Dorothy. "The Bystander Effect." Reprinted by permission.

Barron, Donna. "American Family Life: The Changing Picture." Reprinted by permission.

Bodett, Tom. "Wait Divisions." From *Small Comforts*, copyright © 1987 by Tom Bodett. Reprinted by permission of Addison-Wesley Publishing Company, Inc.

Carson, Ben, M.D., with Cecil Murphey. "Do It Better!" From *Think Big*, copyright © 1992 by Benjamin Carson, M.D. Reprinted by permission of Zondervan Publishing House.

Collier, James Lincoln. "Anxiety: Challenge by Another Name." Reprinted by permission from the December 1986 *Reader's Digest*.

Dillard, Annie. "The Chase." From *An American Childhood*, copyright © 1987 by Annie Dillard. Reprinted by permission of HarperCollins, Publishers, Inc.

Ellerbee, Linda. "Television Changed My Family Forever." From *Move On*, copyright © 1991 by Linda Ellerbee. Reprinted by permission of The Putnam Publishing Group.

Ephron, Delia. "Coping with Santa Claus." From *Funny Sauce*, copyright © 1982, 1983, 1986 by Delia Ephron. Reprinted by permission of Viking Penguin, a division of Penguin Books USA Inc.

Garity, Joyce. "Is Sex All That Matters?" Reprinted by permission.

Greene, Bob. "Handled with Care." From *American Beat*, copyright © 1983 by Bob Greene. Reprinted by permission of John Deadline Enterprises, Inc.

Gregory, Dick. "Shame." From *Nigger: An Autobiography*, copyright © 1964 by Dick Gregory Enterprises, Inc. Reprinted by permission of Dutton Signet, a division of Penguin Books USA Inc.

Haley, Alex. "Thank You." Copyright © 1982 by Alex Haley. Reprinted by permission of John Hawkins & Associates, Inc.

Hamill, Pete. "Crack and the Box." Copyright © 1990 by Pete Hamill. Reprinted by permission of International Creative Management, Inc.

Huttmann, Barbara. "A Crime of Compassion." Reprinted by permission.

Johnson, Beth. "Let's Get Specific." Reprinted by permission.

Jones, Rachel L. "The Price of Hate." Reprinted by permission from the *St. Petersburg Times*, copyright © 1988.

Keegan, Paul. "A Dangerous Party." Reprinted by permission.

Lam, Andrew. "They Shut My Grandmother's Door." Reprinted by permission.

Langella, Frank. "The Monsters in My Head." Copyright © 1986 by The New York Times Company. Reprinted by permission.

Leo, John. "One Poke Over the Line." Reprinted by permission from *U. S. News and World Report*, copyright © October 26, 1992.

Malcolm, Andrew H. "Dad." Copyright © 1984 by The New York Times Company. Reprinted by permission.

Piassa, Bernadete. "A Love Affair with Books." Reprinted by permission.

Rego, Caroline. "The Fine Art of Complaining." Reprinted by permission.

Rooney, Andy. "Tickets to Nowhere." Reprinted by permission of Tribune Media Services.

Sawaquat, Lewis. "For My Indian Daughter." Reprinted by permission.

Sherry, Mary. "In Praise of the F Word." Reprinted by permission.

Soto, Gary. "Living Up the Street." From *Living Up the Street*, copyright © 1985 by Gary Soto. Reprinted by permission of Strawberry Hill Press, Portland, Oregon.

Teague, Bob. "To Get a Story, I Flimflammed a Dead Man's Mother." Reprinted by permission from *TV Guide* ® Magazine. Copyright © 1982 by Triangle/News America Publications Inc.

Ullman, Laura. "Will You Go Out with Me?" Reprinted by permission.

Wine, Bill. "Rudeness at the Movies." Reprinted by permission.

Wong, Jade Snow. "Fifth Chinese Daughter." From *Fifth Chinese Daughter,* copyright © 1950 by Harper and Row. Reprinted by permission of the University of Washington Press.